STAFFING THE
CONTEMPORARY
ORGANIZATION

STAFFING THE CONTEMPORARY ORGANIZATION

A GUIDE TO PLANNING, RECRUITING, AND SELECTING FOR HUMAN RESOURCE PROFESSIONALS

DONALD L. CARUTH
ROBERT M. NOE III
AND
R. WAYNE MONDY

PRAEGER

New York
Westport, Connecticut
London

Library of Congress Cataloging-in-Publication Data

Caruth, Donald L.
  Staffing the contemporary organization.

  Bibliography: p.
  Includes index.
  1. Personnel management. 2. Manpower planning.
3. Recruiting of employees. 4. Employee selection.
I. Noe, Robert M. II. Mondy, R. Wayne, 1940-
III. Title.
HF5549.C296 1990   658.3

ISBN 0-275-93804-2 (alk. paper)

British Library Cataloguing in Publication Data is available.

A hardcover edition of *Staffing the Contemporary Organization*
is available from Quorum Books, an imprint of Greenwood
Publishing Group, Inc. (ISBN 0-89930-236-X).

ISBN: 0-275-93804-2

First published in 1988
Paperback edition 1990

Praeger Publishers, One Madison Avenue, New York, NY 10010
An imprint of Greenwood Publishing Group, Inc.

Printed in the United States of America

The paper used in this book complies with the
Permanent Paper Standard issued by the National
Information Standards Organization (Z39.48-1984).

10 9 8 7 6 5 4 3 2 1

To Marianne
DLC
To Joanie
RMN
To Judy Bandy Mondy, My Staffing Expert
RWM

Contents

Figures and Tables

FIGURES

ix

TABLES

Preface

Staffing the contemporary organization is a challenging, complex endeavor. Economic changes, demographic shifts, increased competition, organizational restructuring, and a host of other factors suggest that this activity will be of crucial importance in the years to come. As organizations enter the last decade of this century, it is rapidly becoming apparent that the acquisition and utilization of human resources is as vital to continued organizational success as the advanced technology required for producing products or providing services. Indeed, technology alone is not enough since its effective usage depends on people—the right kinds of people, in the right numbers, performing the right jobs, at the right times. Whether in the past, present, or future, it is people—the catalytic resource of any institution—that have, do, and will determine organizational success.

The uniqueness of this book is its integration of topics that are usually the subjects of disparate treatment: human resource planning, legal aspects of staffing, recruiting, selecting, performance appraisal, career development, and so forth. It is our contention that the entire range of activities associated with planning for, obtaining, utilizing, and developing human resources must be viewed as an integrated system called "staffing." We firmly believe that unless staffing is conceived of as a system, or perhaps more correctly as a major subsystem of the entire human resource management process, activities performed in one area of staffing may negate activities performed in another area. While there are other books that purport to deal with staffing in general, we have found none that takes the encompassing systems view that we offer to our readers.

This book is written as a working reference for human resource professionals, operating managers, educators, students, and others seeking practical guidance on staffing procedures, policies, techniques, and problems. This work is based not only on thorough research, but also on our experience as managers, consultants, observers, and teachers in the field of human resource management. Our main thrust is practicality—what has worked or will work for organizations—rather than obtuse scholarship.

This book is written generically so that it can be used by practitioners in all types of organizations, profit-making and nonprofit, from manufacturing to service. We trust that it will also be used by our colleagues in academe as well as their students.

Any work such as this one depends upon the assistance, encouragement, cooperation, and inspiration of many people. While it would be impossible to enumerate everyone who has had a hand in influencing us and guiding our thinking in the preparation of this book, we would like to express our thanks to the following individuals: Dr. Frank M. Rachel, Professor of Business, North Texas State University; Dr. Shane R. Premeaux, Professor of Management, NcNeese State University; Dr. Art Bethke, Associate Dean, Northeast Louisiana University; Dr. Harry N. Mills, Professor of Management, East Texas State University; Robert E. Edwards, Senior Vice President, Drake Beam Morin, Inc.; Charles J. Brown, Senior Vice President, Dallas Teachers Credit Union; and Dr. Bill Middlebrook, Assistant Professor of Management, Southwest Texas State University.

Several others were directly instrumental in the completion of this manuscript and without their efforts this book would not have been possible. We are especially indebted to Arlene Ekeland who provided invaluable assistance in typing and editing; Darrell Beauchamp who prepared the artwork; and Dr. Trezzie A. Pressley, Dean, College of Business and Technology, East Texas State University, who not only provided encouragement but also the tangible support needed to turn an idea into reality.

STAFFING THE
CONTEMPORARY
ORGANIZATION

1

Staffing: An Overview

Broadly defined, staffing is the process of determining human resource needs in an organization and securing sufficient quantities of qualified people to fill those needs. It is not, however, as simplistic an activity as that definition might seem to imply. Staffing is actually a complex endeavor involving a number of diverse tasks, ranging from job analysis to performance appraisal, from interviewing to career development, from hiring to termination. Moreover, to execute properly the tasks of staffing, organizational members charged with this responsibility must be knowledgeable of the legal, psychological, and environmental contexts within which staffing takes place. The tasks that must be performed, coupled with the contexts in which they must be carried out, make staffing a difficult and challenging activity in contemporary organizations.

The objective of the staffing process is to ensure that an organization continuously has the right quality and quantity of employees in the right place at the right time to perform successfully the work of the institution. As with the definition, the objective of staffing also appears to be simplistic, but accomplishing it effectively is no easy matter. The diverse tasks must be integrated with each other to create a process that functions smoothly and operates in a timely fashion, and the tasks must be coordinated harmoniously with the environments and contexts in which they occur.

Combining the broad definition of staffing with its objectives, we can now define staffing more specifically as the process through which an organization ensures that it has, on a continuous basis, the proper number of employees with the appropriate skills in the right jobs at the right times to achieve the organization's objectives.

Except in small organizations that do not have a personnel department, the responsibility for staffing is usually shared by line managers and personnel specialists. Personnel professionals develop programs to recruit

1

qualified workers, but operating managers make the final decisions as to who will be hired. Staffing specialists develop the administrative procedures for such activities as promotions, demotions, transfers, layoffs, and the like, but line managers determine which employees will be promoted, demoted, and so on. Personnel professionals design the performance appraisal system, but line managers actually evaluate the workers. Consequently, staffing is best viewed as a joint activity wherein human resource specialists contribute their knowledge, expertise, and counsel and line managers make the final decisions. Both groups must work together in coordinated fashion to ensure that the objective of staffing is fulfilled.

Effective staffing plays a crucial role in the short-run as well as the long-term performance, growth, vitality, and success of contemporary organizations. Indeed, it is only through effective staffing that any institution—regardless of size, industry, scope, or objectives—can remain viable.

WHY STAFFING IS IMPORTANT

The activities performed in the staffing process are important to enterprises of all types and sizes because of the relationship these tasks have to the organization's goals, the direct costs incurred, the indirect costs experienced, the organizational impacts created, and the legal aspects involved.

Organizational Goals

The most carefully formulated plans, the most logical organization structure, the most sophisticated marketing programs, and the most advanced computer systems will not, of themselves, assure an institution of success. Plans, structures, programs, and systems are not self-actuating; they can only be implemented, maintained, and realized through people. It is people—the most crucial of resources—that serve as the catalyst, the activating and energizing force, making possible the utilization of all other resources and enabling an organization to achieve its goals. Without qualified human resources available in the right numbers, at the right place, and at the right time, organizational goals and objectives will not be reached. Even in a completely automated manufacturing plant, it is people who press the buttons, program the computers, and call the shots. It is people who wait on customers, answer telephones, and solicit new accounts in a highly computerized service enterprise. Despite computers and automation, it is still people who accomplish objectives. Increasingly today, the degree of success that any institution enjoys is directly dependent upon the caliber of human resources provided through the staffing process. Only by effective staffing can an organization expect to fulfill its mission and achieve its goals.

Direct Costs

Direct staffing costs encompass such items as salaries of staffing specialists, office and equipment, employment advertising, employment agency fees, tests, physical examinations, relocation expenses, and others. While it is difficult to ascertain with any degree of precision the actual amount of out-of-pocket expenditures directly associated with the staffing process for the average company, one can easily surmise that they are not insignificant. For example, it is estimated to cost some hospitals as much as $12,000 to recruit and orient one nurse;[1] the average cost of relocating an employee is around $32,000;[2] and employment agency fees typically range from one-tenth to one-third of the annual salary of the employee located by the agency.

Further indication of costs related to staffing can be inferred from a survey conducted by the Bureau of National Affairs.[3] According to this survey, budgets for the human resource or personnel departments in surveyed companies represent a median of 2.7 percent of total company payroll and a median of one percent of the total operating budget of these companies. While these figures include all personnel department expenses and not just staffing costs, it would seem safe to assume that the portion of expenses directly attributable to performance of staffing activities is substantial.

To put it very simply, staffing costs represent a sizable outlay for many organizations. Consequently, it is important that staffing activities be performed as effectively as possible to ensure that the organization is deriving maximum benefit from its direct expenditures in this area.

Indirect Costs

The staffing process involves a number of "hidden" or indirect costs. Included in this category are such things as: (1) the time operating managers spend interviewing prospective employees, conducting performance appraisals, making promotion or termination decisions, documenting staffing actions, and so forth; (2) the time supervisors or employees spend training the new worker or orienting the person to the workplace; (3) the amount of productivity lost by the new employee while he or she is in the process of learning to perform the job; and (4) the amount of scrappage or wasted materials resulting from the new employee's mistakes while learning the job. Because costs of these sorts are contained in normal operating budgets they are often overlooked as staffing-related expenses. Nevertheless, they are as real as the direct costs. Little work, unfortunately, has been done to determine just how much indirect cost may be associated with the staffing process. We can, however, assume from their nature that indirect staffing expenditures may be considerable.

Organizational Impacts

Performance of the staffing function affects the overall organization in many ways. Some of the obvious organizational impacts include morale, employee turnover, productivity, customer service, community relations, employee relations, and corporate image. If staffing is performed effectively, morale will be high, turnover will be low, and productivity will be high. If staffing is done ineffectively, customer service will suffer, community relations may be affected, corporate image could be tarnished, and employee relations may be poor. Thus, it is extremely important that staffing activities be carried out in such a manner as to increase positive impacts on the organization and ameliorate negative impacts.

Legal Aspects

While all phases of human resource management have become increasingly legalistic in nature, staffing is the one area that has been most affected. The overwhelming majority of federal employment legislation enacted and court decisions rendered since 1964 have been directed to various parts of the staffing process. Laws and regulations have imposed new requirements on staffing activities. The potential liability for violations of the law have increased tremendously. Staffing can no longer simply concern itself with securing the right number and quality of employees to perform the work of the organization, but must carry out its tasks in conformance with a plethora of statutory guidelines. Procedures, practices, and policies must conform to the law or the organization runs the risk of investigations or legal actions.

In the event that legal action is brought against a company, the costs involved may be substantial. Three examples will illustrate this point. In 1973, American Telephone and Telegraph agreed to pay $15 million in back wages to some 15,000 members of protected classes against whom the company had allegedly discriminated.[4] In 1984, Burlington Northern Railroad agreed to a $60.5 million out-of-court settlement in another case of alleged discrimination. The company agreed to hire 15,000 blacks over a six-year period, using $50.5 million for training, hiring, and promotion. Back pay of $10 million was given to current and former employees.[5] Even if an organization wins its case, the cost of a court battle can be very expensive. In 1986, Sears, Roebuck and Company asked the Equal Employment Opportunity Commission for some $12 million in attorneys' fees after the company's victory in its twelve-year discrimination fight with EEOC.[6]

The importance of effective staffing should not be underestimated. It is critical to the success of the organization; the direct and indirect costs are substantial; the organizational impacts are real; and the legal ramifications are potentially great.

STAFFING AND THE HUMAN RESOURCE
MANAGEMENT SYSTEM

The human resource management system in an organization comprises all those processes, activities, and tasks concerned with the acquisition, utilization, development, and rewarding of people in the workplace. Broadly speaking, all managers in a company are human resource managers because they have direct responsibility for people. The individual specifically designated as human resource or personnel manager is, in reality, the coordinator of the human resource management system, providing advice, expertise, and assistance to the other managers. While the personnel manager has responsibility for the proper functioning of the system, it is the operating managers who implement and use it.

The human resource management system is composed of six major subsystems or processes as shown in Figure 1.1. Staffing is the process that sets the other processes in motion; staffing also influences and in turn is influenced by the other five processes. The relationship between the other five parts of the human resource management system and staffing is described in the following paragraphs.

Compensation

Compensation consists of all of the rewards—tangible and intangible, monetary and non-monetary—that an organization provides its employees

Figure 1.1
Human Resource Management System

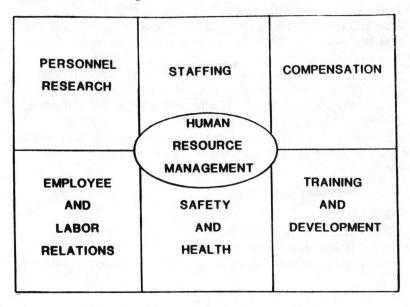

in exchange for the work they perform. This definition suggests that compensation is more than just pay, and it is. The three components of compensation are direct monetary rewards (wages and salaries), indirect financial payments (benefits and services), and psychological satisfactions (status, recognition, good working conditions, meaningful work, and so forth).

The compensation program a firm develops exerts a major influence on staffing. An inequitable compensation program may make constant recruiting necessary because employees leave the organization to take higher paying jobs elsewhere. Moreover, a poor compensation plan may increase the difficulty of finding sufficient numbers of qualified workers. On the other hand, an equitable compensation scheme can facilitate recruiting and increase the likelihood of hiring and retaining well-qualified employees.

How does staffing affect the compensation system? Primarily, through the employees it brings into the firm. If employees are consistently hired at the upper ends of the pay scales, the compensation plan may have to be changed frequently to maintain internal equity and external competitiveness. If employees are consistently hired at the lower ends of the pay scales, the compensation plan will have to be altered less frequently.

Training and Development

Training and development is concerned with improving the productivity of individuals, groups, and the entire organization. Training normally involves the imparting of skills that help workers to perform their present jobs better. Development is concerned with assisting employees to realize their full potential. These two efforts begin when the individual joins an organization and continues throughout the person's tenure with the firm.

Training and development has a significant impact on staffing. A company that has gained a reputation for providing excellent training and development—such as International Business Machines or Electronic Data Systems—may find it easier to attract and retain qualified employees. Turnover also may be reduced because workers are reluctant to leave an organization that provides the needed knowledge, skills, and learning experiences for attaining personal goals. Additionally, productivity is improved because employees are better able to perform their current jobs and to assume positions of higher responsibility when these positions become available.

Safety and Health

Safety and health include those things an organization does to protect employees from on-the-job injuries or work-related illnesses and to promote the general physical and mental well-being of employees, respectively.

While progressive companies have long been concerned with these factors, federal legislation, local regulations, and the development of a health-conscious attitude on the part of a large segment of the population have heightened the interest of organizations in safety and health matters.

How does safety and health relate to staffing? Different organizations project different images in this area. Some merely adhere to the minimum standards regarding safety and health while others respond vigorously to these concerns. The image that an institution projects and the reputation it has can either help or hinder the staffing process. A reputation for being concerned about safety and health facilitates staffing efforts; a reputation for lack of concern increases the difficulty of finding sufficient numbers of qualified employees to carry out the work of the company.

Employee and Labor Relations

Employee and labor relations are concerned with the way a company manages its work force and how it interacts with its union, if it has one.

Vitally important to each of us as employees is the concept of fairness in the employment relationship. Although fairness may not mean the same to each individual, we are all concerned, generally speaking, with equity in the workplace. In matters of discipline, promotion, demotion, layoff, termination, and pay we tend to value equity and consistency of treatment. Certainly, the reputation a firm has in employee relations either facilitates or hinders the staffing process. How management deals with its employees soon becomes public knowledge that either enhances or tarnishes the company's image.

Labor relations refers specifically to the organization's interactions with its union-represented employees. Again, it is reputation or image in this area that impacts positively or negatively on the staffing process.

Personnel Research

Personnel research is that human resource management process concerned with the gathering, analyzing, and interpreting of data. It permeates all of the other processes in the human resource system.

Personnel research provides information that may be used to improve the staffing process. Data on the types of employees who have proven to be the most succesful with the organization, turnover ratios, attitudes, accident frequencies, and productivity are often of assistance in recruiting, selecting, promoting, and planning personnel needs. Information gathered through research may be used to change staffing practices, revise procedures, or develop new policies in an effort to increase the effectiveness of staffing.

Obviously, all parts of the human resource management system must be integrated so that they do, in fact, function as a system. Staffing is affected by everything else that occurs in human resource management. Through the people it brings into the organization, staffing affects all of the other human resource processes. Actions taken in staffing must be carefully thought through to assess their actual or potential impact on other areas of managing people in the workplace.

THE STAFFING PROCESS

Although staffing is closely related to other human resource management functions, it can be viewed for purposes of analysis and study as a separate process with its own activities and objectives. The basic components of staffing are shown in Figure 1.2. Each of these components is briefly described below.

Job Analysis and Design

The activities associated with ascertaining the duties of a job and determining the skills required to perform those duties are referred to as job analysis. Since every process within the human resource management system utilizes and relies upon the information provided by job analysis, it can be considered to be the most fundamental of all personnel tasks and tools.

Job design is primarily concerned with how the work to be performed in an organization should be divided into pieces or "chunks" that can be handled by individual employees. Once work is analyzed to find out what has to be done and the skills required to do it, job design takes over and determines the manner in which specific tasks can be accomplished most effectively.

Job analysis answers the questions of "what specific duties must be performed?" and "what human qualifications are needed to perform these duties?" Job design answers the question of how the work can best be performed. Chapter 5 covers job analysis and design in detail.

Human Resource Planning

Determining the number of employees that an organization will need in the future and the kinds of skills those employees must possess is the task of human resource planning. Before many of the other staffing activities can be undertaken, human resource planning must be successfully completed. Chapter 6 explores this crucial topic.

Figure 1.2
The Staffing System

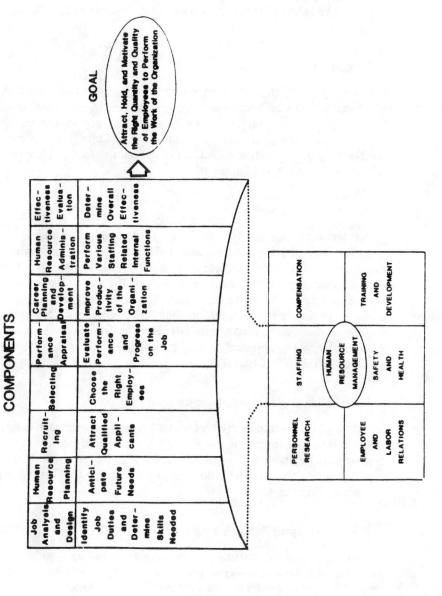

COMPONENTS

Job Analysis and Design	Human Resource Planning	Recruiting	Selecting	Performance Appraisal	Career Planning and Development	Human Resource Administration	Effectiveness Evaluation
Identify Job Duties and Determine Skills Needed	Anticipate Future Needs	Attract Qualified Applicants	Choose the Right Employees	Evaluate Performance and Progress on the Job	Improve Productivity of the Organization	Perform Various Staffing Related Internal Functions	Determine Overall Effectiveness

GOAL

Attract, Hold, and Motivate the Right Quantity and Quality of Employees to Perform the Work of the Organization

PERSONNEL RESEARCH	STAFFING	COMPENSATION
EMPLOYEE AND LABOR RELATIONS	HUMAN RESOURCE MANAGEMENT	TRAINING AND DEVELOPMENT
	SAFETY AND HEALTH	

Recruiting

Recruiting consists of those activities undertaken to encourage sufficient numbers of qualified people to apply for employment with an organization. Its primary purpose is to ensure that there is an adequate supply of applicants available at the appropriate time. Recruiting is the subject of Chapter 7.

Selecting

Choosing the applicant best qualified for a particular position is the goal of selecting. Some basic considerations in selecting are presented in Chapter 8. Because of their actual or potential importance in the selection of employees, employment tests are examined in Chapter 9. Interviewing, the most widely used selection tool and the most imperfectly utilized selection device, is discussed in Chapter 10.

Performance Appraisal

Performance appraisal is basically concerned with determining how well employees are carrying out their assigned tasks. It is also frequently used as a mechanism for identifying candidates for promotion and pay increases. Performance appraisal is an integral part of the staffing process for two reasons. First, it is the means through which employees are most often promoted to positions of higher responsibility. Second, it provides feedback information that can be used to evaluate the effectiveness of recruitment and selection activities, approaches, and procedures. Performance appraisal is explored in depth in Chapter 11.

Career Planning and Development

Career planning and development is a formalized approach taken by an organization to ensure that people with the proper qualifications and experience are available when needed. Its emphasis is on meshing the career aspirations of employees with the needs of the company. This subject is examined in Chapter 12.

Human Resource Administration

This portion of the staffing process involves handling a multitude of administrative details that begin when an employee is hired and continue throughout his or her tenure with the organization. Among the activities included here are promotions, demotions, transfers, resignations, terminations, retirements, layoffs, and the like. Human resource administration is covered in Chapter 13.

Evaluation of Effectiveness

Does the staffing process do what it is supposed to do? How well are the various activities carried out? Is staffing performed in a cost-effective manner? These are the kinds of questions that evaluation seeks to answer. The evaluation of staffing is discussed in Chapter 14.

Interrelationships within Staffing

Referring once again to Figure 1.2, we can see that each of the components of the staffing process is related to successful accomplishment of staffing's objective. Job analysis is the most basic component because it has a direct impact on every other aspect of staffing. Human resource planning is dependent upon job analysis, but it is also affected by the activities that occur in performance appraisal, career planning and development, and human resource administration. These activities determine the numbers and kinds of employees that are available for movement within the organization. Human resource planning forms the basis for recruiting additional employees, thus setting the recruiting activity in motion. Recruiting sets the selecting component in motion. The employees a firm hires then affect performance appraisal, career planning and development, and human resource administration. Evaluation of the effectiveness of staffing is affected by all activities performed in each of the other staffing processes. In short, anything that is done in any of the staffing components has an effect on what is done and how well it is done in the other components. Consequently, staffing must be viewed as an integrated activity if it is to be accomplished effectively. Policies, procedures, programs, and practices used in any particular component cannot be developed or implemented without carefully examining their potential impact on other areas of the staffing process.

THE ENVIRONMENTAL CONTEXT OF STAFFING

The entire human resource management system, which includes staffing, is affected by a series of external and internal environmental forces. The external environment consists of those factors that affect a firm's human resource system from outside the boundaries of the organization. Major external forces include the legal system, the economy, the work force and labor market, competitors, customers, technology, unions, and society at large. The internal environment consists of those factors within the organization itself that affect the human resource system, including the mission and objectives of the organization, corporate policies, organizational climate, management philosophy, and other functional areas within the company such as marketing and finance. Figure 1.3 depicts the various environmental forces.

The basic staffing tasks of an organization remain essentially the same no matter what impact is exerted by the external or internal environment. However, the manner in which these tasks are performed may be altered substantially by either or both environments. The ways in which the various environmental forces affect staffing are briefly examined below.

External Factors

Contemporary organizations are increasingly subject to and influenced by forces operative outside the organization. To a great extent, the way an institution does business and conducts its internal affairs is shaped or even determined by outside influences. Staffing, in particular, is affected by such environmental factors.

Figure 1.3
Environmental Context of Staffing

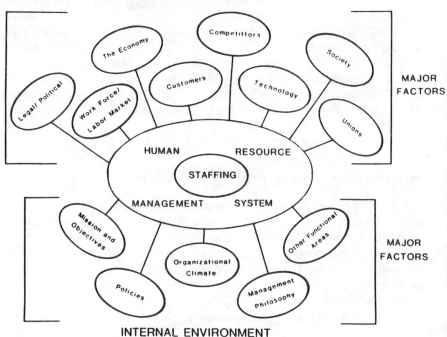

Legal System. The external force that has undoubtedly had—and will continue to have—the greatest effect on staffing is the legal system. Federal, state, and local laws regulate almost every aspect of staffing. Procedures must conform to legally imposed guidelines; policies must reflect the spirit as well as the letter of the law; practices must meet statutory standards. The legal system has dramatically altered the staffing process over the last twenty-five years. While the basic objective of staffing remains the same—securing sufficient numbers of qualified people at the right time—it must now be accomplished in accordance with a number of externally imposed requirements established by law.

Further compounding the effect of various laws and regulations is the increased willingness of employees or would-be employees to sue organizations over alleged violations of employment rights. The courts, too, seem more inclined to look with favor upon the claims of employees as evidenced by the number of cases won by employees and the amounts of settlements that firms have been ordered to pay. The result is that those involved in staffing must be fully cognizant of the legal system and the impact developments in this area are having on the performance of the staffing function.

Economy. The economic health of the country has a direct bearing on the accomplishment of staffing tasks. In times of vigorous economic growth as firms expand, competition for qualified employees intensifies and staffing activities are affected. Job analysis and human resource planning increase in importance with the addition of new jobs and the anticipation of when more employees will be required. Recruitment efforts are accelerated in the quest for qualified applicants. Selection becomes more difficult because of the wider range of employment opportunities open to applicants. Career planning, with its traditional emphasis on upward mobility in the organization, assumes greater importance as a means of attracting, holding, and motivating workers. Human resource administration activities increase as more employees are hired, promoted, transferred, or leave the organization.

In times of poor economic health, staffing is also directly affected. Job analysis and human resource planning activities tend to slow down. Recruitment efforts decrease because of the greater number of jobs applicants available. Selection is improved—at least potentially—due to the availability of a larger pool of applicants from which to choose. Career planning loses some of its emphasis. Layoffs, retirements, and transfers increase the workload for human resource administration.

In short, the state of the economy tends to increase or decrease the level or intensity of staffing activities as well as change the priority or importance attached to these activities.

Work Force/Labor Market. The work force consists of the total number of noninstitutionalized individuals, sixteen years of age and over, who are employed or who are unemployed but actively seeking employment. It represents the total number of individuals potentially available to all employers within this country. The work force also encompasses the mix of skills available as well as other factors of importance to employers.

The work force is dynamic, changing in numbers and characteristics over time. As these changes occur they affect the staffing process. Aggregate shortages of skills make it more difficult to attract and hold sufficient numbers of employees to perform the work of the organization. Surpluses simplify this task. A scarcity of qualified younger workers alters recruitment, selection, and career planning. An abundance of qualified older workers necessitates changes in staffing practices, policies, and philosophies. As will be seen in a later chapter, anticipating shifts in the work force is one of the tasks of human resource planning. Organizations that fail to recognize and plan for changes in the work force will find their staffing activities rendered more difficult.

The labor market is that geographical area—local, regional, national, or international—from which workers are usually recruited by an employer. It is a subset of the work force where supply of and demand for individuals with specific skills interact; consequently, it is of critical importance to an organization. For example, if the demand for particular skills is high relative to supply in a given labor market, an intensive recruiting effort may be required. Conversely, if supply exceeds demand, less vigorous recruiting may suffice. Since labor market conditions change frequently (much more rapidly, in fact, than does the work force), it is necessary to stay abreast of these changes to ensure continued effectiveness of the staffing process.

Competitors. Unless an organization monopolizes the market it serves, it will be forced to compete for sales with other institutions offering similar products or services. Likewise, unless an organization is the only user of particular skills in its labor market, it will be forced to compete with other firms for the talent needed to produce its goods or services. The degree of competition extant in the labor market influences the way staffing is conducted. Intensive competition for workers results in a rigorous approach to staffing; moderate competition produces a much less intensive approach. Moreover, the actions that competing labor market institutions take often suggest that a particular employer modify its staffing practices in order to remain competitive in the skills marketplace.

Customers. The people who actually use a firm's products or services are a vital part of the external environment. An organization has the task of ensuring that its employment practices do not antagonize the members of the market it serves. In some instances consumers have boycotted the products of organizations that paid substandard wages or failed to employ adequate numbers of minority workers.[7] To satisfy the perceptions of customers relative to its employment practices, an organization may have to revise its staffing practices.

Since customers are constantly demanding high-quality products and efficient service, organizations must strive to have employees who can provide these products or services. Product or service quality is directly related to the skills and qualifications of the institution's employees. Sales may be lost or gained depending upon the quality of employees that a firm has. Thus, customers exert pressure on an organization and affect its staffing practices.

Technology. Technology refers to the processes by which an organization converts inputs into goods and services. Computers and automation have drastically changed the conversion processes in most enterprises over the last twenty years and will alter these processes even more in the future. Masses of unskilled or semiskilled workers have been replaced by fewer highly skilled workers who program the computers and monitor the automated equipment. New skills are needed today to meet the demands of a new technology. These skills are typically still in short supply and it is often difficult to recruit sufficient numbers of qualified individuals for the jobs that are available. Competition in high-technology jobs is intense and employee turnover is usually high. Staffing practices, as a result, have to be changed to ensure that an organization has and will continue to have the right kinds of people available when they are needed.

Unions. Unions occupy the anomalous position of being both an external force as well as an internal force. They are perhaps best viewed, however, as an external force because they are a third party in their dealings with a company.

The manner in which staffing is conducted differs markedly in union and nonunion firms. In some few heavily unionized industries recruiting and selecting is done by the union itself. Human resource administration, too, is frequently dramatically altered when a company has a union: seniority is of paramount importance; layoff procedures are rigidly specified; bumping or regression rights are defined; terminations become more difficult. Also affected is performance appraisal—many labor agreements preclude its use altogether.

Although effective staffing is still of great importance in a unionized environment, procedures, practices, and policies may be quite different from those in a nonunionized firm and influence the way staffing is accomplished.

Society. Members of society, too, exert considerable influence on the staffing process in a company. The public at large is no longer content to accept without question the actions of institutions. People have found that changes in organizational practices can be made through the pressure of their voices and votes. This influence is evidenced by the number of regulatory statutes passed since the early 1960s.

The image a firm conveys to the general public can greatly affect the effectiveness of staffing. A reputation for fairness and integrity in dealing with employees can result in more and better qualified applicants seeking employment with a firm. Likewise, a firm that is concerned with producing safe products, of reasonable quality, and at fair prices may find its ability to attract employees increased.

Society generally expects an organization to be a good corporate citizen. To the extent the organization fulfills this expectation, it may facilitate its staffing activities.

The external environment places a great deal of pressure on staffing. There are expectations and demands to be satisfied; there are requirements to be met; there are challenges to be faced. It is important that the pressures brought by external forces be recognized clearly and that staffing activities be carried out in such a manner as to meet these external demands, pressures, requirements, challenges, and expectations in a positive fashion.

Internal Environment

The internal organizational environment has considerable influence on the way in which staffing is accomplished in an enterprise. As indicated in Figure 1.3, significant internal factors include mission and objectives, policies, organizational climate, management philosophy, and the other functional areas in the organization.

Mission and Objectives. Mission refers to an organization's overall reason for existence, its general purpose as an entity. Objectives are specific results to be achieved within a designated period of time. Mission and objectives define what an organization does and how it goes about doing it. They provide direction for an enterprise and thus influence and shape all other institutional activities.

Two very simplified examples will illustrate how mission and objectives relate to staffing. Company A has the goal of being a leader in its industry with respect to technological advances. Growth is expected to occur through the pioneering of new products and processes. Company B, on the other hand, has the goal of conservative growth with little risk taking. Only after another company's products have proven themselves in the marketplace will Company B commit itself to producing similar products.

In Company A, the firm will need a creative environment that encourages new ideas. Highly skilled, imaginative workers will have to be recruited and selected to bring about the desired technological advancement the company desires. On the other hand, the basic staffing tasks remain the same in Company B, but the objectives of the firm dictate that the tasks be altered considerably. A different kind of work force will need to be recruited and selected. Highly creative individuals are not essential to achieving Company B's goals.

As these simple examples show, overall company mission and objectives can and do influence the staffing process.

Policies. A policy is a general statement that guides thinking in decision making. Organizational policies establish parameters that assist managers and employees in the accomplishment of their jobs. Policies set the tone for what is done in a company as well as the manner in which it is done.

In a large organization policies are established for every area of operations—marketing, finance, accounting, production, engineering—but frequently the greatest number of policies relate to human resource management. Human resource policies reflect the tone of other corporate policy statements and set forth the kinds of actions to be taken relative to people. A company's policies say a great deal about the importance or lack of importance attached to staffing. For example, a promotion from within policy underscores an organization's commitment to preparing its present employees for advancement. Absence of such a policy suggests a lack of concern. In either case, policy or lack of policy influences the emphasis given to staffing activities.

Organizational Climate. The psychological atmosphere prevailing in a company is referred to as its organizational climate. An infinite number of possible climates exist. At one extreme is a negative, closed, and threatening climate. At the other extreme is a positive, open, and nurturing climate. The psychological atmosphere has a direct relationship to employee motivation, work quality, employee turnover, and absenteeism. A positive climate enhances motivation, improves work quality, decreases turnover, and reduces absenteeism. A negative climate has the opposite effect. In general, a positive climate makes the task of staffing easier while a negative climate makes it more difficult.

Management Philosophy. The prevailing values of management—often referred to as corporate culture—affect everyone and everything in an organization. The way management feels about people and the actions it takes with them speak much more loudly than platitudinous pronouncements and lofty-sounding policies. Values, philosophy, and culture influence staffing and how it is carried out. Management beliefs and actions that suggest a genuine interest in and concern for people in an organization have a positive impact on staffing. Beliefs and actions that suggest lack of interest and concern have a deleterious effect.

Other Functional Areas. Marketing, finance, production, and all other functional areas in an organization have an effect on the staffing process. For example, if the work performed in the manufacturing area is boring, dirty, or dangerous, staffing specialists may be forced to recruit continuously to ensure that production has sufficient numbers of qualified people because turnover is likely to be quite high. Or, if the product or service of the firm is difficult to sell, constant recruiting may be necessary to keep the marketing function at full strength. Conversely, if the work performed in finance is challenging and exciting, employee turnover is likely to be low and there may be a ready pool of applicants to fill any vacancies that do occur. Thus, the actual work that is performed, the way it is performed, and the conditions under which it is carried out may greatly influence the work of staffing.

The internal environment shapes and molds the way staffing is accomplished in a firm; it influences the importance that is attached to each staffing task; it determines to a large extent the effectiveness with which staffing will be performed.

NOTES

1. *The Nurse Recruiter*, February 1982, p. 1.

2. Arlene A. Johnson, "Relocation: Getting More for the Dollars You Spend," *Personnel Administrator*, April 1984, p. 29.

3. "Personnel Activities, Budgets, and Staffs: 1984-1985," *Bulletin to Management*, May 23, 1985, p. 7.

4. Richard D. Arvey, *Fairness in Selecting Employees* (Reading, Mass.: Addison-Wesley, 1979), p. 1.

5. *Fair Employment Report*, April 9, 1984, p. 59.

6. "Sears Seeking Lawyer Fees: EEOC Appeals," *Resource*, May 1986, p. 9.

7. S. Prakesh Sethi, *Up Against the Corporate Wall* (Englewood Cliffs, N. J.: Prentice-Hall, 1971), pp. 107-28.

2

Staffing Legislation and Regulation

As mentioned in the previous chapter, one of the most important external forces affecting an organization's staffing policies and practices is the legal system. Virtually every phase of staffing—from recruitment to selection, from compensation to termination, from performance appraisal to promotion—is covered in some fashion by federal legislation or administrative regulations. This chapter briefly examines the most prominent affecting staffing.

FEDERAL LEGISLATION

Prior to the 1930s, organizations, with few exceptions, enjoyed wide latitude in employment practices and employee relations. With the coming of the New Deal under President Franklin Roosevelt, specific, but still limited, rights of workers began to receive protection under federal legislation. The civil rights movement of the 1960s ushered in a whole new age of federal protection for employees and job applicants and produced a dramatic revision of staffing practices and employee relations—a revision that is still continuing. Described below in chronological order are the statutes that have made staffing the legalistic challenge that it is today.

Civil Rights Act of 1866

The oldest piece of federal legislation affecting staffing is the Civil Rights Act of 1866, which is based on the Thirteenth Amendment to the U.S. Constitution. Specifically, this Act provides that all citizens have the same right "as enjoyed by white citizens . . . to inherit, purchase, . . . hold, and convey . . . property," and that "all persons . . . shall have the same right to make and enforce contracts . . . as enjoyed by white citizens." As interpreted by the courts, employment as well as membership in a union is a contractual arrangement. Thus, if a black is denied employment, promotion, union membership, or any other employment advantages or opportunities because of his or her race, the courts have held that the right to make a contract has been violated. Whites and Hispanics are also covered by this Act if they are discriminated against on the basis of race. Until 1968 it was assumed that the Act was applicable only when action by a state or state agency and not by private parties was involved. The Supreme Court overruled this assumption and broadened the interpretation of the Act to cover *all* contractual arrangements. Interestingly, the Civil Rights Act of 1866 has no statute of limitations attached to it.[1]

Civil Rights Act of 1871

This Act is based on the Fourteenth Amendment to the U.S. Constitution, which guarantees all citizens the right to equal protection under the law. Originally referred to as the "Ku Klux Klan Act," the Civil Rights Act of 1871 makes it illegal for two or more persons to conspire to deprive any person or class of persons of the right of equal protection under the law. It has been held by the federal courts that where two or more officials of a corporation, the employer and its employees, or two or more employees have conspired among themselves to deny equal rights to a person or persons on the basis of race, a violation of the statute has occurred. The Act applies to private enterprises and parties as well as states and local governments. While the Act has no effective statute of limitations, limitations provided for in Title VII of the Civil Rights Act of 1964 or by those expressed in state tortious conspiracies are normally adhered to.[2]

National Labor Relations Act of 1935

Commonly known as the Wagner Act, this legislation gives employees the right to form unions and requires employers to recognize unions of employees and to bargain with them in good faith relative to wages, hours of work, and other terms and conditions of employment. As specified in the Act, "Employees shall have the right to self-organization, to form, join, or assist labor organizations, to bargain collectively through representatives of their own choosing, and to engage in other concerted activities, for the purpose of collective bargaining or other mutual aid or protection." The rights given to employees are protected against interference by employers. Specifically, employers are prohibited from: (1) interfering with, restraining, or coercing employees in their exercise of the right to form unions; (2) dominating a union or interfering in the affairs of a union; (3) discriminating against employees in regard to hiring, job tenure, or any condition of employment for the purpose of encouraging or discouraging union membership; (4) discriminating against or terminating an employee who has filed an unfair labor charge or has given testimony under the Act; and (5) refusing to bargain in good faith with the chosen representatives of employees.[3]

Also created by the Act was the National Labor Relations Board, which has the responsibility of conducting elections to determine if employees wish to be represented by a union, determining which of two competing unions will be certified as the bargaining agent for a group of employees, preventing unfair labor practices in the area of unionization activities, and investigating reported claims of unfair labor practices.

Social Security Act of 1935, as Amended

This Act created the Social Security Administration and established the existing system of old age, survivors, disability, and unemployment compensation insurance.[4] Employees and employers share equally the cost of old age, survivors, and disability insurance—those items that are commonly described as Social Security. Employers pay the full cost of unemployment insurance, the funding of which is accomplished through a payroll tax. Unemployment benefits are paid through state agencies in each of the fifty states. The Act also created a minimum period of twenty-six weeks of unemployment compensation for employees who meet the qualifications for such compensation.

Fair Labor Standards Act of 1938, as Amended

Popularly known as the Wage and Hour Act, this statute established a minimum wage for the vast majority of workers in the private sector of the economy.[5] Also established was the standard work week of forty hours. Workers covered by this statute are divided into two categories: exempt and non-exempt. Non-exempt workers must be compensated at a rate of one and one-half times their regular hourly rate of pay for hours worked in excess of forty during a given work week. A work week is defined as a recurring period of 168 hours or seven consecutive 24-hour periods. The work week does not have to conform to the calendar week and it may begin at any hour of the day. Exempt employees—managers, administrators, and professionals—are excluded from the overtime pay requirement. Additionally, the Act set the minimum working age for covered employment at sixteen; if the work is considered hazardous, the minimum working age is eighteen.

Labor-Management Relations Act of 1947

This statute, an amendment to the National Labor Relations Act of 1935, was enacted with the express intent of restoring a balance of power between unions and management.[6] Usually referred to as the Taft-Hartley Act, it altered union-management relations by: (1) protecting the right of employees to refrain from as well as engage in union activity; (2) prohibiting the closed shop (an arrangement that required all workers to be union members at the time they were hired); (3) narrowing the freedom of the bargaining parties to authorize the union shop (under a union shop arrangement the employer is free to hire anyone it chooses, but all new workers must join the union within a stipulated period of time or they will be terminated); (4) granting the employer greater freedom of speech when faced with an attempt to unionize workers; (5) granting management the right to refuse to recognize or bargain with unions of supervisory personnel; (6) giving employees the right to initiate decertification proceedings should they no longer desire to be represented by a union; (7) providing for government intervention to halt strikes for an eighty-day "cooling off" period where such strikes would create a "national emergency" detrimental to the welfare of the country; and (8) giving states the power to enact so-called right-to-work laws precluding the union shop arrangement.

A significant feature of the Labor-Management Relations Act was that it extended the concept of unfair labor practices to unions. Previously, such practices had been limited to management alone. Under the Act specific unfair labor practices on the part of unions consist of: (1) restraining or coercing employees in the exercise of their collective bargaining rights, (2) causing an employer to discriminate in any fashion against an employee in order to encourage or discourage union membership, (3) refusing to bargain in good faith with an employer, (4) engaging in certain types of strikes or boycotts, (5) requiring employees to pay initiation fees or dues that are excessive or discriminatory, and (6) requiring an employer to pay for services not performed by workers.

The Act also created the Federal Mediation and Conciliation Service and assigned it the responsibility for assisting employers and unions in negotiating new contracts when the parties have reached an impasse in negotiations and for maintaining a panel of qualified arbitrators to settle union-management grievances.

Equal Pay Act of 1963, as Amended

The Act is an amendment to the Fair Labor Standards Act of 1938 and covers the same employers as FLSA.[7] The statute makes it illegal for an employer to discriminate in pay on the basis of sex where jobs require equal skill, effort, and responsibility and are performed under similar working conditions. Pay differentials between sexes are permitted when such differences are based on seniority systems, merit systems, production-related pay plans (wage incentives), or factors other than sex. Premium pay differences for working undesirable shifts are also allowed. In 1972 the Act was amended to cover employees in executive, administrative, professional, and outside sales positions as well as employees in most state and local governments, hospitals, and schools. Over the years, the Act has become less significant because a violation of the Equal Pay Act is also a violation of Title VII of the Civil Rights Act of 1964, a broader and more powerful statute.

Title VII of the Civil Rights Act of 1964, as Amended

The one statute that has had the greatest impact on human resource management is Title VII of the Civil Rights Act of 1964, as amended by the Equal Employment Act of 1972.[8] Under Title VII it is illegal for an employer to discriminate in hiring, firing, promoting, compensating, or in terms, conditions, or privileges of employment on the basis of race, color, sex, religion, or national origin.

Title VII covers employers engaged in or affecting interstate commerce who have fifteen or more employees for each working day in each of twenty calendar weeks in the current or preceding calendar year. Also included in the definition of employers are state and local governments, schools, colleges, unions, and private employment agencies that procure employees for an employer having fifteen or more employees.

Three notable exceptions to discrimination as covered by Title VII are bona fide occupational qualifications (BFOQ), seniority and merit systems, and testing and educational requirements. According to the Act it is not "an unlawful employment practice for an employer to hire and employ employees . . . on the basis of his religion, sex, or national origin in those certain instances where religion, sex, or national origin is a bona fide occupational qualification reasonably necessary to the normal operation of the particular business or enterprise." Thus, for example, religious institutions such as churches or synagogues may legally refuse to hire individuals whose religious persuasion is different from that of the hiring institution. Likewise, a maximum security correctional institution housing only male inmates may decline to hire females as security guards. The concept of bona fide occupational qualification was designed to be narrowly, not broadly, interpreted and has been so construed by the courts in a number of cases. The burden of proving the necessity for a BFOQ rests entirely on the employer.

The second exception to discrimination under Title VII is a bona fide seniority system such as the type normally contained in a union contract. Differences in employment conditions among workers are permitted "provided that such differences are not the result of an intention to discriminate because of race, color, religion, sex, or national origin. . . ." Even though a bona fide seniority system has a disparate or adverse impact on those individuals protected by Title VII, the system can only be invalidated by evidence that the actual motives of the parties to the agreement was to discriminate.

In the matter of testing and educational requirements, Title VII states that it is not "an unlawful employment practice for an employer to give and to act upon the results of any professionally developed ability test provided that such test, its administration, or action upon the results is not designed, intended or used to discriminate because of race, color, religion, sex, or national origin. . . ." Any employment testing and educational requirements must be job related, and the burden of proof is on the employer to show that a demonstrable relationship exists between actual job performance and the test or educational requirement.

Other exceptions to Title VII include aliens (noncitizens are not protected from discrimination because they are not citizens; however, they are protected from discrimination based on their national origin) and members of the communist party. As an interesting aside, homosexuals are not protected under Title VII either. The courts have consistently ruled that where the term "sex" is used in any federal statute that term refers to biological gender and not to sexual preference.

The Civil Rights Act of 1964 also created the Equal Employment Opportunity Commission and assigned enforcement of Title VII to this agency. The EEO Commission consists of five presidentially appointed members and is empowered to investigate, conciliate, and litigate charges of discrimination arising under provisions of Title VII. Additionally, the commission has the responsibility of issuing procedural regulations and interpretations of Title VII and the other statutes it enforces. The most significant regulation issued by EEOC, to be discussed in the next chapter, is the *Uniform Guidelines on Employee Selection Procedures.*

When a charge is filed under Title VII, EEOC investigates the evidence to determine if there is a possible violation of the statute. Where there is a state or local agency similar to EEOC that meets EEOC standards, the complaint is first referred to that agency.[9] In the event that the complaint is deferred to a state or local agency, the deferral agency has at least sixty days of exclusive jurisdiction over the charge. After sixty days, or if the deferral agency has terminated its proceedings or waived jurisdiction, the EEOC assumes jurisdiction over the complaint. Title VII requires deferral to a state or local agency where one exists, and if EEOC fails to defer, it may lose not only its jurisdiction but also its ability to conduct an investigation.

If EEOC finds no probable cause for a case after its investigation, it ends its involvement and notifies the complainant that he or she has the right to pursue the case in federal court. (However, the complainant retains the right to pursue his or her case in court at any time—before, during, or after EEOC or other agency involvement.) If EEOC's investigation finds that there is probable cause for a discrimination charge, the first attempt at settlement will be through a process called conciliation—a negotiated arrangement between the complainant, the employer, and EEOC that is satisfactory to all parties and adequately compensates the victim or victims of discrimination and meets the standards set by EEOC.

Failing to achieve a settlement by conciliation, EEOC next has the option to file suit in federal district court against the employer in question. Whether EEOC will pursue litigation is usually contingent upon five factors: (1) the number of people affected by the alleged practice, (2) the amount of monetary settlement involved, (3) the number of other discrimination charges brought against the employer, (4) the type of charge involved, and (5) the opportunity to establish legal principle or precedent in discriminatory matters. Because litigation involves the commitment of considerable resources, EEOC's court actions are generally limited to important cases that are likely to be favorable to the agency and have a far-reaching impact on employment practices. In other words, EEOC does not take court action lightly.

Under Title VII, charges may be filed by any of the EEOC commissioners, any aggrieved person, or anyone acting on behalf of an aggrieved person; for example, an attorney. The time limit for filing charges is 180 days after the occurrence of the alleged discriminatory act. If the complainant is first required to file the charge with a state or local agency, the time limit for filing with EEOC is extended to 300 days.

The Civil Rights Act of 1964 also prohibits retaliation against employees who have opposed an allegedly illegal employment practice. Anyone who testifies, assists, or participates in discriminatory proceedings is also protected.

Age Discrimination in Employment Act of 1967, as Amended

This Act protects individuals over the age of forty from discrimination by employers in matters of hiring, job retention, job privileges, and other terms and conditions of employment.[10] Covered under ADEA are employers with twenty or more employees for twenty or more calendar weeks (either in the current or preceding calendar year), unions with twenty-five or more members, employment agencies, and federal, state, or local governments.

A 1986 amendment to ADEA prohibits mandatory retirement of most private sector employees at age seventy; however, high-level executives may be retired at age sixty-five if they are entitled to immediate, nonforfeitable pensions or deferred compensation of at least $27,000 annually. A 1978 amendment had previously eliminated the maximum retirement age of seventy for federal employees.

An exception to the provisions of the Act provides that age may be used as a bona fide occupational qualification in those instances where age is reasonably necessary for business operations or safety factors;[11] for example, actors and actresses required for youthful roles, persons employed to advertise or promote the sale of products designed for youthful consumers, or intercity bus drivers. Age is also a bona fide occupational qualification where federal statutory or regulatory requirements impose a compulsory age limitation as in the case of the Federal Aviation Agency requirement that sets a ceiling of age sixty for commercial airline pilots.

ADEA differs from Title VII in that it provides for trial by jury and there is a possible criminal aspect to an age discrimination charge. Trial by jury has significant implications for employers inasmuch as jurors may have greater sympathy for older persons who allegedly have been discriminated against. The punitive aspect means that an employee may receive more than lost wages if discrimination is proven.

Rehabilitation Act of 1973, as Amended

This statute covers government contractors, subcontractors, or organizations receiving federal monies in excess of $2,500.[12] Individuals are considered handicapped if they have a physical or mental impairment that substantially limits one or more major life activities, have a record of such impairment, or are regarded as having such an impairment. Only physical or mental impairments are covered by the Act. Disadvantages arising from environmental, cultural, or economic factors are not covered. Clearly protected, however, are such diseases and conditions as epilepsy, cancer, cardiovascular disorders, blindness, deafness, mental retardation, emotional disorders, and dyslexia. Under certain circumstances, alcoholism and narcotics addiction are also protected.

The Rehabilitation Act is administered by the Office of Federal Contract Compliance Programs, which investigates and attempts to settle (normally through conciliation where possible, but through litigation if necessary) complaints of discrimination. There is no private right of action under the Act; consequently, the complainant must file a complaint with OFCCP within 180 days of the alleged discriminatory act, at which point OFCCP assumes responsibility for all further action.

There are two primary levels of the Act. All contractors or subcontractors exceeding the $2,500 base are required to post notices that they agree to take affirmative action (that is, positive steps over and above normal practices) to recruit, employ, and promote qualified handicapped individuals. If the contract or subcontract exceeds $50,000, or if the contractor has fifty or more employees, the employer must prepare a written affirmative action plan for review by OFCCP.

Vietnam Era Veterans Readjustment Assistance Act of 1974

This Act, administered by the Department of Labor, covers disabled and other veterans of the Vietnam era.[13] It relates only to government contractors or subcontractors having contracts with the federal government of $10,000 or more. Under the provisions of this statute a contractor is precluded from discriminating against any employee or applicant for employment because he or she is a disabled or other veteran of the Vietnam era. The contractor must take affirmative action to employ, promote, and avoid discrimination against covered individuals in all areas of employment practices. Honorably discharged veterans and other veterans of the Vietnam era who served more than 180 days on active duty between August 5, 1964 and May 7, 1975 are covered. Disabled veterans are defined as those individuals with a compensable disability rated at 30 or more percent by the Veterans Administration. Also included are those persons whose discharge or release from active duty was for a disability incurred or aggravated in the line of duty. In addition, the person must have separated from the military service within forty-eight months prior to the alleged violation.

A major provision of the Act is that covered organizations must list virtually all job openings with the local state employment office. These listings must be provided concurrently with the utilization of other recruiting sources. Organizations with fifty or more employees who have received contracts for over $50,000 must maintain an affirmative action program. Because of the affirmative action requirement, contractors must provide a schedule for review of all physical and mental job qualifications. This requirement is intended to ensure that all job specifications are actually job related.

Pregnancy Discrimination Act of 1978

Passed as an amendment to Title VII of the Civil Rights Act of 1964, as amended, the Pregnancy Discrimination Act prohibits discrimination in employment based on pregnancy, childbirth, or related medical condition such as an abortion.[14] The basic premise of the Act is that women affected by pregnancy or related conditions must be treated the same as other applicants and employees not so affected but similar in their ability or inability to work. A pregnant woman or one affected by a related condition is therefore protected from being refused a job, denied a promotion, or being fired merely because she is pregnant, has recently delivered, or has had an abortion. An employer generally cannot cause a woman to take a leave of absence as long as she, under the advice of her physician, is able to work.

Likewise, the employer cannot require a woman who has delivered to remain off work for a set period of time after the delivery. If other employees on a disability leave are entitled to return to their jobs when they are able to work again, the same right must be granted to women who have been unable to work because of pregnancy and subsequent delivery.

In the benefits area—health insurance, sick leave, and disability coverage—the same principle applies. A woman unable to work for pregnancy-related reasons is entitled to disability benefits or sick leave on the same basis as employees unable to work for other medical reasons. Also, any health insurance provided must cover expenses for pregnancy-related conditions on the same basis as expenses for other medical conditions. However, health insurance for expenses arising from abortion is not required except where the life of the mother would have been endangered if the fetus were carried to term or where medical complications have arisen from an abortion.

The net effect of the pregnancy discrimination amendments to Title VII has been to raise the cost of employee benefit plans and penalize employers who have vigorously pursued affirmative action plans to increase their numbers of female employees.

As the foregoing review has indicated, the field of human resource management has become quite legalistic in nature. Consequently, a general awareness of the statutory framework is imperative for human resource personnel—and especially staffing specialists—in order to avoid employment practices that are proscribed by law.

EXECUTIVE ORDERS

An Executive Order is a directive issued by the president of the United States, without legislative authority, stipulating the terms and conditions under which the federal government will do business with private sector employers or regulating the employment practices of the government itself. Executive Orders cover only those private employers who do business with the government and have thus entered into a contract whereby they agree, as a condition of the contract, to abide by the terms and conditions set forth by the government.

The two Executive Orders that have had a significant impact on employment practices of firms doing business with the federal government are Executive Order 11246 and Executive Order 11375, an amendment to the former Order.

Executive Order 11246, as Amended by Executive Order 11375

Executive Order 11246 was signed by President Lyndon Johnson on September 24, 1965.[15] This Executive Order made it the policy of the government to provide equal opportunity in federal employment for all qualified persons. Discrimination in employment because of race, creed, color, or national origin was prohibited. The Order also required promoting the full realization of equal employment opportunity in the federal sector through a positive, continuing program of affirmative action in each executive department and governmental agency. The policy of equal opportunity applies to every aspect of federal employment policy, procedure, and practice.

A major provision of Executive Order 11246 requires that all executive departments or agencies that issue contracts to employers or that administer a program involving federal financial assistance to employers must make certain that employers adhere to a policy of nondiscrimination in employment as a condition for the approval of a contract, grant, loan, insurance, or guarantee. The "equal opportunity clause" in the contract or grant stipulates that the employer: (1) will not discriminate against any applicant or employee because of race, creed, color, or national origin; (2) will take affirmative action to increase the number of minorities or protected classes in the employer's work force; (3) agrees to follow the rules, regulations, and requirements set forth by the Executive Order 11246; (4) will furnish all information that may be required; (5) state its policy of nondiscrimination in employment advertisements; (6) notify any union with which it has a labor agreement of its policy of nondiscrimination and its intention to follow the requirements of the Order; and (7) include an equal opportunity clause in each subcontract that it issues.

Employment practices covered by this regulation include recruiting, employment advertising, selecting, promoting, demoting, transferring, layoffs, terminations, rates of pay and other compensation, and selection for training, including apprenticeship programs. Employers are also required to post notices, in conspicuous places such as employee bulletin boards, relative to their nondiscriminatory policies.

In the event of non-compliance, contracts can be cancelled, terminated, or suspended in whole or part, and the contractor may be declared ineligible for further government contracts.

In 1968, Executive Order 11246 was amended by Executive Order 11375. The word "creed" was changed to "religion" and sex discrimination was added to the other prohibited forms of discrimination.

All first or second tier government contractors with contracts in excess of $10,000 are covered under this regulation. Contractors with contracts of $50,000 or more must also file EEO-1 reports (to be discussed in Chapter 4) and develop a written affirmative action plan. It is interesting to note that these affirmative action requirements are not established by the Executive Order itself, but by OFCCP regulations. Contractors having contracts of $1 million or more must meet all of the previous stipulations and must undergo an on-site pre-award compliance review.

The Secretary of Labor established the Office of Federal Contract Compliance Programs and gave it the power and responsibility for administering and enforcing Executive Order 11246.[16] The OFCCP has set forth regulations that apply to both federal contractors and subcontractors. Under Executive Order 12086 issued by President Carter in 1978, OFCCP has the responsibility for conducting equal employment opportunity compliance reviews for contracts issued by the Department of Defense, the General Services Administration, Housing and Urban Development, the Department of Transportation, the Department of the Interior, the Environmental Protection Agency, the Treasury Department, the Department of Commerce, and the Small Business Administration. When there is reason to believe that a contractor has violated the equal opportunity clause in a contract, the director is empowered to institute proceedings to correct the violation. The contractor in question must be given a full hearing in front of an administrative law judge before OFCCP can impose any sanctions against the contractor. As previously stated, OFCCP can cancel or suspend contracts for failure to comply with equal opportunity requirements. OFCCP also has the power to prohibit federal agencies from entering into new contracts with contractors that have been declared ineligible.

STATE AND LOCAL LAWS

In addition to federal legislation and administrative regulations governing staffing practices, there are numerous state and local laws that affect human resource management.[17] Highly industrialized states such as Michigan, Wisconsin, Illinois, New York, and California frequently serve as trendsetters, passing state statutes on employment rights well before Congress enacts similar federal legislation. At times, state legislation is even more stringent than that at the federal level. For example, in New York the protected age group is from eighteen to sixty-five and an employer cannot discriminate against anyone in that group on the basis of age. Age-based retirement is illegal except in a few occupations. In California there is no top limit on age. However, in the majority of instances, federal legislation sets the pattern for subsequent state statutes.

A number of states and even some cities have passed fair employment practice laws that prohibit discrimination on the basis of race, color, religion, sex, or national origin. Several states also have anti-discrimination laws protecting the handicapped. When federal legislation conflicts with state or local fair employment practices regulations, the law that most favors the employee or the protected class of employees is the one that will be followed. This means that federal statutes are the ones adhered to in the vast majority of cases.

Because state and local laws vary greatly, it is outside the scope of this book to attempt to examine or compare them. It is important, though, that human resource personnel (and staffing specialists in particular) familiarize themselves with the numerous state and local regulations relative to employment practices in the locales where their companies do business. Failure to do so may make an already complicated legal environment even more difficult to contend with.

SUMMARY

This chapter has dealt with a number of federal laws and regulations that are often confusing. To alleviate some of this confusion and to help the human resource professional sift through some of the complexity involved, Table 2-1 presents a capsule summary of the legislation and Executive Orders that have been discussed. This table shows the major provisions of each regulation, who is covered by each regulation, and the federal agency responsible for enforcement of the regulatory provisions.

Table 2.1
Summary of Major Staffing Legislation

Law	Major Provisions	Coverage	Enforcement Agency
CIVIL RIGHTS ACT OF 1866	Gives all citizens the same rights as "white citizens."	All employers other than the federal government; unions.	Federal court system after individual files suit.
CIVIL RIGHTS ACT OF 1871	Guarantees all citizens the right to equal protection under the law. Makes it illegal for two or more persons to conspire to deprive any person or class of persons of the right of equal protection under the law.	All employers other than the federal government; unions.	Federal court system after individual files suit.
NATIONAL LABOR RELATIONS ACT OF 1935	Gives employees the right to form union, bargain collectively, and engage in other activities for their mutual aid and protection. Requires employers to bargain in good faith with unions in matters of wages, hours of work, and other terms and conditions of employment. Establishes mechanism and procedures for conducting elections to determine if employees wish to be represented by a union or which of two competing unions will be certified as bargaining agent.	Most employers and non-managerial employees in private sector.	National Labor Relations Board

	Defines unfair labor practices on part of employer. Establishes the National Labor Relations Board.		
SOCIAL SECURITY ACT of 1935, AS AMENDED	Creates system of old age, survivors, disability, and unemployment insurance. Levies federal tax to fund social security benefits. Creates minimum period of 26 weeks unemployment compensation. Establishes Social Security Administration.	All employers and employees.	Social Security Administration
FAIR LABOR STANDARDS ACT OF 1938, AS AMENDED	Sets minimum wage for most workers. Establishes standard 20-hour workweek. Requires time and half payment for hours worked in excess of 40 per week. Exempts certain classifications of employees from overtime pay requirement. Sets minimum age for employment. Sets minimum hourly wage rate.	Employers involved in interstate commerce with two or more employees and annual revenues greater than $362,500.	Wage and Hour Division of the Employment Standards Administration, Department of Labor.

Table 2.1 (continued)

LABOR-MANAGEMENT RELATIONS ACT OF 1947	Protects right of employees to refrain from as well as engage in union activity.	Most employers and non-managerial employees in private sector.	National Labor Relations Board
	Prohibits the closed shop.		
	Allows states the right to enact legislation banning the union shop.		
	Gives employers the right to refuse to recognize unions of supervisory personnel.		
	Defines unfair labor practices on part of unions.		
	Defines national emergency strikes and empowers the President to impose an 80-day "cooling off" period to postpone such strikes.		
	Creates the Federal Mediation and Conciliation Service to assist employer and union in negotiating new contracts and arbitrating grievances.		
EQUAL PAY ACT OF 1963, AS AMENDED	Prohibits discrimination in pay on basis of sex where jobs are performed under similar conditions and require equal skill, effort, and responsibility.	Same as Fair Labor Standards Act of 1938, As Amended.	Equal Employment Opportunity Commission

34

Law	Provisions	Coverage	Enforcement Agency
TITLE VII, CIVIL RIGHTS ACT OF 1964, AS AMENDED	Permits pay differentials between sexes where such differences are based on seniority systems, merit systems, wage incentive plans, or factors other than sex. Prohibits discrimination in hiring, firing, promoting, compensating, or in terms, conditions, or privileges of employment on the basis of race, color, sex, religion, or national origin. Permits discrimination in employment on the basis of race, religion, sex, or national origin where any of these factors are bona fide occupational qualifications necessary to the operation of an enterprise. Permits bona fide seniority, merit, or incentive systems that have the effect of discriminating provided such systems are not the result of an intention to discriminate.	Employers with 15 or more employees; unions with 15 members; employment agencies; state and local governments.	Equal Employment Opportunity Commission
AGE DISCRIMINATION IN EMPLOYMENT ACT OF 1967, AS AMENDED	Prohibits discrimination in hiring, job retention, job privileges, and terms and conditions of employment for	Employers with 20 employees; unions with 25 members; employment agencies; federal,	Equal Employment Opportunity commission

35

Table 2.1 (continued)

	individuals over the age of 40. Eliminates mandatory retirement of employees at age 70.	state, and local governments.	
REHABILITATION ACT OF 1973, AS AMENDED	Prohibits discrimination in employment on basis of physical or mental impairment that limits one or more major life activities. Requires affirmative action by employers to hire the handicapped.	Federal contractors and subcontractors with contracts of $2,500 or more; other organizations receiving federal assistance of $2,500 or more; federal government.	Office of Federal Contract Compliance Programs, Department of Labor
VIETNAM ERA VETERANS READJUSTMENT ASSISTANCE ACT OF 1974	Prohibits discrimination in employment against veterans of Vietnam era. Requires affirmative action by employers to hire and promote Vietnam veterans.	Federal contractors or subcontractors with contracts of $10,000 or more.	Office of Federal Contract Compliance Programs, Department of Labor
PREGNANCY DISCRIMINATION ACT OF 1978	Prohibits discrimination in employment based on pregnancy, child, birth, or related medical condition.	Employers with 15 employees; unions with 25 members; employment agencies; federal, state, and local governments	Equal Employment Opportunity Commission
EXECUTIVE ORDERS 11246 AND 11375	Prohibits discrimination in employment on basis of race, religion, color, national origin, or sex.	Federal contractors and subcontractors with contracts of $10,000 or more; federal government.	Office of Federal Contract Compliance Programs, Department of Labor

NOTES

1. Howard C. Lockwood, "Equal Employment Opportunities," in Dale Yoder and Herbert G. Heneman, eds., *Staffing Policies and Strategies* (Washington, D.C.: Bureau of National Affairs, 1974), pp. 4-252.

2. Barbara Lindemann Schlei and Paul Grossman, *Employment Discrimination Law*, 2nd ed. (Washington, D.C.: Bureau of National Affairs, 1983), p. 692.

3. R. Wayne Mondy and Robert M. Noe, *Personnel: The Management of Human Resources*, 3rd ed. (Boston: Allyn and Bacon, 1987), p. 545.

4. Donald L. Caruth, *Compensation Management for Banks* (Boston: Bankers Publishing Company, 1986), pp. 252-53.

5. Ibid., p. 253.

6. Mondy and Noe, *Personnel*, pp. 546-48.

7. Caruth, *Compensation Management*, p. 254.

8. Mondy and Noe, *Personnel*, pp. 63, 68.

9. Kenneth J. McCulloch, *Selecting Employees Safely under the Law* (Englewood Cliffs, N.J.: Prentice-Hall, 1981), pp. 182-83.

10. Mondy and Noe, *Personnel*, pp. 66-67.

11. Schlei and Grossman, *Employment Discrimination Law*, pp. 507-17.

12. Mondy and Noe, *Personnel*, p. 67.

13. Schlei and Grossman, *Employment Discrimination Law*, p. 276.

14. Mondy and Noe, *Personnel*, pp. 68-69.

15. Ibid., p. 71.

16. Ibid., pp. 71-72.

17. Ibid., pp. 69-70.

3

Significant Federal Court Decisions

Because law is a dynamic thing that changes as the courts interpret and apply it in various cases, personnel practitioners must know much more than just the letter of the law as expressed in the statutes that affect them. They must also understand the spirit of the law as defined by the courts. Interpretation of the law is revised continuously as court decisions are rendered, even though the statutes in question have not been altered by further legislative action. Consequently, it is imperative for human resource professionals to understand how the courts have applied and interpreted the law in previous situations. Thus, it is appropriate to review some of the more significant federal court decisions and indicate the requirements imposed by these decisions.

SUPREME COURT DECISIONS

As the final interpreter of the law, the Supreme Court actually decides how the various federal statutes will be applied. Decisions rendered by the Court become, in effect, the "law of the land" and are binding on all entities in the country. It is vitally important, therefore, to understand how the Court has ruled on the application of federal statutes relative to staffing. A review of several major cases will illustrate the Court's interpretation of the spirit of the law in employment situations.

Griggs v. *Duke Power Company* (3 FEP 175)

Decided by the Supreme Court in March 1971, *Griggs* is the landmark case in human resource management and has had the most far-reaching impact on employment practices of any case decided by the Court. At issue was the question of whether the company could use a high school diploma and a passing score on a standardized intelligence test as bona fide requirements for employment or promotion. The plaintiff was able to demonstrate that in the relevant labor market for the company 34 percent of the white males had a high school diploma as opposed to only 12 percent of the black males. The plaintiff was also able to establish that there were people who were successfully performing the job in question who did not have a high school diploma. Additionally, the plaintiff was able to prove that there was no demonstrable relationship between test scores and job performance.

As it often does, the Court used *Griggs* to interpret existing laws broadly and specify legal principles.[1] The decision affirmed the following points:

- It is not necessary to prove that an employer intended to discriminate in order to substantiate the existence of discrimination. The result of an employment practice and not the employer's intention is sufficient to establish the existence of discrimination.

- Employment practices that appear neutral on the surface or that appear neutral in intent are illegal if their effect on protected classes is unequal.

- Tests or other employment practices must be removed if they discriminate on the basis of race or any other protected classification.

- Tests or other measuring devices can be used only when they can be shown to have a demonstrable relationship to actual job performance.

- It is the responsibility of the employer to show that tests are job related.

The immediate impact of the *Griggs* decision was felt in the area of pre-employment testing. Many employers abandoned the use of tests altogether; others retained industrial psychologists to establish a statistical relationship between employment tests and actual job performance. Concomitantly, employers began to examine other pre-employment practices that had a tendency to eliminate higher percentages of minorities and women than of white males from hiring consideration.

Overlooked to a great extent in the immediate concern with pre-employment practices was the fact that the Court had laid down requirements for *all* employment practices. Any employment practice, as clarified in later Court decisions, must meet job relatedness and non-discriminatory standards.

Phillips v. Martin Marietta Corporation (3 FEP 40)

In another 1971 decision, the Court ruled that the company had discriminated against a female because she had young children. This was the first decision involving the issue of "sex-plus" discrimination.

The company had a rule of not hiring women with school-age children; no such rule was imposed on males. The company argued that it did not preclude all women from job consideration; in fact, the company's workforce was 75 percent female. Martin Marietta contended that the rule was a business necessity because women with school age children were likely to be absent more frequently than those without children.

The Court rejected the company's argument and ruled that an employer cannot have one hiring policy for women and another hiring policy for men. The major implication of this decision is that hiring standards must be uniform for both sexes and that the employer cannot use a subset of sex (such as having children) unless it is applied equally to both men and women.

Espinoza v. *Farah Manufacturing Company* (11 FEP 696)

In 1973 the Court ruled that Title VII does not prohibit discrimination on the basis of lack of citizenship. The Equal Employment Opportunity Commission had previously said that it was discriminatory to refuse to hire anyone who was a noncitizen since this selection standard was likely to have adverse impact on individuals of foreign national origin. Inasmuch as 92 percent of the employees at the Farah facility in question were Mexican-Americans or native Mexicans who had become American citizens, the Court held that the company had not discriminated on the basis of national origin when it refused to hire a Hispanic who was not a U.S. citizen.

Albermarle Paper Company v. *Moody* (10 FEP 1181)

In this 1975 case, the Court reaffirmed its position on the use of employment tests by ruling that:

- Any test used in selection or promotion must be validated if its use has been shown to discriminate against a protected class.
- The burden of proof for demonstrating that a test is valid rests entirely upon the employer.
- Any selection device used by an employer must be shown to measure actually what it alleges to measure.
- Performance appraisals that do not have a job-related content base have a built-in bias.
- A job analysis conducted by an employer is admissible as evidence that the employer has made an attempt to validate selection and promotion tests.
- Performance appraisals by supervisors that are based on vague and inadequate standards of job relatedness are open to subjective interpretations and do not meet the guidelines for test validity.

The decision in this case makes it clear that : (1) tests must be job related, (2) performance appraisal is an employment test and the system of appraisal used must be validated in terms of actual job content, (3) it is the employer that must substantiate the job relatedness of any test, and (4) job analysis can be used as evidence to show that performance appraisal or any other test measures what it actually purports to measure.[2]

Washington v. Davis (12 FEP 1415)

In 1970 two black police officers in the District of Columbia filed suit alleging that the promotion policies of the District's police department were racially discriminatory. To be accepted by the department and to enter an intensive seventeen-week training program, a police recruit was required to satisfy certain physical and character standards, to be a high school graduate or the equivalent, and to receive a grade of at least forty on "Test 21," an examination developed by the Civil Service Commission and widely used throughout the federal service.[3]

The validity of Test 21, designed to measure verbal ability, vocabulary, reading, and comprehension, was the issue in question. However, the District Court in trying the case noted that since August 1969, 44 percent of the new police force recruits had been black. This percentage represented the proportion of blacks on the police force and was roughly equivalent to the percentage of twenty- to twenty-nine-year-old blacks residing in the department's fifty-mile recruiting radius. The District Court rejected the contention that Test 21 was culturally biased to favor whites over blacks. It found the test to be reasonable and directly related to the requirements of the police recruit training program and that it was neither designed nor operated so as to discriminate against blacks. The test sampled material that recruits would be exposed to in the training program. Moreover, a positive relationship was found to exist between success in the training program and success on the job. However, it was also found that blacks and women failed the test at a much higher rate than did white males.

The Court of Appeals overturned the District Court ruling and held that lack of discriminatory intent was irrelevant since four times as many blacks as whites failed the test—a disproportionate impact that evidenced the existence of discrimination.

In 1976 the Supreme Court reversed the decision of the Court of Appeals and upheld the decision of the District Court. It ruled that there was no indication that the test was racially biased or that it had been used for the purpose of excluding blacks from the police force. A major conclusion in this case is that if a test is specifically job related and racially neutral, it may be used as a selection device even though it has a disproportionate impact on protected classes.

Dothard v. *Rawlingson* (15 FEP 10)

In this 1977 case the Court addressed minimum height and weight requirements. Rawlingson, a twenty-two-year-old female college graduate whose major course of study had been correctional psychology, was denied employment as a correctional counselor trainee because she failed to meet the state of Alabama's minimum weight requirement of 120 pounds for the position of correctional counselor. The Court held that minimum height and weight requirements have a discriminatory impact on females where there is no evidence to attest to the necessity of these requirements for satisfactory job performance.

Regents of the University of California v. *Bakke* (17 FEP 1000)

This highly publicized 1978 case addressed the issue of reverse discrimination.[4]

The medical school at the University of California at Davis had an admissions program wherein a minimum number of places in the first year medical class were reserved for racial minorities. Allen Bakke, a while male, was denied admission to the medical school even though he scored higher on the admission criteria than some minority group members who were admitted. Bakke filed suit in state court charging that he had been discriminated against because of his race. In 1976, ruling in Bakke's favor and issuing a decree requiring his admission to the medical school, the California Supreme Court held that a preferential selection program was unconstitutional. The U.S. Supreme Court, acting on a request from the regents of the University of California, agreed to review the state court's decision.

The Court reached its decision on June 28, 1978. In a five-to-four decision, Bakke was ordered to be admitted to medical school. He received his degree in 1982.

Even though deciding in Bakke's favor, the Court failed to clarify the issue of reverse discrimination. On the question of whether or not the racial quota system at the university was acceptable in deciding who should be admitted, four of the Justices said yes. On the question of whether or not an applicant's race can ever be considered in admission decisions, five of the Justices said yes. Apparently, affirmative action programs that require government contractors covered by Executive Order 11246 to utilize racial hiring goals and timetables to correct the past effects of discriminatory practices are acceptable, but individual decisions to discriminate against specific white applicants in order to remedy past effects of employment practices are not. Rather than saying that no consideration of race is acceptable in hiring or admission programs, the Court seemed to suggest that race may be taken into consideration as a factor as long as it is not the *sole* factor in making a selection decision.

Weber v. *Kaiser Aluminum Corporation* (21 FEP 1643)

In 1974 the United Steelworkers of America and Kaiser Aluminum and Chemical Corporation entered into a master collective bargaining agreement covering the terms and conditions of employment at fifteen Kaiser plants. The agreement contained an affirmative action plan designed to eliminate racial imbalances in Kaiser's almost exclusively white craft work force. Hiring goals for black craft workers were set at each Kaiser plant. The hiring goals were equal to the percentages of blacks in each of the respective labor markets for the fifteen plants. To enable the plants to meet these goals, on-the-job training programs were initiated to train unskilled production workers, both black and white, in the skills needed to become craft workers. The plan agreed to reserve 50 percent of the openings in these newly created in-plant training programs for blacks.

In 1974 only 1.83 percent of the skilled craft workers at the Gramercy, Louisiana plant were black, although the work force in the local labor market was approximately 39 percent black. Thirteen craft trainees were selected from Gramercy's production work force for the new training program—seven blacks and six whites. The most junior black selected for the program had less seniority than several of the white workers whose bids for admission were rejected. Brian Weber subsequently filed a class action suit alleging that Kaiser and the United Steelworkers had discriminated against him and other white workers.

Although the lower courts agreed with Weber's allegation of discrimination, the Supreme Court did not and reversed the rulings of the lower courts. In reaching its decision, the Court relied heavily upon what it considered to be the underlying intent or spirit of Title VII—the opening of job opportunities for blacks. The Court recognized that while there was no history of discrimination against blacks at the company, there was a serious underutilization of blacks in the craft work force. Also, the plan had been voluntarily entered into by Kaiser and the United Steelworkers and did not, per se, create a bar to employment or advancement of white workers. Moreover, the plan was temporary in nature and would terminate when the percentage of black workers in the crafts equalled the percentage of blacks in the labor market. Under these conditions, the Court felt that there was no violation of Title VII.[5]

American Tobacco Company v. *Patterson* (28 FEP 713)

This 1982 decision allows seniority and promotion systems established under Title VII to stand although they unintentionally affect minority workers adversely. Under *Griggs* a prima facie violation of Title VII may be established by policies or practices that are neutral on their face and neutral in intent but that nevertheless discriminate against a particular protected group. A seniority system would fall under the *Griggs* rationale were it not for Section 703(h) of the Civil Rights Act of 1964. That section provides that:

Notwithstanding any other provision of this subchapter, it shall not be an unlawful employment practice for an employer to apply different standards of compensation, or different terms, conditions, or privileges of employment pursuant to a bona fide seniority or merit system . . . provided that such differences are not the result of an intention to discriminate because of race, color, religion, sex, or national origin, nor shall it be an unlawful employment practice for an employer to give and to act upon the results of any professionally developed ability test provided that such test, its administration or action upon the results is not designed, intended, or used to discriminate because of race, color, religion, sex, or national origin. . . .

Thus, the Court ruled that a bona fide seniority system adopted after Title VII may stand, even though it has a discriminatory impact. It should be noted that the Supreme Court has generally taken a "hands off" position where bona fide labor agreements between company and union are involved as long as the agreement does not intend to discriminate.

Connecticut v. *Teal* (29 FEP 1)

In a 1982 decision in which the Court split five to four, the majority opinion stated "that Connecticut's non-discriminatory 'bottom line' was no answer, under the terms of Title VII, to respondents' prima facie claim of employment discrimination." In this case, four black employees of the Department of Income Maintenance of the State of Connecticut had been promoted provisionally to positions as Welfare Eligibility Supervisors and had served in that capacity for almost two years. To attain permanent status as supervisors, however, these individuals had to participate in a selection process that required, as the first step, a passing score on a written examination. On the examination, 54.17 percent of the black candidates passed while 79.54 percent of the white candidates passed. The four blacks who had been promoted provisionally failed. In April 1979, the four individuals filed suit alleging that Title VII had been violated by the state's imposing, as an absolute condition for consideration for promotion, that applicants pass a written test which excluded blacks in a disproportionate number. They further alleged that the test was not job related.

More than a year after the suit was filed, and approximately one month before the case went to trial, promotions were made from the eligibility list generated by the written examination. In choosing persons for that list, past work performance, recommendations from the candidates' supervisors, and seniority were considered. After the selection process was completed this time, 22.9 percent of the identified black candidates were promoted and 13.5 percent of the identified white candidates were promoted. Connecticut argued that it is this "bottom line" result, more favorable to blacks than to whites, that should be considered.

The Court ruled against Connecticut and stated that each step of the hiring process is open to scrutiny and that the final result of the selection process—the bottom line—is not sufficient evidence to prove non-discrimination. In short, the Court ruled that each step in the selection process could be examined to show adverse impact on protected classes.[6]

SIGNIFICANT FEDERAL CIRCUIT COURTS OF APPEALS DECISIONS

After a case is tried in federal district court, if any party to the case is dissatisfied with the decision, normally the next step is to appeal the decision to a federal circuit court of appeals. There are twelve such courts in this country and each state is assigned to one of the circuits. Rulings at this level have a significant effect on employment practices since the Supreme Court hears only the cases it elects to hear. Thus, a circuit court ruling may or may not be open to further appeal. Some of the more important decisions to come from these courts are discussed below.

Diaz v. Pan American World Airways (3 FEP 337)

This 1971 decision ruled that being a female is not a bona fide occupational qualification for the position of flight attendant. This case established the concept of business necessity as the basis for a BFOQ as opposed to business convenience or customer preference. Discrimination based on sex is valid only when the essence of the business operation would be undermined by not hiring members of one sex exclusively.

According to the Court:

The primary function of an airline is to transport passengers safely from one point to another. While a pleasant environment, enhanced by the obvious cosmetic effect that female stewardesses provide as well as, according to the finding of the court trial, their apparent ability to perform the non-mechanical functions of the job in a more effective manner than most men, may all be important, they are tangential to the essence of the business involved. We do not mean to imply, of course, that Pan Am cannot take into consideration the ability of individuals to perform the non-mechanical functions of the job. What we hold is that . . . Pan Am cannot exclude all males simply because most males may not perform adequately.

In general, the Court stressed the importance of making judgments about the qualifications of people as individuals, not as members of a group.

Spurlock v. *United Airlines, Inc.* (5 FEP 17)

In this case the 10th Circuit Court held that United Airlines could use as selection criteria a college degree and a minimum of 500 hours flying experience even though these requirements eliminated a greater percentage of black applicants than white applicants. United's contention, supported by statistics, was that applicants who have a greater number of flight hours are more likely to succeed in its rigorous training program. The Court agreed. The Court also accepted United's argument that the high cost of the training program rendered it necessary to have as many individuals as possible who enter the program complete it. The Court also agreed with this line of reasoning as an example of business necessity. Moreover, United was able to show a direct correlation between having a college degree and successfully completing the training program. The Court ruled that the airline "met the burden of showing that its requirement of a college degree was sufficiently job related to make it a lawful pre-employment standard."

Spurlock illustrates that the courts will accept fairly rigorous pre-employment requirements if those requirements are logical and supported by factual evidence; they will not, however, accept requirements based on subjectivity, intuition, and generalizations.

Richardson v. *Hotel Corporation of America* (5 FEP 323)

This case, decided by the 5th Circuit Court in 1972, addressed the matter of considering conviction records for specific crimes as a selection criterion. The Court found that the hotel did not discriminate on the basis of race when it discharged Richardson, a newly hired black bellhop, after learning that he had previously been convicted of theft and receiving stolen property. The hotel had a policy of rejecting applicants for employment in "security sensitive" positions if they had been convicted of a serious crime. As a bellhop the complainant would have had keys to the rooms in the hotel. The Court ruled for the hotel on grounds of business necessity, in spite of the contention that more blacks than whites are convicted of serious crimes and that discharge based upon criminal record is therefore inherently racially discriminatory.

According to the Court: (1) people who have been convicted of serious crimes are more likely to engage in future criminal conduct than those who have never been convicted, (2) it is reasonable for the company to require persons having access to valuable property of others to be relatively free from convictions related to theft of property, (3) the hotel applied its policy to both blacks and whites, (4) similar requirements are not imposed on employees who do not have access to property, and (5) the hotel has had an excellent record of providing equal opportunity in jobs at all levels to minority group members.

In short, conviction records can be used as selection criteria or grounds for dismissal if they are job related.

Rowe v. General Motors Corporation (4 FEP 445)

This 1972 case decided by the 5th Circuit Court involved performance appraisal. The company's evaluation system was used as the basis for determining promotions, with the immediate supervisor's recommendation on promotability the key factor in deciding whether the employee would be promoted. The appraisal standards used were vague and supervisors were given no written instructions for conducting the appraisals. The decision reached in this case emphasized the following points:

- Subjective, unstructured evaluation systems that result in a disparate adverse effect on minorities have been unanimously condemned by the courts and found discriminatory.
- Objective measures of performance accomplish the goals of performance appraisal better than subjective means such as interviews or vague evaluations by supervisors.
- Written instructions on the use of appraisal criteria and the qualifications for promotion should be furnished to the evaluators.
- Where all of the appraisers are white and all of those being appraised are minority group members, the appraisers cannot be expected to evaluate fairly the performance of those being evaluated. As the Court stated, "We and others have expressed a skepticism that black persons dependent on decisive recommendations from whites can expect non-discriminatory action."
- A review process whereby evaluations given by supervisors are examined by the next level of management provides a safeguard in performance appraisal that may avert discriminatory practices.

Interpreting *Rowe* broadly, it would appear that a firm's performance appraisal system, if it is to avoid potential discrimination, must be objective, provide written instructions to appraisers, establish a review procedure by another level of management, and exercise care to see that evaluators are not all from one group while those being evaluated are all from another, protected group.[7]

Brito v. Zia Company (5 FEP 1207)

In this 1973 case performance appraisals were used as the basis for laying off employees. Fifteen employees were laid off in a reduction in force at the company on the basis of unsatisfactory performance. Twelve of those laid off were Spanish-surnamed individuals and three were white.

The decision by the Court indicated that:

- Performance appraisals were based on the best judgments and opinions of the evaluators and not on any identifiable quality or quantity of work criteria.
- The subjective appraisal system adversely affected a protected class in determining who would be laid off.
- No performance records were maintained by the company and there was no documentation to substantiate the ratings given to employees.
- Performance of the employees was not observed on a daily basis by the evaluators.
- Evaluations were neither administered nor scored in a controlled and standardized fashion; thus, they were susceptible to subjective interpretation.
- The company failed to validate its performance appraisal system under the EEOC guidelines for test validation.

It is apparent from *Brito* that face or even content validity is not sufficient evidence to demonstrate the validity of a performance appraisal system; the system must be validated in terms of job requirements and content.

Hodgson v. Greyhound Lines, Inc. (7 FEP 460)

In 1974 the 7th Circuit Court ruled that Greyhound did not violate the Age Discrimination in Employment Act when it refused to hire persons thirty-five years of age or older as intercity bus drivers. The Court found that Greyhound had a rational basis in fact to believe that the elimination of its hiring age policy would increase the likelihood of risk or harm to its passengers. The company provided statistical evidence showing that the company's safest driver is one who has between sixteen and twenty years of driving experience with the company and is between fifty and fifty-five years of age—a blend of experience with the company and age that could never be attained in hiring applicants forty or older. Greyhound also presented evidence concerning degenerative physical and sensory changes that humans undergo at about age thirty-five that have a detrimental effect upon driving skills and that are not detectable by physical tests. Thus, age can be a bona fide occupational qualification where it is reasonably necessary to the essence of the business and the employer has a rational or factual basis for believing that all or substantially all people within the age class would not be able to perform satisfactorily.

Wade v. *Mississippi Cooperative Extension Service* (39 FEP 460)

Unlike most discrimination cases, *Wade* was not filed under contemporary employment statutes; it was filed under the equal protection clause of the Fourteenth Amendment. At issue was the Extension Service's performance appraisal system. In its decision the 5th Circuit Court ruled that:

- In a performance appraisal system, general characteristics such as "leadership, public acceptance, attitude toward people, appearance and grooming, personal conduct, outlook on life, ethical habits, resourcefulness, capacity for growth, mental alertness, loyalty to organization" are "susceptible to partiality and to the personal taste, whim, or fancy of the evaluator" as well as "patently subjective in form and obviously susceptible to completely subjective treatment" by those conducting the appraisals.

- The agency had not used performance evaluation ratings consistently as a basis for promoting employees or adjusting their salaries.

- Trait-rating performance appraisal systems are subjective and biased because they are not usually based on a study of job content.

- Where a trait is used in an appraisal system there must be a clear relationship between that trait and the work performed in the job.

- When subjected to legal challenge, the employer must be able to demonstrate the relationship between the performance appraisal instrument used and job content.

Wade, as with other cases, emphasizes the requirement for specifically relating performance appraisal factors to actual job content. Broadly speaking, this case also stresses the importance of job analysis, since it is through job analysis that job content is determined.[8]

SUMMARY

This chapter has presented a number of court decisions that illustrate how the law has been applied in specific staffing situations. Table 3.1 summarizes the Supreme Court cases reviewed, showing the key points of each decision and its implications for staffing. Table 3.2 shows the same things for the Circuit Courts of Appeals cases. These two summaries should help the reader in reviewing and comparing the various decisions of the federal courts.

Table 3.1
Summary of Significant Supreme Court Cases

Case	Key Points of Decision	Implications for Staffing
GRIGGS V. DUKE POWER COMPANY	It is not necessary to show intent to discriminate in order to substantiate existence of discrimination.	Increases the importance of a systematic, periodic review of all employment practices and policies to ensure that they are free of discriminatory impact.
	Employment practices that appear neutral on the surface or in intent are illegal if their impact on protected classes is unequal.	Necessitates the validation of tests, measuring devices, and selection requirements in terms of actual job performance or relationship to job content.
	Tests or other measuring devices can be used only when they have a demonstrable relationship to actual job performance.	Requires maintaining adequate documentation to demonstrate that tests and other employment practices are nondiscriminatory.
	Employer bears the burden of proof in showing that tests are job related.	Increases the need for recognizing that tests are not limited to pencil-and-paper examinations, but include any selection requirements or standards.
PHILLIPS V. MARTIN MARIETTA CORPORATION	Employer cannot have one hiring policy for females and another hiring policy for males.	Increases the importance of a systematic, periodic review of all employment practices, policies, and hiring standards to ensure that they are uniform for both sexes.
	Employer cannot use a subset of sex as a selection criterion unless applied equally to both sexes.	

51

Table 3.1 (continued)

ESPINOZA V. FARAH MANUFAC-TURING COMPANY	Title VII of the Civil Rights Act of 1964 does not prohibit discrimination against individuals who are not citizens.	Allows employers to use a requirement of citizenship as a selection criterion.
ALBERMARLE PAPER COMPANY V. MOODY	Any test used in selection or promotion must be validated if its use has been shown to discriminate against a protected class.	Necessitates the validation of tests in terms of actual job performance or relationship to job content.
	The burden of proof for demonstrating test validity rests entirely upon the employer.	Increases the importance of job analysis as a means of validating selection or promotion tests.
	Performance appraisals that do not have a job related content basis possess a built-in bias.	Requires that performance appraisal systems or instruments be recognized as tests that are subject to the same validation requirements used on other kinds of tests.
	Job analysis studies are admissible as evidence in support of an attempt to validate selection and promotion tests.	
	Performance appraisals based on inadequate standards of job relatedness do not meet the guidelines for test validity.	
WASHINGTON V. DAVIS	A test that is specifically job related and racially neutral may be used as a selection device even though it adversely affects protected classes.	Requires that tests be specifically job related and racially neutral. Allows employer to use job related and racially neutral tests even if

Case	Key Points of Decision	Implications for Staffing
		such tests have an adverse impact on minorities.
		Necessitates the validation of tests in terms of actual job performance, relationship to job content, and racial neutrality.
		Increases the need for job analysis to determine necessity for or to validate height and weight requirements as selection criteria.
DOTHARD V. RAWLINGSON	Minimum height and weight requirements for jobs have a discriminatory impact on females.	
	Employer must prove necessity of minimum height and weight requirements for successfully performing jobs where these requirements are used as selection criteria.	
REGENTS OF THE UNIVERSITY OF CALIFORNIA V. BAKKE	Affirmative action plans favoring minorities are acceptable if used to correct the effects of past discriminatory practices.	Allows employer to use racial hiring goals and timetables in affirmative action plans designed to correct the effects of past discriminatory practices.
	Race may be taken into consideration in selection decisions provided it is not the sole factor used.	Precludes discrimination against specific white applicants in order to remedy effects of past discriminatory practices.
		Permits employer to take minority status into consideration as a selection criterion provided it is not the only criterion used.

53

Table 3.1 (continued)

WEBER V. KAISER ALUMINUM COMPANY	Affirmative action plans entered into by a company and its union are permissible even if there is no evidence of past discrimination.	Permits companies and unions to enter into mutually agreed upon affirmative action plans even though there is no past history of discrimination.
	Affirmative action plans that do not create a bar to employment of or advancement of white workers are acceptable.	Requires careful design of affirmative action plans to avoid the possibility of creating a barrier to employment of or advancement of whites.
	Affirmative action plans intended to correct underutilization of minorities are permissible.	
AMERICAN TOBACCO COMPANY V. PATTERSON	Bona fide seniority, promotion, and merit systems enacted after passage of Title VII of the Civil Rights Act of 1964 are permissible even though they may unintentionally discriminate against protected classes.	Permits companies and unions to enter bona fide labor agreements that may have a discriminatory impact provided it was not the intention of the parties to discriminate.
	Intention to discriminate must be absent for a labor agreement to be considered bona fide.	
CONNECTICUT V. TEAL	The "bottom line" is not sufficient evidence to refute a charge of discrimination by a protected class.	Increases the importance of a systematic, periodic review of each step in the selection and promotion process to ensure that there is no discriminatory impact at any step.
	Each step in the selection and promotion process is subject to examination and may be used to evidence adverse impact on protected classes.	Invalidates the use of the "bottom line" defense as the sole factor attesting to absence of discrimination in the total selection and promotion process.

54

Table 3.2
Summary of Significant Circuit Courts of Appeals Cases

Case	Key Points of Decision	Implications for Staffing
<u>DIAZ v. PAN</u> <u>AMERICAN WORLD</u> <u>AIRWAYS</u>	Discrimination based on sex is valid only when it is necessary to the essence of business operations.	Increases importance of job analysis as a means of determining and validating bona fide occupational qualifications as business necessities.
	Business necessity is the basis for establishing a bona fide occupational qualification.	Requires employer to substantiate a bona fide occupational qualification in terms of job duties or performance, not convenience or customer preference.
	Business convenience or customer preference do not constitute business necessity.	Severely limits the use of sex as a bona fide occupational qualification.
	Selection judgments relative to people must consider people as individuals not as members of a group.	
<u>SPURLOCK v. UNITED</u> <u>AIRLINES, INC.</u>	Rigorous selection requirements are permissible if those requirements are logical and supported by factual evidence as to their necessity.	Requires employers to substantiate selection requirements with factual evidence demonstrating their business necessity and job relatedness.
	Selection requirements based on subjectivity, intuition, and generalizations are not acceptable.	Precludes the use of selection requirements based on subjectivity, intuition, and generalizations.
	Selection standards must be sufficiently job related and supported by evidence to that effect for them to constitute legally usable standards.	Increases importance of job analysis as a means of determining and supporting selection requirements.

Table 3.2 (continued)

RICHARDSON V. HOTEL CORPORATION OF AMERICA

Criminal convictions may be used as selection criteria or grounds for dismissal if they can be shown to be sufficiently job related.

Allows the use of criminal conviction records as selection criteria or grounds for termination where previous convictions are reasonably related to a particular job.

Requires employer to demonstrate the relationship between previous convictions and the job in question.

ROWE V. GENERAL MOTORS CORPORATION

Subjective, unstructured performance appraisal systems that have a disparate adverse impact on minorities are discriminatory.

Evaluators should be given written instructions on the use of performance appraisal criteria.

Where all of the appraisers are white and all of the appraisees are minority group members, the appraisals are likely to be discriminatory.

Performance appraisals should be subject to review by the next higher level of management as a safeguard against discriminatory practices.

Stresses the importance of developing objective, job related performance appraisal systems and instruments.

Points out the need for building a review or audit procedure into the performance appraisal system.

Indicates the necessity of formalizing a performance appraisal system in writing and furnishing these guidelines to appraisers so as to avoid possible subjectivity and discrimination.

Suggests that care be taken to assure that appraisers are not all from one group while appraisees are from a different or protected group.

BRITO V. ZIA COMPANY	Face or content validity are not sufficient evidence to demonstrate the validity of a performance appraisal system.	Requires employers to recognize that performance appraisal is a form of employment test that must be validated, as are other tests, in terms of job requirements and job content.
	Performance appraisal systems must be validated in terms of job requirements and content under EEOC guidelines for test validation.	
HODGSON V. GREYHOUND LINES, INC.	Age may be used as a bona fide occupational qualification where it is reasonably necessary to business operations and can be rationally or factually supported.	Permits an employer to use age as a bona fide occupational qualification where the employer can factually or rationally support it as a business necessity.
		Increases importance of job analysis as a means of determining and validating the use of age as a bona fide occupational qualification.

57

Table 3.2 (continued)

WADE V. MISSI-
SSIPPI COOPER-
ATIVE EXTENSION
SERVICE

Trait rating performance appraisal
systems are generally suspect because they lack a job content basis.
The burden of proof for demonstrating the relationship between a
performance appraisal system and
actual job content rests entirely
on the employer.

Suggests very strongly that employers
develop performance appraisal systems
and instruments that have a job content basis.

Indicates the necessity for closely
examining trait rating performance
appraisal systems to determine their
relationship to job content.

Places the burden of proof for demonstrating the relationship between the
performance appraisal and actual job
content on the employer.

Increases the importance of job
analysis as a means of determining
job content for use in performance
appraisal.

NOTES

1. Donald L. Caruth, *Compensation Management for Banks* (Boston: Bankers Publishing Company, 1986), pp. 222-23.

2. Ibid., pp. 225-26.

3. Richard D. Arvey, *Fairness in Selecting Employees* (Reading, Mass.: Addison-Wesley, 1979), pp. 74-76.

4. Barbara Lindemann Schlei and Paul Grossman, *Employment Discrimination Law,* 2nd ed. (Washington, D.C.: Bureau of National Affairs, 1983), pp. 786-802.

5. R. Wayne Mondy and Robert M. Noe, *Personnel: The Management of Human Resources,* 3rd ed. (Boston: Allyn and Bacon, 1987), p. 78.

6. Ibid., p. 80.

7. Caruth, *Compensation Management,* pp. 223-24.

8. Ibid., pp. 226-27.

4

The Uniform Guidelines, Adverse Impact, and Affirmative Action Programs

While an understanding of employment legislation, Executive Orders, and federal court decisions is imperative for staffing specialists, additional knowledge is required to ensure that employment practices, policies, and procedures are implemented and followed in a manner that reflects not only the letter but the spirit of the law as well. The additional knowledge that staffing specialists must have is a thorough understanding of the Equal Employment Opportunity Commission's guidelines for lawful employment practices, the definition and interpretation of adverse impact, and the meaning and application of affirmative action programs. These three broad areas are the subject of this chapter.

UNIFORM GUIDELINES ON EMPLOYEE SELECTION PROCEDURES

Prior to 1978, employers had to comply with several different sets of employment and selection guidelines promulgated by different federal agencies. To eliminate this confusing situation and provide employers with a single set of standards, in 1978 the Equal Employment Opportunity Commission, the Civil Service Commission, the Department of Justice, and the Department of Labor adopted and issued the *Uniform Guidelines on Employee Selection Procedures*. The *Guidelines* cover the major federal equal opportunity statutes and Executive Orders. They do not apply to the Age Discrimination in Employment Act of 1967, as Amended, or to the Rehabilitation Act of 1973. While the courts are not bound by the *Guidelines*, they do tend to afford these interpretive rules substantial deference in the decisions they make.

The *Guidelines* set forth a single set of principles designed to assist employers, labor organizations, employment agencies, and licensing and certification boards in complying with requirements of federal law prohibiting employment practices that discriminate on the basis of race, color, religion, sex, and national origin. They are designed to provide a framework for determining the proper use of tests and other selection devices and procedures. The *Guidelines* provide a basis for making lawful employment decisions relative to hiring, promotion, demotion, referral, retention, licensing, and certification. Recruiting procedures, under the *Guidelines*, are not considered selection procedures and are therefore not covered;[1] however, inferences can be made from the *Guidelines* that suggest what is proper or improper practice in recruiting.

One of the most important clarifications contained in the *Guidelines* is the definition of an employment test as:

Any measure, combination of measures, or procedures used as a basis for any employment decision. Selection procedures include the full range of assessment techniques from traditional paper and pencil tests, performance tests, training programs, or probationary periods and physical, educational, and work experience requirements through informal or casual interviews and unscored application forms.[2]

Under this broad, comprehensive definition, virtually *any* factor used in making *any* employment decision is a test. From the time a person's resume or application crosses the organization's threshold to the time that person retires thirty years later, any evaluation for any purpose—hiring, promoting, rewarding, terminating—is, in fact, an employment test under the *Guidelines*. It is unfortunate that many organizations apparently have not fully grasped EEOC's all-inclusive definition of employment test.

Prior to the issuance of the *Guidelines*, the only means for establishing the job relatedness of a test was through validation of each test used. The *Guidelines* do not require validation in all cases. The fundamental principle underlying the *Guidelines* is that employer policies or practices that have an adverse impact on employment opportunities on classes of individuals protected under Title VII or Executive Orders are illegal unless justified by business necessity. Adverse impact occurs when members of a protected class receive unequal consideration for employment. As specifically defined by the *Guidelines*, adverse impact occurs if protected groups are not hired at the rate of at least 80 percent of the rate for the best achieving group. This 80 percent selection factor is also known as the four-fifths rule. Groups identified for analysis in determining if adverse impact has occurred are: (1) blacks, (2) American Indians, (3) Asians, (4) Hispanics, (5) females, and (6) males.

Assuming that adverse impact has been shown, employers have two avenues available to them if they still desire to use a particular selection device, procedure, or standard. First, the employer may validate the selection device used to show that it is indeed a predictor of success on the job. When the device has been proven to be a valid, reliable indicator of on-the-job performance, the employer has established business necessity as the basis for its use. In the event that the firm's selection tool has not been validated, business necessity may be demonstrated in another manner. The employer can show that there is a strong relationship between the selection device and job performance and that, without using this specific selection procedure, the firm's training costs would become prohibitive.

The second avenue available should adverse impact be shown is the bona fide occupational qualification defense. The BFOQ defense means that certain qualifications are needed for job performance and that the majority of the members of one or more protected classes cannot reasonably be expected to possess the necessary qualifications. The BFOQ defense has been narrowly interpreted by the courts because it has often been based on stereotyping and vague generalizations. For example, the courts have rejected the contention that since most women cannot lift 150 pounds all women can be excluded from consideration for a job involving such lifting requirements. Employers electing to use the BFOQ defense for their selection procedures must have significant evidence to substantiate their position.

Creators of the *Guidelines* adopted, in essence, a "bottom line" approach in assessing whether a firm's employment practices are discriminatory. If a number of selection procedures are used in making a selection decision, for example, the enforcement agencies are likely to focus (*Connecticut* v. *Teal* notwithstanding) on the result of the combined practices to determine the existence of adverse impact. Essentially, EEOC is more concerned with what is occurring—the bottom line—as opposed to how it occurred. Admitting that discriminatory practices may exist that cannot be validated by an employer, EEOC's focus tends to be on the net effect produced by the procedures that are used.

ADVERSE IMPACT

There are three approaches that have been developed to determine the existence of adverse impact. These three are the four-fifths rule, the standard deviation method, and the Chi-Square Test.

The four-fifths or eighty-twenty rule is outlined in the *Guidelines* and should generally be used first since it is accepted in most instances by both EEOC and OFCCP. If adverse impact is shown under the four-fifths rule, other statistical methods may then be used. It should be remembered that the eighty-twenty rule is itself a rule of thumb; it is not a hard-and-fast criterion. A second method for assessing adverse impact is the standard deviation approach. This method was tested in the Supreme Court decision in the case of *Hazlewood School District* v. *United States* (15 FEP 1). The Chi-Square Test has not yet received judicial acceptance but is a widely accepted test of statistical significance that may be used by employers.

Establishing Job Pools

The first step in conducting an adverse impact analysis is to establish job pools. A job pool is a group of jobs having essentially the same minimum level of qualifications. An organization may decide to create separate pools for accountants, computer programmers, machine operators, or salespeople. The key to establishing a reliable job pool is the similarity of minimum qualifications for each job in the pool. Computer operator and computer programmer jobs, for example, would not be placed in the same pool because qualifications required for these two types of jobs are dissimilar.

Once pools have been identified, the second step is to collect data on: (1) the total number of qualified applicants for jobs in the pool, (2) the number of applicants selected, (3) the number of applicants classified as to minority or majority status, and (4) the number of applicants selected by minority or majority status. These data are then analyzed to determine the existence or nonexistence of adverse impact.

Four-Fifths Rule

The general formula for computing adverse impact using the four-fifths or eighty-twenty rule is:

$$\frac{\text{Protected Group Selection Rate}}{\text{Best Achieving Group Selection Rate}} = \text{Protected Group Selection Ratio}$$

The selection rate for protected group applicants is determined by dividing the number of protected group members hired by the total number of qualified protected group applicants within a given period of time. Selection rates should be calculated for blacks, American Indians, Asians, Hispanics, and females. Separate selection rates would be determined for each identified job pool. The selection rate for the best achieving group, typically white males, would be determined in the same manner for the same time period.

To illustrate how the four-fifths formula for calculating adverse impact works, assume that during a twelve-month period 400 individuals were hired for the job of machine operator. Of the total number hired, 300 were white males and 100 were blacks. There was a total of 1,500 applicants: 1,000 white males and 500 blacks. The selection rate for white males is 30 percent (300 ÷ 1,000 = .30), and the selection rate for blacks is 20 percent (100 ÷ 500 = .20). Applying these numbers to the formula for calculating adverse impact we arrive at a selection ratio of 66.67 percent for the protected group.

$$\frac{\text{Protected Group Selection Rate}}{\text{Best Achieving Group Selection Rate}} = \text{Protected Group Selection Ratio} = \frac{20\%}{30\%} = 66.67\%$$

Inasmuch as the selection ratio for blacks is 66.67 percent of the selection ratio for white male machine operators, adverse impact exists under the four-fifths rule that requires a selection ratio for protected classes of 80 percent of the selection ratio for the best achieving group.

Evidence of adverse impact is, obviously, more than the total number of protected group workers hired. The total number of applicants is also important. Assume, for instance, as a second example of the four-fifths rule, that 300 black applicants were hired and 300 white applicants were hired, but that 1,500 blacks and 1,000 whites applied for job openings. Using these numbers we see that adverse impact still exists:

$$\frac{300}{1,500} = 20\% \text{ Black Selection Rate}$$

$$\frac{300}{1,000} = 30\% \text{ White Selection Rate}$$

$$\frac{20\%}{30\%} = 66.67\% \text{ Protected Group Selection Ratio}$$

Even though 200 more blacks were hired in the second example as compared to the first example, there were 1,000 more black applicants. Thus, the selection ratio indicates that black applicants still are not hired at a rate that approaches 80 percent of the selection rate for white males. The total number of minorities or women hired is insufficient evidence to refute a claim of adverse impact. EEOC is concerned with the comparative rate, not the sheer numbers, at which protected class members are hired.

It must be emphasized that the four-fifths rule is intended to be a guideline, not a hard-and-fast measure of adverse impact. Protected class selection ratios well below 80 percent may be acceptable in some cases, while selection ratios considerably above 80 percent may not be acceptable in other cases. According to the *Guidelines*:

Smaller differences in selection rate may nevertheless constitute adverse impact, where they are significant in both statistical and practical terms or where a user's actions have discouraged applicants disproportionately on grounds of race, sex, or ethnic group. Greater differences in selection rates may not constitute adverse impact where the differences are based on small numbers and are not statistically significant, or where special recruiting or other programs cause the pool of minority or female candidates to be atypical of the normal pool of applicants from that group.[3]

For all practical purposes, EEOC reserves the "right to excuse an employer that fails the four-fifths rule or hold in violation an employer that satisfies the four-fifths rule."[4]

What determines how the rule will be applied? In essence, it is the number of applicants involved. When the numbers are small, statistical chance alone may produce a violation of the four-fifths rule. But, when large numbers of applicants are involved, adverse impact may exist even if the selection ratio for protected classes is considerably above 80 percent.[5] In the latter instance, EEOC may conclude that systemic discrimination is present in the organization and adversely affects a significant number of minorities and women. An employer must, consequently, pay attention not only to the rate at which protected group members are selected but also to the overall numbers hired, using the four-fifths rule as a basic guideline for the likely acceptance of selection practices by EEOC.

Standard Deviation Formula

As previously indicated, the standard deviation formula has been court tested as a method for determining adverse impact. The standard deviation approach uses the following formula:

$$\text{Standard Deviation} = \sqrt{\frac{\text{Total Black Applicants}}{\text{Total Applicants}} \times \frac{\text{Total White Applicants}}{\text{Total Applicants}} \times \frac{\text{Total Number of Workers Selected}}{}}$$

This formula is known as a two-tailed standard deviation formula in that it indicates whether there has been discrimination against either the protected group or the group used as the basis for comparison.[6] The expected number, plus or minus two standard deviations, constitutes the acceptable hiring range for employers. Two standard deviations are used because, statistically speaking, the possibility of error due to chance is reduced to 4.6 times out of 100 occurrences. The *Guidelines* suggest that at least a .05 error rate be used; consequently, two standard deviations is within the suggested range of error.

An example will illustrate how this formula is applied in actual practice. Assume that there were 300 applicants for a particular job. Of the total number of applicants, 100 were black and 200 were white. Assume also that 90 individuals were hired: 25 blacks and 65 whites. Inserting these numbers into the formula we would arrive at the following:

$$\text{Standard Deviation} = \sqrt{\frac{100}{300} \times \frac{200}{300} \times 90}$$

$$= \sqrt{20}$$

$$= 4.47$$

The number of blacks we would expect this employer to hire, on the basis of the indicated selection ratio, is 30. ($100 \div 300 \times 90 = 30$). Therefore, the acceptable hiring range would be $30 \pm (2 \times 4.47)$, or 21.06 to 38.94. Since the actual number of blacks hired was 30, a number that falls within the acceptable range, no adverse impact exists. If the number hired was less than 21, the conclusion would be that adverse impact exists. Because two standard deviations are used, if the number of blacks hired was outside the range of 21.06 to 38.94, there would be less than a 5 percent probability that it was due to chance.

Chi-Square Test

When the Chi-Square Test of adverse impact is used, the selection rates of various subgroups are compared. This test assists in determining if differences exist between the selection rates for subgroups. An advantage of the Chi-Square approach is that it is sensitive to differences in sample size. Unfortunately, the four-fifths rule does not distinguish between a selection rate of 10 out of 20 or 1,000 out of 2,000.[7]

In using Chi-Square, a contingency table is prepared that shows the number of individuals in the various subgroups. Such a table might look like the following:

	Selected	Not Selected
Men	A	B
Women	C	D

The formula for calculating Chi-Square would be:

$$\text{Chi-Square} = \frac{N(AD - BC)^2}{(A + B)(C + D)(A + C)(B + D)}$$

Assume that for the position of machine operator fifty men and fifty women apply. Of this total number of applicants, nine men and six women are hired. Using these figures in the Chi-Square Test would result in the following:

	Selected	Not Selected	Total
Men	9	41	50
Women	6	44	50
Totals	15	85	100

$$\text{Chi-Square} = \frac{100 \, (396 - 246)^2}{(50) \, (50) \, (15) \, (85)} = 0.71$$

The value calculated must be interpreted based upon the degrees of freedom that may be found in most textbooks on statistics. For one degree of freedom, Chi-Square values less than 3.84 are not considered to be statistically significant at a .05 level since 5 times out of a 100 the difference may be due solely to chance. Because the *Guidelines* advocate a .05 significance level and the Chi-Square value in this example is less than 3.84, it is apparent that the selection rates for men and women are not significantly different. Therefore, there is no indication of adverse impact.

ADDITIONAL GUIDELINES

After the publication of the *Uniform Guidelines* in 1978, a number of modifications were made to the stipulated regulations. Some of these changes resulted from Supreme Court decisions; others were made in an attempt to clarify further or add to the interpretation of the *Guidelines*. Topics covered in these modifications include sexual harassment, discrimination based on national origin, and religious discrimination. Each of these three subjects is addressed in a separate set of *Guidelines*.

Interpretive Guidelines on Sexual Harassment

The Equal Employment Opportunity Commission published its *Guidelines on Discrimination Because of Sex* in 1980. The Office of Federal Contract Compliance Programs issued similar guidelines in 1981. The EEOC developed the sex discrimination guidelines because of the belief that sexual harassment is a widespread problem in the workplace.[8] Attesting to this problem is one study that reported that 59 percent of the female employees interviewed in the study indicated experiencing one or more incidents of sexual harassment in the workplace.[9] This particular issue is one of growing concern today and is anticipated to remain a major area of importance in the years to come.

Sexual harassment is defined by EEOC as:

Unwelcome sexual advances, requests for sexual favors, and other verbal or physical conduct of a sexual nature . . . when (1) submission to such conduct is made either explicitly or implicitly a term or condition of an individual's employment, (2) submission to or rejection of such conduct by an individual is used as the basis for employment decisions affecting such individual, or (3) such conduct has the purpose or effect of unreasonably interfering with an individual's work performance or creating an intimidating, hostile, or offensive working environment.[10]

According to the *Guidelines*, employers are totally responsible for the acts of their supervisors with respect to sexual harassment regardless of whether the employers were aware of such acts. Where coworkers are concerned, the employer is responsible for acts of sexual harassment if it knew or should have known of the harassment conduct, unless the employer can show that it took immediate and appropriate corrective action to deal with the problem once it was made known.

Another interesting aspect of the *Guidelines* is that employers may also be responsible for sexual harassment acts committed in the workplace by non-employees. To be held responsible for the acts of non-employees, however, the employer or its supervisors must have knowledge of the conduct or should have known that such conduct was occurring and failed to take immediate corrective action. In determining the liability of the employer for the acts of non-employees, EEOC will take into consideration "the extent of the employer's control and any other legal responsibility which the employer may have with respect to the conduct of such nonemployees."[11]

There have been a number of court cases involving sexual harassment in the workplace. In *Miller* v. *Bank of America* (20 FEP 462), the U.S. Court of Appeals for the Ninth Circuit held the employer to be liable for a supervisor's sexually harassing behavior even though the employer had a policy prohibiting such conduct and had no knowledge of the harassment. The Court "reasoned that, just as an employer is liable for the negligence of its employees in operating motor vehicles, an employer should be held liable for adverse action taken by its supervisors because of sexual harassment. . . ."[12] In *Barnes* v. *Costle* (15 FEP 345), the Circuit Court for the District of Columbia ruled that the employer was not entitled to exoneration because the supervisor's behavior was, in the eyes of the employer, a "personal escapade." The importance of immediate and appropriate action in dealing with sexual harassment once the employer has knowledge of it was underscored in *Tomkins* v. *Public Service Electric & Gas Co.* (16 FEP 22). The Third Circuit Court held that the employer's failure to take action was a sufficient basis to establish a claim against the company. In general, the courts have held that sexual harassment in and of itself is a violation of Title VII. The victim, moreover, is not required to prove that she resisted sexual harassment or that she was penalized if she did offer resistance.[13]

The need for company policy statements and training programs dealing with sexual harassment is essential. According to the *Guidelines*:

Prevention is the best tool for the elimination of sexual harassment. An employer should take all steps necessary to prevent sexual harassment from occurring, such as affirmatively raising the subject, expressing strong disapproval, developing appropriate sanctions, informing employees of their right to raise and how to raise the issue of harassment under Title VII, and developing methods to sensitize all concerned.[14]

Firms must investigate all complaints, either formal or informal, alleging sexual harassment and, after investigation, take prompt and appropriate action to correct the situation.[15]

Interpretive Guidelines on National Origin Discrimination

Guidelines on Discrimination Because of National Origin was issued by the Equal Employment Opportunity Commission in 1980. Title VII, while establishing national origin as a protected class, does not define what is meant by that term; thus, between 1964 and 1980 there was some confusion as to discrimination on the basis of national origin. It was this confusion that EEOC sought to eliminate with its new interpretive *Guidelines*.

National origin discrimination is defined:

broadly as including, but not limited to, the denial of equal employment opportunity because of an individual's, or his or her ancestor's, place of origin; or because an individual has the physical, cultural, or linguistic characteristics of a national origin group.[16]

Both EEOC and the courts have interpreted national origin protection under Title VII as extending far beyond discrimination against individuals who came from or whose forebears came from a particular country. National origin protection also includes:

(1) marriage or association with a person of a specific national origin; (2) membership in, or association with, an organization identified with or seeking to promote the interests of national groups; (3) attendance at, or participation in, schools, churches, temples, or mosques generally used by persons of a national origin group; (4) use of an individual's or spouse's name which is associated with a national origin group.[17]

Because height and weight requirements used as selection criteria tend to exclude applicants on the basis of national origin, employers must evaluate these items for adverse impact. In effect, height and weight requirements are exceptions to the bottom-line concept normally adhered to by EEOC.

Two other selection procedures that may be discriminatory on the basis of national origin are fluency in English and training or education requirements.

Certainly, a questionable practice is denying employment opportunities to individuals because of their accent or inability to communicate fluently in English. In instances where this practice is continually followed by employers, EEOC's position is that the practice is a presumed violation of Title VII warranting further investigation. An employer may require, however, that employees speak only in English at certain times if it is necessary to the performance of the employee's duties and thereby constitutes a business necessity.

Denying employment opportunities to individuals because of their foreign training or education or requiring individuals to be foreign trained or educated may also be the basis for discrimination on grounds of national origin if adverse impact on a particular national origin group can be shown and if the requirements are not job related.

Harassment on the basis of national origin such as ethnic slurs or derogatory remarks is also interpreted to be a violation of Title VII if such conduct has the purpose or effect of creating an intimidating, hostile, or offensive working environment, interferes with an individual's performance of his or her job, or adversely affects an individual's employment opportunities with an organization.[18] Generally speaking, the same standards are applied to national origin harassment as are used in sexual harassment.

Interpretive Guidelines on Religious Discrimination

The third set of guidelines issued by the Equal Employment Opportunity Commission in 1980 was *Guidelines on Discrimination Because of Religion.* Under the 1972 amendments to Title VII, "The term 'religion' includes all aspects of religious observance and practice, as well as belief. . . ." EEOC's position is that it will define religious practices as including moral or ethical beliefs that are held with the strength of traditional religious views.[19]

The 1972 amendments to Title VII also require that employers make reasonable accommodations for employees' religious practices and observances unless the employer can demonstrate that accommodation would place undue hardship on the conducting of the employer's business.

In determining whether an accommodation would constitute undue hardship, EEOC will give consideration to the size and operating costs of the employer as well as the number of individual employees who actually need the accommodation. The *Guidelines* recognize that regular payment of premium wages in the form of overtime compensation would constitute undue hardship whereas such payments on an infrequent or temporary basis would not. Undue hardship would likewise exist if the accommodation required the employer to deviate from its seniority system under the terms and conditions of a bona fide union contract.

The *Guidelines* identify several methods for accommodating religious practices. Some of the methods suggested are: (1) voluntary substitutes (one employee electing to work in the place of another employee who needs time off for religious purpose); (2) flexible scheduling that allows an employee to take a particular day off and work another day in its place; (3) lateral transfers to units where work schedules do not interfere with religious observances; and (4) changes in job assignments.

Some collective bargaining agreements include a provision that each employee must join the bargaining unit or pay the union a fee equivalent to the amount of dues for the bargaining services the union renders. Where an employee's religious practices or beliefs do not permit compliance with this provision, the labor union should make an attempt to accommodate the employee by allowing him or her to donate an equivalent amount, in lieu of union dues, to a charitable organization of the individual's choosing.

DISPARATE TREATMENT AND ADVERSE IMPACT

Unlawful employment discrimination, as established through various Supreme Court decisions, can be divided into two broad categories: disparate treatment and adverse impact. Disparate treatment is the most easily understood form of discrimination. An employer simply treats some people less favorably than others because of race, religion, sex, national origin, or age; for example, males are treated differently than females, whites are treated differently than blacks. The crux of disparate treatment is different treatment on the basis of some non-allowable criterion. It may be thought of as direct discrimination. Common forms of disparate treatment include selection rules with a racial, sexual, or other premise, prejudicial actions, unequal treatment on an individual basis, and different hiring standards for different groups.

McDonald v. *Santa Fe Trail Transportation Company* (12 FEP 1577) offers an excellent example of disparate treatment. Three of the company's employees, two whites and one black, had allegedly misappropriated sixty gallons of antifreeze. Santa Fe took disciplinary action against the workers by terminating the two whites, but not the black employee. The discharged white workers filed suit against the company, charging that their termination violated both Title VII and the Civil Rights Act of 1866. The Supreme

Court, in a 1977 decision, agreed with the plaintiffs that they had been the recipients of unequal treatment on the basis of their race.

Central to disparate treatment is the matter of proof. The plaintiff must first be able to establish a prima facie case, and, second, be able to establish that the employer was acting on the basis of a discriminatory motive.

Adverse impact, as previously discussed in this chapter, occurs when facially neutral or neutrally applied employment procedures affect different groups differently. Unlike disparate treatment, adverse impact does not require proof of a discriminatory motive or intent on the part of the employer. It is only necessary to show that employment practices affect different groups differently.

RECORD-KEEPING REQUIREMENTS

Employers are required to maintain considerable records as a result of the *Uniform Guidelines*. Even if no adverse impact exists, employers with 100 or fewer employees are required to have certain records available for each year. As specified in the *Guidelines*, the following data must be maintained and available:

(a) The number of persons hired, promoted, and terminated for each job, by sex, and where appropriate by race and national origin; (b) The number of applicants for hire and promotion by sex, and where appropriate by race and national origin; (c) The selection procedures utilized (either standardized or not standardized).[20]

Employers with more than 100 employees are required to maintain records showing whether their selection process has had an adverse impact on any job groups. Adverse impact analysis must be conducted annually for each protected class that constitutes at least 2 percent of the labor force in the relevant labor market or 2 percent of the applicable workforce. However, it is not necessary to maintain records by race or national origin if one race or one national origin group in the relevant labor market does not comprise at least 2 percent of the labor force.

EEOC suggests that required records be kept for a minimum of two years. Certainly, it is in the best interest of an employer to have adequate documentation on hand that can be used to refute a discrimination claim in the event that a charge is filed.

Simply because certain records must be maintained for a stipulated period of time does not mean that the employer has to keep these records under active consideration or in an active file. For example, employment applications must be retained, but the employer has no obligation to continue active review of these applications beyond its customary period of thirty to sixty days.

Moreover, because documents must be maintained does not mean that all of the documents "should be made available to any investigator from any agency."[21] An EEOC investigator who is examining a claim of sex discrimination is not automatically entitled to see company records pertaining to racial composition of the workforce, promotion rates by race, and so forth.

AFFIRMATIVE ACTION

An affirmative action plan is a program undertaken by an organization to improve job opportunities for and increase the utilization of protected classes in its workforce. Such a program may be originated voluntarily by a company (or a company and its union) or it may be imposed mandatorily by federal regulations, court order, or EEOC action.

An organization may elect, on its own, to initiate an affirmative action plan to correct conspicuous imbalances in its work force such as underutilization of minorities in certain jobs or occupations. By doing so, the organization is not admitting to discriminatory practices, rather, it is attempting to correct deficiencies in the hiring and promotion of women and minorities that have resulted from legitimate selection procedures. A voluntary program is likely to be based on an employer's recognition of its social responsibility to the community in which it operates.

There is, however, a risk attached to a voluntary affirmative action plan: the possibility of reverse discrimination. While the Supreme Court has, as discussed in Chapter 3, addressed the issue of reverse discrimination twice (*Regents of the University of California* v. *Bakke* and *Weber* v. *Kaiser Aluminum Corporation*), it has yet to give a clear-cut answer on this issue. Nevertheless, the majority opinion in *Weber* would appear to lay down certain principles to which voluntary affirmative action plans must adhere:

- The plan must be remedial in nature and designed to open job opportunities in occupations that have traditionally been closed to minorities.
- The plan must not "trammel" the interests of white employees.
- The plan must not create a bar to the advancement of white employees.
- The plan must not require the discharge of whites to create job openings for minorities.
- The plan must be temporary in nature.

Inasmuch as *Weber* addressed the issue of reverse racial discrimination, the terminology used by the Court in specifying plan requirements reflects racial considerations. It seems clear, however, that the guidelines promulgated in the majority opinion apply equally as well to other protected classes.

While the potential for charges of reverse discrimination exist in any voluntary affirmative action plan, the charges are almost certain to come from majority employees since ". . . employers can be sure the federal government is not going to prosecute them for reverse discrimination because it has never done so."[22]

The vast majority of affirmative action plans are originated under mandatory requirements. There are three situations that require employers to develop such plans: (1) the employer is a government contractor with a contract of $50,000 or more, (2) the employer has been found guilty of discrimination and ordered by a federal court to develop and implement a plan, or (3) a discrimination suit brought against the employer by EEOC shows the existence of discrimination, and the employer has entered into a consent decree with EEOC whereby the employer will establish an affirmative action plan.

CONTENT OF AN AFFIRMATIVE ACTION PLAN

The procedures established by the Office of Federal Contract Compliance Programs for developing and implementing affirmative action programs were published in the *Federal Register* on December 4, 1974. These regulations are known as Revised Order Number 4. OFCCP is very specific as to what should be included in an affirmative action plan. Although the following discussion is based on the requirements for affirmative action outlined by OFCCP, the same requirements would generally apply to plans mandated under different regulations or by other agencies.[23]

Development or Reaffirmation of Equal Opportunity Policy

The organization's policy statement should reflect the employer's attitude regarding equal employment opportunity, assign overall responsibility for EEO within the company, and provide for monitoring and reporting procedures. The policy should state the firm's intentions to recruit, hire, train, and promote persons in all job titles without regard to race, color, religion, sex, or national origin, except where sex is a bona fide occupational qualification. It should also state that all employment decisions will be made consistent with equal employment opportunity principles. Moreover, the policy should ensure that promotion decisions impose only valid requirements. The policy, finally, should guarantee that all personnel actions involving such areas as compensation, benefits, transfers, layoffs, return from layoff, company-sponsored training, education, tuition assistance, and social and recreational programs will be administered without regard to race, color, religion, sex, or national origin.

Dissemination of Policy

Revised Order No. 4 is quite specific with regard to dissemination of an organization's equal employment opportunity policy.

The policy should be disseminated internally as follows:

- Include it in the company's policy manual.
- Conduct special meetings with executive, management, and supervisory personnel to explain the intent of the policy and individual responsibility for effective implementation, making clear the chief executive officer's attitude on equal opportunity.
- Schedule special meetings with all other employees to discuss the policy and explain individual employee responsibilities.
- Discuss the policy thoroughly in both employee orientation and management training programs.
- Meet with union officials to inform them of the policy and request their cooperation.
- Include non-discrimination clauses in all union agreements and review all contractual provisions to ensure that they are non-discriminatory.
- Publish articles covering EEO programs, progress reports, promotions, and so forth of minority and female employees in company publications.
- Post the policy on company bulletin boards.
- When employees are featured in product or consumer advertising, employee handbooks, or similar publications, both minority and non-minority men and women should be pictured.
- Communicate to employees the existence of the organization's affirmative action program and make available such elements of the program as will enable employees to know of and avail themselves of its benefits.

There are also additional requirements for disseminating the policy externally. These are as follows:

- Inform all recruiting sources, verbally and in writing, of the organization's policy, stipulating that these sources actively recruit and refer minorities and women for all positions listed.
- Incorporate the equal opportunity clause in all purchase orders, leases, contracts, and so on covered by Executive Order 11246, as amended, and its implementing regulations.
- Notify minority and women's organizations, community agencies, community leaders, secondary schools, and colleges of company policy, preferably in writing.
- Communicate to prospective employees the existence of the organization's affirmative action program and make available such elements of the program as will enable such prospective employees to know of and avail themselves of its benefits.

- When employees are pictured in consumer or help wanted advertising, both minority and non-minority men and women should be pictured.
- Send written notification of company policy to all subcontractors, vendors, and suppliers, requesting appropriate action on their part.

Responsibility for Implementation

An executive should be appointed as director or manager of the organization's equal employment opportunity program. This individual should be given the necessary top management support to accomplish the assignment effectively. Revised Order No. 4 specifies the minimum level of responsibility associated with the task of EEO manager. These tasks include:

- Developing policy statements, affirmative action programs, and internal and external communication techniques.
- Assisting in the identification of problem areas.
- Assisting line management in arriving at solutions to problems.
- Designing and implementing audit and reporting systems.
- Serving as liaison between the organization and the enforcement agencies.
- Serving as liaison between the company and minority organizations, women's organizations, and community action groups concerned with employment opportunities for minorities and women.
- Keeping management informed of latest developments in the area of equal employment opportunity.

Revised Order No. 4 also imposes some requirements on an organization's line management. These include:

- Assistance in the identification of problem areas and establishment of local and unit goals and objectives relative to equal employment.
- Active involvement with local minority organizations, women's organizations, community action groups, and community service programs.
- Periodic audit of training programs, hiring and promotion patterns to remove impediments to the attainment of goals and objectives.
- Regular discussions with local managers, supervisors, and employees to ensure that the company's equal opportunity policies are being followed.
- Review of the qualifications of employees to ensure that minorities and women are given full opportunities for transfers and promotions.
- Career counseling for all employees.
- Periodic audit to ensure that each location or company facility is in compliance.

- Ensuring that supervisors understand that their work performance is being evaluated on the basis of their equal employment opportunity efforts and results as well as other criteria.

- Ensuring that supervisors understand that it is their responsibility to take actions to prevent harassment of employees assigned to their units through affirmative action efforts.

Utilization Analysis

An acceptable affirmative action program must include an analysis of areas where the organization is deficient in its utilization of minorities and women. The first step in conducting a utilization analysis is to complete a work force analysis. To do this, each job title is listed as it appears in applicable collective bargaining agreements or payroll records and ranked from the lowest paid job to the highest paid job within each department or other similar organizational unit. For each job title, the total number of incumbents for each of the following groups must be given: blacks, Spanish-surnamed Americans, American Indians, Orientals, and females. The wage rate or salary range for each job title must also be given.

The second step involves an analysis of all major job groups at each facility or location at which the company operates, with an explanation if minorities or women are currently being underutilized. A job group, for this purpose, is defined as one or more jobs or groups of jobs having similar content, wage rates, and opportunities. Underutilization is defined as having fewer minorities or women in a particular job group than would reasonably be expected by their availability in the labor market. Utilization analysis is important to the affirmative action concept because the percentage figure calculated will determine whether underutilization exists. For example, if the utilization analysis determines the availability of blacks for a certain job group to be 30 percent, then the organization must have 30 percent blacks in that job group. If 30 percent of the job group is not black, underutilization exists and the company must set a goal of reaching the level of 30 percent blacks in that job group.

In determining whether there is underutilization of minorities, the Office of Federal Contract Compliance Programs states that the organization should consider the following factors:

1. The minority population of the labor market surrounding the facility.

2. The amount of minority unemployment in the surrounding labor market.

3. The percentage of the minority work force, as compared to the total work force, in the immediate labor areas.

4. The general availability in the immediate area of minorities having requisite skills.

5. The availability of minorities having requisite skills in an area from which the company can be reasonably expected to recruit.

6. The availability of promotable and transferable minorities within the organization.

7. The existence of training institutions capable of training people in the requisite skills.

8. The degree of training the company is reasonably able to undertake as a means of making all job classes available to minorities.

In determining whether there is underutilization of women, OFCCP takes a slightly different approach and considers the following factors:

1. The size of the female unemployed work force in the labor area surrounding the facility.

2. The percentage of the female work force as compared to the total work force in the immediate area.

3. The general availability in the immediate area of women having requisite skills.

4. The availability of women having requisite skills in an area from which the company can reasonably be expected to recruit.

5. The availability of women seeking employment in the labor market or recruiting area of the organization.

6. The availability of promotable and transferable female employees within the organization.

7. The existence of training institutions capable of training people in the requisite skills.

8. The degree of training the company is reasonably able to undertake as a means of making all job classes available to women.

If underutilization of minorities or women is occurring, a further study should be made to identify the cause of the problem. Revised Order No. 4 identifies nineteen possible causes of underutilization. These are as follows:

• Underutilization of minorities or women in specific job groups.

• Lateral and/or vertical movement of minority or female employees occurring at a rate lower than that of non-minority or male employees.

• A selection process that eliminates a significantly higher percentage of minorities or women than non-minorities or men.

• Application forms or other preemployment forms not in compliance with federal legislation.

• Position descriptions that are inaccurate in relation to actual job duties and functions.

- Formal or scored selection procedures that are not validated as required by the *Uniform Guidelines.*
- Test forms that are not validated by location, work performance, and failure to include minorities and women in the sample.
- Referral ratio of minorities or women to the hiring supervisor or manager that indicates that a significantly higher percentage are being rejected as compared to non-minority or male applicants.
- Minorities or women are excluded from or are not participating in company-sponsored activities or programs.
- De facto segregation that is still in existence in some facilities.
- Seniority provisions that contribute to overt or inadvertent discrimination; that is, a disparity by minority group status or sex exists between length of service and types of jobs held.
- Nonsupport of company policy by managers, supervisors, or employees.
- Minorities or women underutilized or significantly underrepresented in training or career improvement programs.
- No formal techniques established for evaluating the effectiveness of EEO programs.
- Lack of access to suitable housing that inhibits recruiting efforts or employment of qualified minorities.
- Lack of suitable transportation, either public or private, to the workplace.
- Labor unions and subcontractors not notified of their responsibilities in affirmative action efforts.
- Purchase orders not containing an EEO clause.
- Equal employment opportunity posters not prominently displayed.

Establishment of Goals and Timetables

Central to any affirmative action program is the concept of goals and timetables. These goals and timetables represent minority and female hiring or promotion levels that are realistic and attainable in terms of the organization's utilization deficiencies and its affirmative action program. In establishing goals and setting timetables, the organization should consider the results that it can reasonably expect to achieve by putting forth good faith, positive efforts to increase the size and utilization of its minority and female work force.

Both human resource managers and line managers should be involved in the process of developing goals and timetables. There are two goals that must be established regarding underutilization: an annual goal and an ultimate goal. The annual goal is one that moves toward elimination of underutilization, whereas the ultimate goal is, of course, the abolishment of any underutilization. Both of these goals should be specific in terms of planned results and related to realistic timetables for their accomplishment. However, goals should not be so rigid that inflexible quotas are established. Rather, they should be reasonably attainable targets that can be met through positive action by the employer.

Development and Execution of Programs

Employers should conduct detailed analyses of job descriptions to ensure that these documents accurately reflect job requirements and content. In other words, an effective affirmative action program requires that a comprehensive job analysis program be in place and operating. Additionally, all job specifications should be validated in terms of the job. Special attention should be given to academic, experience, and skills requirements. If a job specification screens out a disproportionate number of minorities or women, the requirement must be validated in accordance with the procedures specified in the *Uniform Guidelines*.

When a job opening occurs, all members of management who are involved in the recruiting, screening, selecting, and promotion process should be notified. Also, any individual involved in recruiting, screening, selecting, promotion, disciplinary, and related processes should be carefully trained so as to eliminate bias in any personnel action.

The organization's entire selection and employment process should be carefully evaluated to ensure freedom from discrimination or bias. Any procedures that adversely affect the hiring of minorities or women must be scrutinized and revised or eliminated if there is a possibility that such procedures result in unfair discrimination or exclusion of protected classes from employment opportunities.

Particularly important in an effective affirmative action program are efforts to increase the number of minorities and females who apply for job openings. Revised Order No. 4 suggests some techniques that are designed to improve recruitment efforts and increase the flow of minority and female applicants. These actions include:

- Identifying referral organizations for minorities and women.
- Holding formal briefing sessions with representatives of referral organizations.
- Encouraging minority and female employees to refer applicants to the company.
- Including minorities and women on the human resource staff.
- Permitting minorities and women to participate in career days, youth motivation programs, and related activities in their community.
- Actively participating in job fairs and giving company representatives the authority to make on-the-spot commitments to qualified minorities and women.

- Actively recruiting at schools having predominantly minority or female enrollments.

- Recruiting efforts at other schools that utilize special approaches to reach minorities and women.

- Using special employment programs such as co-op programs, after school jobs, work-study jobs, summer employment, and so forth that increase employment opportunities for minorities and women.

- Pictorially presenting minorities and women in recruiting brochures.

- Placing help wanted ads in minority news media and women's interest media.

To ensure that minorities and women are given equal opportunity for promotion within the organization, OFCCP suggests that companies do the following:

- Post or otherwise announce promotional opportunities.

- Inventory current minority and female employees to determine academic, skill, and experience levels of individual employees.

- Initiate necessary remedial, job training, and work-study programs.

- Develop and implement formal employee evaluation programs.

- Validate all job specifications in terms of job-related performance criteria.

- Require supervisory personnel to submit written explanation when apparently qualified minorities or females are passed over for promotion.

- Establish formal career counseling programs.

- Review seniority practices and seniority clauses in union agreements to ensure that such practices or clauses are non-discriminatory and do not have a discriminatory effect.

- Ensure that facilities and company-sponsored social and recreational activities are integrated and actively encourage all employees to participate in all company-sponsored events and activities.

- Encourage child care, housing, and transportation programs appropriately designed to improve employment opportunities for minorities and women.

Internal Audit and Reporting System

Organizations should monitor records of referrals, placements, transfers, promotions, and terminations at all levels to ensure that a non-discriminatory policy is carried out. Additionally, the company should require formal reports from unit managers on a regularly scheduled basis as to the degree to which corporate or unit goals and timetables relative to affirmative action are met. Report results should be reviewed with all levels of management.

NOTES

1. Kenneth J. McCulloch, *Selecting Employees Safely under the Law* (Englewood Cliffs, N.J.: Prentice-Hall, 1981), p. 24.

2. *Uniform Guidelines on Employee Selection Procedures*, Section 1607.16Q.

3. Ibid., Section 1607.4D.

4. James Ledvinka, *Federal Regulation of Personnel and Human Resource Management* (Belmont, Calif.: Kent Publishing Company, 1982), p. 107.

5. Ibid.

6. McCulloch, *Selecting Employees*, p. 68.

7. Robert J. Haertel, "The Statistical Procedures for Calculating Adverse Impact," *Personnel Administrator*, January 1984, pp. 56-58.

8. Michelle Hoyman and Ronda Robinson, "Interpreting the New Sexual Harassment Guidelines," *Personnel Journal*, December 1980, p. 996.

9. Barbara Hagler, Testimony before House Judiciary II Committee, State of Illinois, March 4, 1980, p. 5.

10. *Guidelines on Discrimination Because of Sex*, Section 1604.11.

11. Ibid.

12. Barbara Lindemann Schlei and Paul Grossman, *Employment Discrimination Law*, 2nd ed. (Washington, D.C.: Bureau of National Affairs, 1983), p. 423.

13. R. Wayne Mondy and Robert M. Noe III, *Personnel: The Management of Human Resources* 3rd ed. (Boston: Allyn and Bacon, 1987), p. 83.

14. *Discrimination Because of Sex*, Section 1604.11.

15. Mondy and Noe, *Personnel*, p. 83.

16. *Guidelines on Discrimination Because of National Origin*, Section 1606.1.

17. Schlei and Grossman, *Employment Discrimination Law*, p. 306.

18. Mondy and Noe, *Personnel*, p. 84.

19. Schlei and Grossman, *Employment Discrimination Law*, p. 207.

20. *Uniform Guidelines*, Section 1607.15A.

21. McCulloch, *Selecting Employees*, p. 300.

22. Ibid., p. 72.

23. Discussion of affirmative action programs is based on material extracted from Office of Federal Compliance Programs' Revised Order No. 4, Revised Order No. 14, and OFCCP Compliance Manual.

5

Job Analysis

Broadly defined, job analysis is the process of collecting, interpreting, and reporting pertinent facts about the nature of a specific job. This process encompasses determining the duties and responsibilities that comprise the job; identifying the skills, abilities, knowledge, and experience required of a worker to be able to perform the job; and preparing job descriptions and job specifications.

Job analysis is the most fundamental of all human resource management activities because all other personnel functions, but most especially staffing, depend to a large extent on the successful execution of this one activity.[1] Human resource planning requires job analysis data to determine the types of jobs and skills that will be needed by the organization in the future. Recruiting needs job analysis information to be able to attract people with the proper experience and skill mix. Since selection of employees, for logical as well as legal reasons, must be based on job-related criteria, job analysis is essential to effective selection. Career planning and development, performance appraisal, and human resource administration all require information furnished by job analysis.

OVERVIEW OF THE JOB ANALYSIS PROCESS

Before considering the job analysis process, an explanation of some of the terminology used in this activity is necessary. Three terms that warrant definition are task, position, and job.

A *task* is a duty; it exists whenever effort must be expended for a specific purpose such as typing a letter. A *position* is a group of tasks assigned to one employee. In any organization, there are as many positions as there are workers. A *job*, on the other hand, is a group of positions that are identical as far as their major or significant tasks are concerned. In a small organization, where every position differs from every other position, a position is also a job.[2]

Job analysis, in essence, consists of four major components: (1) identification of each job in the organization; (2) collection of information about the duties, responsibilities, and working conditions of the job; (3) determination of the human qualifications needed to perform the job; and (4) preparation of job descriptions and job specifications.

Job Identification

Before any job can be analyzed, it is necessary to determine what and how many jobs exist in the organization. To do this, a list of all positions is compiled. In a large organization the list would be assembled department by department; in a small organization, the list would be compiled for the total company. There are several ways this list can be constructed: by studying the organizational chart, by reviewing payroll records, by examining personnel directories, by talking to supervisors and managers, or by observing the actual work performed in each organizational unit. The final list of positions should equal the total number of employees in each department, if it has been compiled department by department; or it should equal the total number of employees in the organization if it has been compiled in aggregate fashion.

Once the list of positions has been completed, the next step is to develop a list of jobs. If, for example, an organization has six employees who function as accounting clerks and they all perform the same duties, it is clear that "accounting clerk" constitutes one job. But, if an organization has three individuals designated as "engineer" and one performs electrical engineering duties, one carries out mechanical engineering duties, and the other performs industrial engineering duties, it is clear that there are three separate jobs, not one. Should any doubt exist as to whether two or more positions are actually similar in nature, they should be listed as separate jobs until further analysis can be done to clarify the situation.

After the tentative list of jobs has been completed, it is good practice to standardize job titles so that they conform to universally accepted and recognized titles. Frequently, organizations create job titles that are unique to the organization and have little or no meaning outside the institution. The *Dictionary of Occupational Titles*, a publication of the U.S. Department of Labor, contains a list of standardized, commonly used, and widely accepted job titles. Wherever possible, these titles should be used.

Collection of Data Relative to Job Duties and Responsibilities

After determining which jobs exist in an organization, the major task of job analysis begins—ascertaining the specific duties and responsibilities of each job. This is the most time consuming of all job analysis activities. Techniques for accomplishing this vital function are examined in subsequent sections of this chapter.

Determination of Needed Human Qualifications

One of the most difficult parts of job analysis is determining the skills, abilities, experience, and other qualifications needed to perform a job. Here, a great deal of judgment, discretion, and expertise is required by the individual performing the job analysis. While input from supervisors and managers is helpful, there is a tendency for these people to describe the qualifications that an ideal job incumbent should possess. Employees, especially those who have been performing a job for a while, also tend to overstate the qualifications needed. The task of the job analyst is to sort through preferred qualifications and determine the minimally appropriate level of skills needed for successful job performance.

Preparation of Job Descriptions and Job Specifications

The final phase of job analysis is to prepare written documents that enumerate the duties and responsibilities of the job—job descriptions—and specify the skills, abilities, and other qualifications needed to perform the job—job specifications.

With this overview of the job analysis process in mind, let us now shift our attention to the purposes or uses of job analysis information. In later sections we will examine in greater detail how the information is gathered and reported.

PURPOSES AND USES OF JOB ANALYSIS

As a basic tool of human resource management, job analysis provides information that can be used in a number of ways to satisfy organizational purposes. The information provided through this activity can be used to:

- Assist in human resource planning. Through job analysis data relative to future skills needs are determined. The organization knows not only what jobs will be needed in the future, but also the qualifications individuals will need to fill these jobs successfully.

- Establish definitive criteria for making staffing decisions. Under the provisions of Title VII, all selection standards and procedures used must be job related. Job analysis is the vehicle through which this is accomplished.

- Indicate the need for training of present as well as future job incumbents in the performance of job duties and responsibilities.

- Establish a basis for appraising the performance of employees in terms of actual job duties.
- Assist in the career planning and development process by identifying the qualifications employees must have to progress to positions of higher responsibility.
- Reallocate work from one job to another if the workload is too heavy in one job or if it could be performed better in another job.
- Correct unsafe or undesirable working conditions in a job before such conditions have a deleterious effect on workers.
- Redesign work flows or organizational relationships where these are currently inappropriate.
- Determine which jobs are exempt from the payment of overtime compensation and which jobs are not.
- Evaluate jobs relative to each other, thereby establishing a system of internal equity that can be used for compensation purposes.
- Establish groups or classes of similar jobs for compensation or performance appraisal purposes.
- Create a factual basis for determining promotions, transfers, terminations, or demotions.
- Establish a basis that assists in research efforts attempting to distinguish successful from less successful employees.
- Protect the organization in the event of legal challenge. The courts have typically held that job analysis made in good faith is admissible as evidence that the organization has attempted to validate certain of its personnel procedures and practices.[3]

As the preceding list, which is intended to be illustrative rather than exhaustive, indicates, there are a number of reasons why any organization should engage in job analysis. Not only is this process a useful tool for human resource management, it is also a vital defense mechanism for legal challenges to employment practices.

TYPES OF JOB ANALYSIS INFORMATION

A wealth of information can result from a thorough, effectively performed job analysis. Table 5.1 presents examples of the types of data, by various categories, that can be gathered.[4] The specific information generated depends largely upon the uses to which it will be put. As a general rule, however, it is preferable to collect as much in the way of job facts as possible so as not to overlook any items that may be important.

Certainly, job duties and responsibilities are the most crucial items that must be identified, but it is also important to identify job qualifications as well as the relationships and contexts in which the job is performed.

TRADITIONAL JOB ANALYSIS METHODS

Over the years, four traditional methods of job analysis have evolved. These are: (1) questionnaires, (2) interviews, (3) observation, and (4) some combination of the preceding methods. These approaches, despite their deficiencies, are still the ones most commonly used by the majority of institutions that conduct job analysis.

Questionnaires

One of the simplest and quickest ways to collect a substantial amount of data on many jobs simultaneously is to administer a structured questionnaire to employees. Questionnaires may also be the most economical data collection method. With this approach each employee in a job—or if there are many employees performing the same job, a representative sample of employees—is given a questionnaire and instructed to provide certain kinds of information about his or her job. While the specific types of data requested depend upon how the organization plans to use the job analysis information, the worker is typically asked to elaborate on the kinds of things previously shown in Table 5.1.

Administering a job analysis questionnaire to employees is done in one of three ways: (1) the job analyst meets with all employees of a work unit and explains how to complete the questionnaire, (2) the job analyst meets with work unit supervisors to explain how to complete the instrument and the supervisors, in turn, explain it to their employees, or (3) the questionnaire is distributed with an accompanying memorandum that contains the needed instructions. From an effectiveness standpoint, the first approach would seem to be the best since it offers the greatest opportunity to answer questions, provide clarification, and eliminate problems that may affect the quality or quantity of the information garnered by questionnaires.

Once the employee completes the questionnaire, it is usually reviewed by his or her supervisor for completeness and accuracy, and then returned to the job analyst.

Designing a questionnaire that will produce the data needed for a thorough analysis of jobs is not an easy matter. The types of information needed, how the information will be used, and other factors must be considered before a sound instrument can be constructed. In many instances, one questionnaire cannot be used for all the jobs in an organization; several may be required. It may be necessary, for example, to design one questionnaire for production workers, another for clerical employees, another for technical personnel, and so on.

Obviously, the questionnaire approach to job analysis has some disadvantages: (1) it may interfere with normal work routine since employees will

Table 5.1
Types of Information Collected by Job Analysis

1. Job Duties
- General purpose of the job.
- Duties performed on a daily basis and the approximate amount of time spent on each.
- Duties performed only at stated periods such as weekly or monthly and the approximate amount of time spent on each.
- Duties performed on an infrequent or irregular basis, such as filling-in for another worker, and the approximate amount of time involved.
- Most difficult or complex parts of the job and why they are difficult or complex.

2. Job Responsibilities
- Nature and extent of responsibility for money, property, equipment, or other types of assets.
- Nature and extent of responsibility for materials or supplies.
- Nature and extent of responsibility for people.
- Number of workers supervised, directly or indirectly.
- Job titles of workers supervised, directly or indirectly.
- Nature and extent of access to or usage of classified, confidential, or proprietary information.
- Nature and extent of decision making authority.

3. Machines, Equipment, Tools, and Materials Used
- Machines and equipment operated and degree of proficiency required.
- Tools used and degree of proficiency required.
- Types of materials used, how they are used, and what is done to them.

4. Controls Over Work
- Type of instructions received regarding how work is to be performed and from whom they are received.
- Tasks performed that must be checked by others and by whom and how they are checked.
- Decisions that must be referred to supervisor
- Policies or procedures used.

5. Performance Standards or Output Expectations
- Output requirements.
- Quality requirements.
- Time schedules, deadlines, or other time requirements that must be met.

6. **Interactions with Others**
   - Nature and frequency of contacts with co-workers or other organizational personnel.
   - Nature and frequency of contacts with people outside the organization.
   - Types of circumstances under which contacts within or outside the organization are normally made.
   - Number of people contacted in a typical workday.

7. **Organizational Relationships**
   - Job title of immediate supervisor.
   - Department and unit to which job is assigned.
   - Type of supervision received.
   - Type of supervision given.
   - Job from which individual is typically promoted to present job.
   - Job to which individual is typically promoted from present job.

8. **Physical Factors and Job Environment**
   - Percentage of time spent sitting, standing, and walking.
   - Amount and type of physical exertion required.
   - Environmental conditions in which work is performed.
   - Typical work schedule, including overtime requirements.
   - Job factors that produce fatigue.

9. **Education, Training, Experience, and Personal Requirements**
   - Minimum level of education needed.
   - Specialized courses required.
   - Licenses or certifications required.
   - Minimum level of experience required.
   - Types of jobs in which required experience is usually gained.
   - Personal requirements needed such as oral or written communication skills, mathematical or mechanical aptitude, etc.
   - Other qualifications, skills, characteristics, or requirements needed.

91

typically complete it during working hours, (2) it may produce inaccurate information due to the tendency of employees to overstate the importance of their jobs, (3) it may generate insufficient data if employees completing the instrument are not verbally facile, (4) it may be viewed by some employees as an imposition or interference with their work efforts, and (5) it may, if used on a large number of jobs at once, produce a mass of data for a job analyst to examine, interpret, synthesize, and report in meaningful fashion.[5] Nevertheless, the questionnaire remains a widely used job analysis method.

Interviews

The second traditional method of conducting a job analysis is to interview employees performing the work. When this method is used, a structured interview guide is utilized so that the same questions are asked of each job incumbent and the same areas are covered in every interview conducted. Such a guide is especially critical when several individuals will be doing the interviewing. In effect, the interview method is much like the questionnaire approach except that the information is given to the analyst orally instead of in writing.

Job analysis interviews may be conducted in several different ways. They may be held with an individual employee, a group of employees performing the same job, the supervisor of a section or department, the individual employee and then the supervisor, or a group of employees and then the supervisor.[6] The most common procedure is to interview the job incumbent individually and then verify the information received by interviewing the worker's supervisor.

Interviews can be a very effective means of collecting job analysis information inasmuch as most workers enjoy talking about what they do. A skillful interviewer who knows what information is needed can often probe a job in much greater depth than could ever be achieved through a questionnaire approach.

Interviews do have certain limitations: (1) they are time consuming and therefore more expensive than questionnaires, (2) the quality of the information gathered is highly dependent upon the interviewer's skill, (3) they are often disruptive to the work routine because they take employees away from their assigned tasks, (4) they may be viewed as somewhat threatening by employees, and (5) even though the interviewer may be highly skilled, the quality and quantity of information obtained may suffer if the employee is not orally expressive.[7] Yet in most instances, the information provided by interviews may be far superior to that that can be collected by questionnaires.

Observation

Job analysis can also be conducted by observing employees as they perform their jobs. The analyst simply watches the worker and records information about the various tasks being performed and the kinds of skills used to perform them. In order not to miss infrequent or irregular tasks, it may be necessary to observe many work cycles over an extended period of time.

The biggest advantages of observation are that the analyst can see firsthand the conditions under which the work is performed, note the level of complexity or difficulty involved, and gain greater insight into the job than might be possible through other methods.

On the other hand, relying solely upon observation as a job analysis method has serious drawbacks: observation requires a highly trained individual who can recognize task difficulties and variations of skill requirements; it is easy to overlook infrequently performed job duties that require greater skill and effort than those performed on a daily basis; observation can be very time consuming and thus expensive; observation can be threatening to employees; and observation may disrupt normal work routine, not only for the worker being observed but also for others in the work unit who are uncomfortable with an outside observer in their midst.

Certainly, there is a place for observation in the collecting of job analysis information, but its place would appear to be secondary rather than primary.

Combination

Of all the traditional approaches to job analysis, a combination method is probably the best in that it minimizes the disadvantages and maximizes the advantages of any one approach used by itself. Of the possible combination approaches, the two used most often are questionnaires and interviews and questionnaires, interviews, and observations.

As indicated earlier, one of the advantages of the questionnaire is that it produces a great deal of data rather quickly. But the job analyst often encounters difficulty in analyzing or interpreting questionnaire data. Employees may use jargon, shop talk, or technical terms that mean little to the person who has to analyze the data. In addition, employees may provide very sketchy information that has little or no value to an outsider who has to make sense of it. Interviews, conducted with the questionnaire in hand, give the analyst an opportunity to seek clarification or obtain additional job information.

The interview itself can be conducted more expeditiously when workers have already supplied written material since the analyst does not have to cover every aspect of each job, but only those parts where additional explanation is needed. Interview time is likely to be 50 percent less when the discussion with the worker is conducted from a completed job analysis questionnaire.[8]

Combining questionnaires, interviews, and observation of the job and physical environment results in the most complete information possible.

Observation often reveals factors about a job that are not necessarily un-covered through questionnaires or interviews; for example, poor lighting, inefficient work station layout that causes a worker to spend more time walking than is necessary, excessive or irritating noise, or unusual physical motions required for task performance.

Utilizing questionnaires, interviews, and observations provides the ad-vantage of seeing a job from different perspectives; consequently, the infor-mation obtained in this fashion not only tends to be more complete, but also more valid.

THE PRODUCTS OF JOB ANALYSIS

Two major written documents result from job analysis: a job description and a job specification. The job description delineates duties and respon-sibilities, and the job specification sets forth the human skills and qualifica-tions needed to be able to perform a specific job. In actual practice job specifications are commonly included as a section in the description itself. However, it is beneficial from a conceptual viewpoint to envision these two end products as separate items that serve different purposes. By doing so, greater emphasis is placed on both describing the job, and accurately speci-fying the skills required for job performance.

Job descriptions and job specifications are crucial to effective staffing; they serve as guidelines for hiring that ensure that the organization is selec-ting the right kinds of individuals to perform the work of the institution. Additionally, job descriptions establish a factual basis for determining rates of pay and establishing performance standards.

Job Descriptions

"Writing a good job description is not a simple matter. A job description must be specific, concise, complete, accurate, meaningful, and readable."[9] Whoever writes the description—job analyst, manager, or supervisor—must have an understanding of the content needed, the manner in which the information is to be presented, and effective writing techniques.

Content. The specific content of a job description varies from company to company, depending upon the uses to be made of the description, the format selected, and the nature of the job being described. Despite content differences, three requisites must be satisfied: job identification, job defini-tion, and job delineation.

Job identification consists of information that differentiates one job from another. Commonly used identifiers include job title, departmental location of the job, specific unit to which the job is assigned, and title of the position to which the job reports. In large organizations additional identifiers may also be used; for example, job number, labor grade, exempt or non-exempt status, and number of job incumbents.

Careful thought should go into selecting a job title since it is the primary job identifier. The title chosen should reflect as clearly as possible the nature of the work performed, be distinct enough to differentiate the job from other similar jobs, and be consistent with other titles used in the organization. Job titles, unfortunately, are often misleading. An "executive secretary" in one organization may be little more than a highly paid typist while a job with the same title in another organization may identify an incumbent who is an administrative assistant to a chief executive officer and does little or no typing. One source of information that can be of invaluable assistance in standardizing job titles is the *Dictionary of Occupational Titles* published by the U.S. Department of Labor. This book contains more than 20,000 standardized job titles as well as job descriptions. Each job title includes a numeric code that categorizes a job by different dimensions such as major job category, subsection of the major category, the job's relationship to data, people, and things, and an alphabetical listing within the job category. Wherever possible, an organization should use the titles and codes contained in the *DOT*.

Job definition is usually accomplished by means of a summary of the job that sets forth the purpose or nature of the job, why it exists, and how it relates to other organizational jobs. A good job summary provides a succinct statement of the job's function and assists in differentiating it from other jobs in the company.

Job delineation is the actual heart of the job description; it is the section of the job description in which duties, responsibilities, reporting relationships, and other tasks or functions are enumerated. It is, obviously, the longest part of the overall description. It is important that sufficiently detailed information be provided about actual job duties, but at the same time, the temptation to become verbose or pompous must be vigorously resisted. The job should be described in such a manner that duties and responsibilities can be clearly understood by those who will use the job description.

Format. There is no universal job description format; nevertheless, the three requisites for content—job identification, job definition, and job delineation—provide a reasonable indication of the basic format that should be followed.

Variations in job description format are most frequently found in the job delineation portion. Often, duties and responsibilities are subdivided in several sections to provide clarity and call attention to important job factors—financial responsibility, decision-making authority, controls over work, and interactions with others, for example. This practice would seem to be a sound one because it not only clarifies duties and responsibilities, but also increases the readability of the job description.

Whatever format is used should be consistent from job to job for each particular group of jobs; that is, all production jobs should be described according to the same format, all managerial jobs should be described according to the same format, and so forth. Also, the format used should parallel the use for which the description is intended. If the job description is to be used as the basis for job evaluation, each compensable factor in the job evaluation plan must be clearly addressed in the job description; if the job description is meant to be used as a basis for performance evaluation, each performance factor must be indicated.

Writing Techniques. Many of the job descriptions in use in industry today are poorly written; they are excessively wordy, imprecise, or difficult to read. A job description should be an action-oriented document that states precisely, concisely, and clearly the duties performed and responsibilities carried out in a particular job. Careful attention to clarity of expression is absolutely essential. The following guidelines should be followed when writing a job description:

- Start each duty or responsibility statement with an action verb such as analyze, calculate, compute, file, issue, prepare, reconcile, sort, tabulate, or transmit. Words of this kind identify what is actually done in a job.
- Avoid imprecise terminology. Words such as "handles," "coordinates," or "deals with" are vague and open to different interpretations by different readers.
- Avoid shop talk, jargon, or acronyms wherever possible because they are confusing to people who are not intimately familiar with the job.
- Use short, easy-to-read sentences.
- Use a style that specifies "who" does "what," "when" it is done, "why" it is done, "where" it is done, and "how" it is done.
- Be detailed, but not wordy. Excessive verbiage not only tends to confuse, but may also imply a degree of complexity that does not exist in a job.
- Use an outline form. With the exception of the job summary, which is normally in paragraph form, a job description is not a narrative. Each job duty or responsibility statement should make a specific point.
- Enumerate each duty and responsibility in the general order of its overall importance to the job.
- Keep the user in mind. In the staffing process one of the key users of the job description is likely to be the screening interviewer who must make a quick decision as to whether an applicant is sufficiently qualified for further consideration. If the job description is not clear to this person, qualified candidates may be eliminated and unqualified candidates may be recommended for further consideration.[10]

Figure 5.1 presents a job description that follows the preceding guidelines. While the job described is, admittedly, a simple one, the same style and format can be used for more complex or difficult jobs.

Figure 5.1
Job Description

Job Title: Records
Job Grade: 02
Job Number: 12
Effective: January 31, 19xx

Administrative Information

Reports to: Loan Operations Manager
Division: Consumer Loans
Department: Loan Operations
Section: Files & Records

Job Summary

Returns all consumer paid loan documents to customers. Supervises daily activities of two file clerks.

Duties and Responsibilities

1. Receives monthly data processing listing and printed address labels for accounts that have been paid in full and require the return of contracts, mortgage documents, auto titles, and other documents.
   (a) Pulls customer files.
   (b) Determines by codes on the data processing list which documents are to be returned.
   (c) Removes documents from files and prepares them for mailing to customer.
2. Answers telephone inquiries from customers or loan officers concerning documents hel in safekeeping.
3. Maintains tickler file on temporary auto titles until permanent title is received.
4. Files permanent auto titles, contrcts, mortgage documents, and other documents in customer files on a daily basis.
5. Supervises two file clerks who maintain correspondence and other general files.
6. Performs file clerk duties as needed.
7. Performs other duties, as required, on a temporary basis, to maintain section or departmental operations and services.

Controls Over Work

1. Pulls and returns only documents indicated on data processing listing.
2. Adheres to organizational policies and procedures concerning the filing, safekeeping, and return of documents.
3. Performs duties under limited supervision by immediate supervisor.

Other Job Facts

1. Engages in bending over, squatting, and reaching approximately forty percent of the time.
2. Has complete access to confidential information maintained in customer files.
3. Operates an IBM Selectric typewriter.

Job Specifications

Job specifications outline the minimum qualifications, such as education, experience, or skills, a person should possess to perform a job satisfactorily. Job specifications should always reflect the minimum, not the ideal qualifications for a particular job. In many instances there is probably a tendency for organizations to overstate qualifications. Why? Essentially, because the information on job qualifications is usually gathered from supervisors or employees—supervisors may describe the ideal candidate while employees may describe their own skills. Several problems may result if specifications are inflated. First, if specifications are set so high that they systematically eliminate minorities or women from consideration for jobs, the organization runs the risk of discrimination charges. Second, compensation costs will increase because ideal candidates will have to be compensated more than candidates with minimum skills. Third, job vacancies will be harder to fill because ideal candidates are more difficult to find than minimally qualified candidates.

Ascertaining the appropriate qualifications for a job is undoubtedly the most difficult part of job analysis. It requires a great deal of probing on the part of the job analyst as well as a broad understanding of the skills needed to perform varieties of work. Because of the problems associated with job specifications, it would appear to be safer for an organization to underspecify than to overspecify qualifications.

Figure 5.2 shows the specifications for the position of "Records Clerk" that was described in Figure 5.1.

OTHER JOB ANALYSIS METHODS

Although the majority of organizations in the United States use the traditional approaches to job analysis described earlier in this chapter, there have been attempts to develop more systematic, standardized approaches to improve the quality and consistency of job analysis information. Three of these approaches—the position analysis questionnaire, the job analysis schedule, and functional job analysis—will be described in this section to illustrate the efforts being made to increase the effectiveness of job analysis. By no means are these three the only newer approaches that have been developed. There are others, but PAQ, JAS, and FJA are the most widely recognized and used of the nontraditional job analysis methods.

Position Analysis Questionnaire

The PAQ was developed at Purdue University. It is the result of more than ten years of research by psychologists who studied thousands of jobs.[11]

Figure 5.2
Job Specification

Job Title: Records Clerk
Job Grade: 02
Job Number: 12
Effective: January 31, 19xx

Administrative Information

Reports to: Loan Operations Manager
Division: Consumer Loans
Department: Loan Operations
Section: Files & Records

Education

High school diploma preferred, but not required.

Experience

Six months or more in a financial institution and familiarity with various loan documents.

Machine Skill Requirements

Ability to operate electric typewriter at approximately 35 words per minute.

Other Skills

1. Ability to communicate in a courteous fashion and use correct grammar.
2. Ability to supervise others on a limited basis.

99

The PAQ is a structured job analysis questionnaire that uses a checklist approach to identify job elements. There are 194 job descriptors that relate to job-oriented or worker-oriented elements. Proponents of the PAQ believe that the ability of the checklist to identify job elements, behaviors required of job incumbents, and other job characteristics makes it possible to use this procedure for virtually any type of job.[12]

The 194 job elements used in the PAQ are grouped into twenty-seven division job dimensions and five overall job dimensions. These thirty-two dimensions are further divided into six major job activities: information input, mental processes, work output, relationships with other persons, job context, and other job characteristics. Each job descriptor is evaluated on a specified scale such as "extent of use," "amount of time," "importance of job," "possibility of occurrence," and "applicability."

With a computer, each job being studied can be scored relative to the thirty-two different job dimensions. The score derived represents a profile of the job that can be compared with standard profiles to group the job into known job families; that is, jobs of a similar nature. In essence, the PAQ identifies significant job behaviors and classifies jobs.

Using the PAQ, job descriptions can be prepared based on the relative importance and emphasis placed on various job elements.

The PAQ is completed by an employee or employees familiar with the job being studied—typically an experienced job incumbent or the immediate supervisor. The profiles and job descriptions are then prepared by job analysts.

As can be deduced from this brief description, the PAQ is a comprehensive, complex form of job analysis that requires an individual trained in its use if it is to produce the desired results.

Department of Labor Job Analysis Schedule

The U.S. Department of Labor has long been involved in developing and refining a systematic means of analyzing and classifying job content. The instrument or methodology that it has developed is called the Job Analysis Schedule.[13] Many federal, state, and local governmental agencies as well as private enterprises use this approach or some variation of it.

The basic thrust of the JAS is centered on gathering data relative to five categories that define satisfactory performance of a worker in a given job: worker functions; work fields; machines, tools, equipment, and work aids; materials, products, subject matter, and services; and worker traits.

Worker functions describes what workers do in the performance of a job with regard to data, people, and things. A scale of values that identifies the varying complexities of what is done with data, people, and things has been developed for the three categories. The twenty-four identifying activities for the three worker function areas are shown in Table 5.2. The highest combination of the three areas establishes the relative importance of the job. Normally, each successive function reading down a column would include or involve each of the other functions that follow. For example, in the column "Data" if the highest activity identified was compiling, it would be assumed that the job also involved computing, copying, and comparing. Note that the numerical values assigned the functions are the reverse of what might be expected in a typical value scale. With JAS, the lower the numerical value, the higher the level of activity.

The work fields identify the characteristics of the mechanical, technological, or socioeconomic requirements of the job. These fields are classified into ninety-nine different categories. Machines, tools, equipment, and work aids identify the instruments and devices of a mechanical nature that are used to carry out the job. Materials, products, subject matter, and services describe the types or kinds of materials worked on, the end products, knowledge used in performing the job, and the nature of the services rendered in the job. Worker traits are primarily concerned with job requirements or, perhaps more appropriately, job specifications. Traits are divided into five components: training time, aptitude, temperament, interests, and physical demands. Obviously, use of the JAS requires a highly trained and skilled job analyst if it is to be utilized effectively.

Table 5.2
Job Analysis Schedule Worker Functions

Data	People	Things
0 Synthesizing	0 Mentoring	0 Setting up
1 Coordinating	1 Negotiating	1 Precision Working
2 Analyzing	2 Instructing	2 Operating-Controlling
3 Compiling	3 Supervising	3 Driving-Operating
4 Computing	4 Diverting	4 Manipulating
5 Copying	5 Persuading	5 Tending
6 Comparing	6 Speaking-Signaling	6 Feeding-Offbearing
	7 Serving	7 Handling
	8 Taking instruction and Helping	

Functional Job Analysis

This approach to job analysis, a modification of the JAS, is a comprehensive approach that concentrates on the interactions among the work, the worker, and the work organization.[14] FJA is a worker-oriented approach to job analysis that identifies what a worker actually does rather than what the worker is responsible for.

FJA utilizes a modified version of the worker functions scales contained in the job analysis schedule. In fact, the two scales are almost identical except that FJA adds a "no significant relationship" to the data, people, and things categories of worker functions and reverses the numerical coding.

The basic premises or fundamental elements of FJA are:

1. A distinction is made between what gets done and what a worker must do to get it done. As far as job analysis is concerned, it is probably more important to know the latter. For example, an airline pilot does not fly passengers; he or she performs a multitude of tasks to take an airplane from one location to another.

2. What a worker does in a job is related to only three basic elements: data, people, and things. These are, in fact, the materials as well as the results of all work that is performed.

3. In relation to data, people, and things, workers function in unique ways. In essence, "data" draws on mental resources; "people" draws on interpersonal resources; and "things" draws on physical resources.

4. Any job requires that a worker relate to data, people, and things in some manner.

5. Although worker behavior or task performance can be described in an almost infinite number of ways, there are only a few definite and identifiable functions connected with data, people, and things. These basics are those shown in Table 5.2.

6. The functions performed by workers proceed from the simplest to the most complex. For instance, the least complex form of "people" would be "serving" while the most complex would be "monitoring." Consequently, if an upper level function is required, all of the preceding lower level functions are also required.

7. The three hierarchies for data, people, and things provide two measures for a job: level and orientation. Level is a measure of complexity in relation to data, people, and things. Orientation is a measure of involvement with data, people, and things.[15]

Proponents of the FJA claim that in addition to being a useful means of analyzing jobs, it also establishes criteria that can be used to evaluate the worth of a job (set compensation rates) and appraise the performance of workers in each job.[16]

As with the other newer approaches to job analysis, FJA is more complex than the traditional methods and requires a well-trained job analyst.

NOTES

1. R. Wayne Mondy and Robert M. Noe III, *Personnel: The Management of Human Resources*, 3rd ed. (Boston: Allyn and Bacon, 1987), pp. 93-95.

2. Donald L. Caruth, *Compensation Management for Banks* (Boston: Bankers Publishing Company, 1986), pp. 37-38.

3. Mondy and Noe, *Personnel*, pp. 93-95, and Caruth, *Compensation Management*, p. 37.

4. Adapted from Caruth, *Compensation Management*, pp. 256-262.

5. Caruth, *Compensation Management*, p. 40.

6. Ibid.

7. Ibid., p. 41.

8. Ibid., p. 43.

9. Ibid., p. 44.

10. Adapted from Caruth, *Compensation Management*, pp. 46-47.

11. Ernest J. McCormick, Paul R. Jeanneret, and Robert Mecham, "A Study of Job Characteristics and Job Dimensions as Based on the Position Analysis Questionnaire (PAQ)," *Journal of Applied Psychology*, August 1972, pp. 347-368.

12. Joseph Tiffin and Ernest J. McCormick, *Industrial Psychology*, 6th ed. (Englewood Cliffs, N.J.: Prentice-Hall, 1974), p. 53.

13. U.S. Department of Labor, Manpower Administration, *Handbook for Analyzing Jobs* (Washington, D.C.: U.S. Government Printing Office, 1972).

14. Monday and Noe, *Personnel*, pp. 108, 110.

15. Ernest J. McCormick, "Job Information: Its Development and Application," in Dale Yoder and Herbert S. Heneman, editors, *Staffing Policies and Strategies* (Washington, D.C.: Bureau of National Affairs, 1974), pp. 4-58.

16. Richard I. Henderson, *Compensation Management: Rewarding Performance*, 3rd ed. (Reston, Va.: Reston Publishing Company, 1979), p. 145.

6

Human Resource Planning

According to one corporate president, "The human resource is perhaps the last great cost that is relatively unmanaged."[1] While this may be an overstatement, it is unfortunately true that human resources often do not receive the same meticulous attention that management devotes to other organizational resources. Nowhere is this more evident than in planning for future personnel needs. Physical and financial resources are usually planned for well in advance. The need for new facilities, equipment, or capital may be anticipated years ahead of the time they will actually be required. Costs will be calculated, sources will be determined, rates of return will be computed, and other analyses will be performed. But when it comes to people resources, it is not unusual to find many organizations relying on the "faith principle"—the assumption that sufficient quantities and qualities of human resources will be available as they are needed to staff the new facilities and operate the new equipment. In most cases, people planning occurs after the fact. The new plant is opened, the new machinery is installed and the scramble is on to find employees to staff the facility and operate the equipment. To neglect planning for human resources, however, is to invite disruptions and delays if sufficient properly trained people do not materialize when they are needed.

Fortunately, a number of organizations have recognized, and others are beginning to recognize, the essentiality of planning for personnel needs. According to one author, ". . . we have entered a new era: the era of human resources planning."[2]

DEFINITION OF HUMAN RESOURCE PLANNING

Human resource planning may be defined in several ways. It may be thought of as: (1) ". . . the process of analyzing an organization's human resource needs under changing conditions and developing the activities necessary to satisfy these needs,"[3] (2) ". . . a systematic process for setting policies governing the acquisition, use, and disposition of personnel in order to achieve organizational objectives,"[4] or (3) ". . . the process which ensures that a sufficient number of employees possessing appropriate skills are available for achieving the firm's goals."[5] Some common threads are apparent in each of these definitions. One, human resource planning is a process; that is, an ongoing activity. Two, the purpose of human resource planning is to aid the organization in reaching its goals and objectives. Three, human resource planning is a systematic, analytical activity, not a haphazard one. And four, the goal of human resource planning is to have the right people in the right jobs at the right times.

Combining the definitions and their common threads, we can now more specifically define human resource planning as a systematic, ongoing activity that ensures that an organization has the right numbers and kinds of people in the right jobs at the right time so that the organization can achieve its stated objectives.

STRATEGIC BUSINESS PLANNING AND HUMAN RESOURCE PLANNING

The determination of future personnel requirements logically stems from the organization's strategic business plan—the document that identifies the direction in which the firm intends to move, in the long run as well as the short run.

Through strategic business planning the institution clarifies its mission and purpose, sets its goals and objectives, and develops courses of action that it hopes will lead to goal accomplishment and mission fulfillment. In the past, it was not unusual for the human resource manager to be left out of the strategic planning process or for human resource planners to forecast personnel requirements without referring to the business plan. Nor was it unusual for management to formulate goals and strategies without explicit information on the potential availability of human resources to carry out the firm's plans. Today, this situation is changing. More organizations are recognizing that well-formulated business plans cannot be developed without input from human resource professionals. Strategic planning and human resource planning are being increasingly viewed as interactive processes that rely heavily upon each other. Strategists need information on the quantitative and qualitative availability of personnel to construct viable plans; human resource planners need information on anticipated expansions or contractions of the organization to forecast requirements and availability of personnel. Only through an interactive linkage can both strategic planning and human resource planning become truly effective.

THE HUMAN RESOURCE PLANNING PROCESS

Figure 6.1 shows a generalized model of the human resource planning process. After the organization's strategic plan has been developed—with the full participation of the human resource department—the determination of specific future personnel needs can begin.

As the model indicates, there are three basic phases involved in human resource planning. The first phase is concerned with identifying the number and kinds of employees the firm will need in the future. This is the requirements forecasting stage. The strategic business plan may necessitate the creation of new jobs, the elimination of existing jobs, no changes in jobs, or call for increases or decreases in organizational positions (that is, numbers of employees). Additionally, the requirements forecast must consider the numbers of employees who will be lost through normal attrition such as termination, retirement, and so forth. After all of the various factors that influence requirements have been considered and the human resource planners have ascertained the personnel required to accomplish the business plan, the anticipated organizational structure of the future is created.

The second phase of human resource planning entails the determination of the availability of qualified people to staff the organization of the future. Here planners must look inside the enterprise to identify individuals who could be promoted or transferred to new jobs or positions; they must also look outside the firm, through the examination of demographic data and other factors, to forecast the number of qualified individuals who will be available to meet the future staffing needs of the organization. Personnel requirements are then matched with personnel availability. Although all steps in the human resource planning process are crucial, comparing needs and availability is especially important because it identifies the staffing situation that will confront the organization in the future and suggests actions that will have to be taken to equate the demand for and supply of human resources.

The final phase of human resource planning is the development of specific courses of action to assure the institution that it will have the appropriate number and kinds of people in the right places at the right time to carry out the strategic business plan.

Each phase in the human resource planning process requires careful thought and analysis. Some steps involve a great deal of complexity and the use of statistical methods. Other steps are highly subjective in nature and depend upon the exercise of creativity. Different approaches to planning may be used at different times or by different organizations. In some instances, planning may be carried out entirely by specialists in the field. In other cases, operating management may bear the bulk of the responsibility. The following sections examine the human resource planning process in greater detail.

Figure 6.1
The Human Resource Planning Process

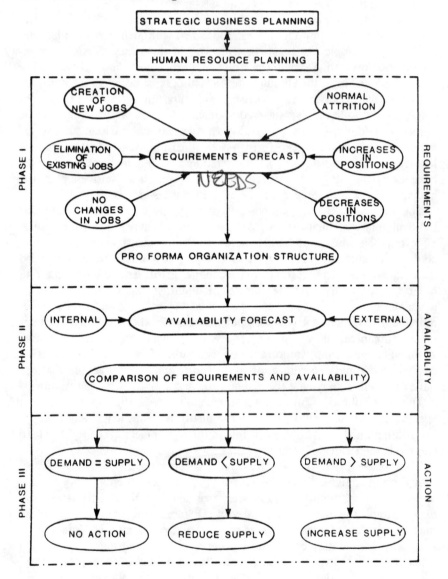

REQUIREMENTS FORECASTING

A requirements forecast is an estimation of the numbers and kinds of employees the organization will need at future dates in order for the firm to realize its stated objectives. It is important to remember two points about forecasting personnel requirements. One, while estimating the total number of employees that will be needed is necessary, a forecast that provides only a total number and does not furnish a breakdown of that number job by job is an incomplete forecast. It is the mix of jobs that is critical; it is the combination of needed skills that lays a foundation upon which effective staffing activities can be built. Although the discussion of forecasting presented in this chapter will tend, for the sake of clarity and simplicity of presentation, to center on obtaining a single number, it should be borne in mind that what is actually involved in forecasting is arriving at a series of job-by-job numbers that reflect the diversity of future personnel requirements. Two, forecasting is, even with the use of sophisticated statistical techniques and computers, an imprecise endeavor, at best. There is no generalized procedure or set of techniques that automatically generates results that any organization can use.[6] Judgment plays a sizable role in forecasting and influences the usefulness of the results obtained.

Human resource forecasting techniques may be divided into two broad categories: subjective and quantitative. Subjective techniques rely heavily on qualitative information supplied by managers, supervisors, human resource planners, and others to develop an estimation of personnel needs. Quantitative approaches utilize statistical or computerized procedures to predict requirements.

Subjective Techniques

Managerial estimates, the Delphi Technique, and zero base forecasting are three subjective approaches used by organizations to forecast human resource requirements. Of these, the most widely used is managerial estimates. While each of these techniques depends on informed judgment, quantitative data may also be employed to substantiate or support the judgment involved.

Managerial Estimates. This is essentially a "bottom up" approach to determining personnel requirements. It is based on the premise that each individual manager in an organization is the person most knowledgeable about the numbers and kinds of people needed to run that unit effectively at various levels of activity. Beginning with the lowest level work units in the organization, each unit manager makes an estimate of personnel needs for the period of time encompassed by the planning cycle. As the process moves upward in the company, each successively higher level of management in turn makes its own estimates of needs, incorporating the input from each of the immediately preceding levels. The result, ultimately, is an aggregate forecast of needs for the entire organization. This process is often highly interactive in that estimated requirements from the previous level are discussed, negotiated, and reestimated with the next level of management as the forecast moves upward through the institution. The interactive aspect of managerial estimating is one of the advantages of this procedure because it forces managers to justify their anticipated staffing needs.

Figure 6.2 shows an illustration of a typical form used at the work unit level to estimate personnel needs. This example deals only with total requirements. In actual practice, estimates would be made for each job in the unit and then combined into one document that enumerates job by job as well as total work unit requirements. The supervisor or manager, in order to make realistic estimates, will have to have information concerning future production levels, changes in products or functions, turnover rates, and the like. The needed information will normally come from the strategic business plan and from human resource specialists.

Examining the illustration, we can see that the supervisor of the unit in question anticipates losing seven employees over the course of the planning period—six through normal attrition and one through a reduction in the number of positions in the unit. The supervisor anticipates gaining two employees through transfer and promotion into the section. Consequently, the unit has a net hiring need of five new employees. At the same time, however, changes in products or services will result in the creation of two new jobs and produce total hiring needs of seven employees.

Admittedly, this example is very simplistic, but it does indicate the basic thrust of managerial estimating. If supervisors and managers have sufficient information on which to base their anticipated requirements and the procedure functions in an adequately interactive manner that requires justification of staffing levels, this approach can provide an organization with reasonably accurate forecasts of human resource requirements.

Delphi Technique. Originally developed by the Rand Corporation, the Delphi Technique is used primarily to forecast future technological advances.[7] Its usefulness in predicting human resource requirements is greatest where technology will dramatically alter the kinds and numbers of employees needed by an organization.

The Delphi Technique is a successive approximation procedure that utilizes a panel of experts or highly knowledgeable individuals to predict future events and their impacts.[8] Ideally, the people participating in the panel do not know the identity of other panel participants—a method that prevents respondents from being influenced by the personalities or opinions of others in the organization. When used in ascertaining human resource requirements, each member of the group is sent a questionnaire that requests

Figure 6.2
Human Resource Forecasting Form

I. <u>CURRENT STAFFING</u> | 35 |

II. <u>ANTICIPATED LOSSES</u>

    1. Normal Attrition

        (1). Terminations   − 1
        (2). Retirements   − 3
        (3). Deaths   − 0
        (4). Lateral Transfers out of unit   − 0
        (5). Promotions out of unit   − 2
        (6). Demotions out of unit   − 0

                 Attrition Losses   − **6**

    2. Changes in Staffing

        (1). Reductions in Positions   − 1
        (2). Job Eliminations   − 0

                 Staffing Losses   − **1**

    3. Total Losses   − **7**

III. <u>ANTICIPATED GAINS</u>

    1. Attrition replacements: internal

        (1). Lateral transfers into unit   + 1
        (2). Promotions into unit   + 1
        (3). Demotions into unit   + 0

                 Internal Gains   + **2**

IV. <u>NET HIRING NEEDS</u> | +5 |

V. <u>POSITION AND JOB INCREASES</u>

    1. Increases in positions   + 0
    2. Anticipated new jobs   + 2

                                 + **2**

VI. <u>TOTAL HIRING NEEDS</u> | +7 |

VII. <u>PROJECTED STAFFING LEVEL</u> | 37 |

111

the individual to estimate, based on perceived changes in technology, the future personnel requirements of the company. The initial results of the survey are then tabulated and returned to the panel members, and they are requested to review and reestimate their forecasts based on the data from the total group. Successive iterations are continued until there is a general consensus on the number and kinds of people the organization will need in the future.

The Delphi Technique is time consuming and expensive. Its use requires the participation of individuals who are thoroughly knowledgeable in the impacts of technology on personnel requirements. Moreover, a great deal of coordination and cooperation are required to produce usable results. Consequently, its use in human resource planning has been fairly limited. The technique can be helpful, however, in anticipating future technological trends and developments that affect personnel requirements in organizations facing a dynamic environment.

Zero Base Forecasting. This technique uses the organization's current staffing level as the starting point for estimating future requirements.[9] The key to zero base forecasting is the necessity of justifying, quantitatively or otherwise, the filling of any vacant position or the creation of any new positions or jobs. If any employee leaves the organization for any reason, the vacant position is not automatically filled. The supervisor or manager must conduct an analysis and offer substantive justification for filling the position. Likewise, when a new position is created, justification for its existence must be provided or the position will not be approved. The primary advantage to this approach is the thorough analysis of human resource needs required for additions to staff or replacements to current staffing.

As yet, this technique has not become a major procedure for forecasting human resource requirements. It is more commonly used in combination with other approaches.

Quantitative Techniques

Although the use of judgment in forecasting human resources requirements has been pointed out in this chapter, quantitative approaches can provide a solid basis for making good judgments. The primary quantitative technique used in organizations is correlation and regression analysis. Some large institutions, because of the number of jobs and the complexity of forecasting requirements, may use computer simulation models to predict personnel needs.

Correlation and Regression Analysis. Correlation measures the relationship between two or more variables, and regression analysis measures the value of one variable in terms of the value of another variable. Because there is often a direct relationship between a firm's sales, output, or assets and employment levels, correlation and regression analysis can be used to determine the degree of relationship and forecast the number of employees that will be required at different amounts of sales, output, or assets.

An example will show how these statistical procedures work. Assume that a firm believes its staffing requirements are dependent upon total sales. The first step is to test that assumption to determine whether there is a direct relationship between the dependent variable (number of employees) and the independent variable (sales). This is done through correlation. The degree of relationship is expressed as a coefficient of correlation (r) in terms of a value of 1.0. A coefficient of 0 would indicate no relationship whatever exists between the variables while a coefficient of $+1.0$ or -1.0 would indicate a perfect relationship—the first a completely positive one and the second a completely negative one.

Table 6.1 contains all of the data that will be used in this correlation and regression analysis example. In the first two columns we see that the firm has compiled data on the number of employees and sales volume for ten periods. The other columns contain calculations that will be used in the correlation and regression formulas.

Table 6.1
Correlation and Regression Analysis Data

Period	Number of Employees Y	Sales in (00,000) X	XY	X^2	Y^2
1	10	15	150	225	100
2	16	19	304	361	256
3	20	30	600	900	400
4	28	22	616	484	784
5	32	41	1,312	1,681	1,024
6	42	40	1,680	1,600	1,764
7	42	50	2,100	2,500	1,764
8	47	53	2,491	2,809	2,209
9	49	45	2,205	2,025	2,401
10	61	53	3,233	2,809	3,721
Σ	347	368	14,691	15,394	14,423

The statistical formula for calculating the coefficient of correlation is:

$$r = \frac{n\,(\Sigma XY) - (\Sigma X)(\Sigma Y)}{\sqrt{[n\,(\Sigma X^2) - (\Sigma X)^2][n\,(\Sigma Y^2) - (\Sigma Y)^2]}}$$

Inserting the values from Table 6.1 into this equation would result in: $r = +0.91488$. Inasmuch as a perfect positive correlation has a value of $+1.0$, we now know that there is an extremely strong positive relationship between sales and the number of employees; that is, the number of employees the firm needs is linked very closely to variations in sales volume. Thus, sales dollars are likely to be a good predictor of total human resource requirements for this organization.

Having established the usefulness of sales as an indicator of personnel needs, the next step is to calculate a regression line that establishes the linear relationship between changes in sales and employee requirements. To do this, a scatter diagram such as the one shown in Figure 6.3 is constructed.

Figure 6.3
Scatter Diagram

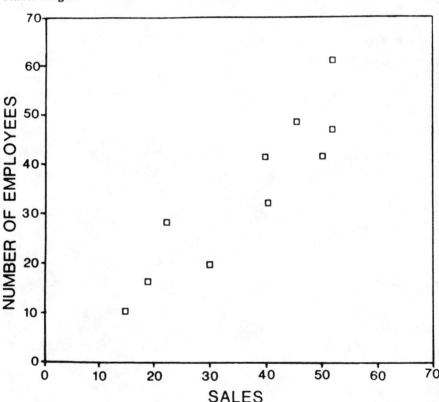

Then a line of "best fit" is computed to show graphically the relationship of employees to sales. The most frequently used method for determining this line is the "least squares" method, which attempts to minimize the sum of the squares of the distance between each unit of data and its corresponding point on the assumed line. The basic formula for a straight line is:

$$Y = a + bX$$

where:

Y = number of employees
a = the point of origin of the line
b = the rate of change
X = sales

To solve for a and b the following formulas are used:

$$a = \frac{\Sigma Y - b\Sigma X}{n}$$

$$b = \frac{n\,(\Sigma XY) - (\Sigma X)(\Sigma Y)}{n\,(\Sigma X^2) - (\Sigma X)^2}$$

Using the data in Table 6.1 to solve these equations, we would find that:

$$a = -3.48725$$
$$b = 1.037697$$

A line can now be drawn through the data as shown in Figure 6.4.

The usefulness of the regression line in forecasting human requirements is that once the line has been statistically fitted to historical data it can then be extrapolated into the future to show potential staffing needs at different levels of sales. In Figure 6.5 we can see that when sales reach $6 million, 60 employees will probably be needed.

Although the calculations involved in correlation and regression analysis seem laborious (in fact, they are if done manually), software packages for personal computers put this approach to forecasting human resource requirements within the reach of organizations of any size. All of the calculations used in the preceding example, including the scatter diagram and the regression line, were generated on a personal computer and reproduced in hard copy form within a matter of minutes through the use of a commercially available statistical software package.

The principal disadvantage of correlation and regression analysis as a forecasting technique is that staffing projections are based on the assumption

Figure 6.4
Scatter Diagram with Regression Line

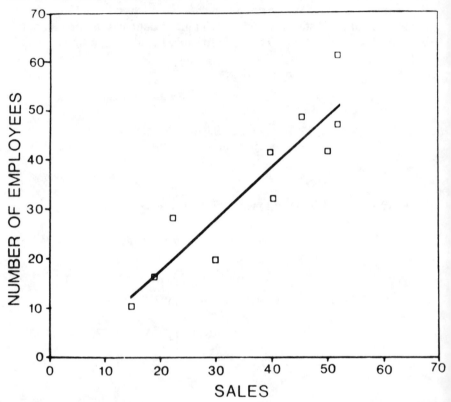

that the future will resemble the past. In many cases, because of technological changes, economic conditions, strategic maneuvers, and a host of other factors, this may not be a valid assumption for organizations. Yet statistical forecasting does establish a sound point of departure upon which anticipated personnel changes can be based.

Simulation

Simulation relies on the use of models to forecast human resource requirements. A model, defined quite simply, is a representation of reality that includes key features or variables of what it purports to represent. In simulation, a computer is used to assist in duplicating a real-world situation through mathematical logic and manipulating important variables so that an approximation of reality under varying conditions can be predicted and

Figure 6.5
Extrapolated Regression Line

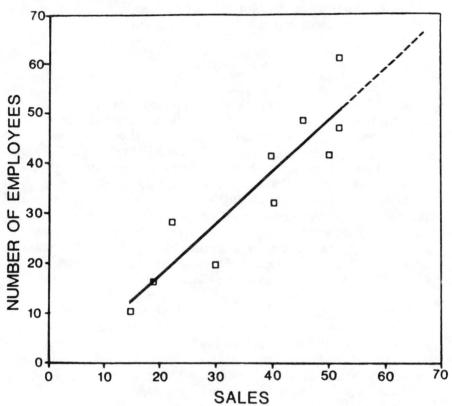

analyzed. Simulation assists human resource planners in answering "What if . . ." questions. Typical questions of this nature are: "What if sales increase by 15 percent . . .," "What if 20 percent of the work force is put on overtime . . . ," "What if the organization adds two new plants in California . . . ," "What if a policy of no new hiring is implemented . . . ?" By developing a model that shows the many complex interrelations between a variety of variables, human resource planners can obtain insights into many staffing situations and possibilities before they actually occur. However, the quality of these insights depends on the sophistication of the model and the identification and quantification of the variables that influence staffing levels.

Simulation is not an approach that can be used by all organizations. In addition to a large-scale computer to manipulate a number of variables under different conditions, the process of building an accurate model is time consuming, expensive, and requires the expertise of individuals skilled in both human resources and computer programming. More widespread use of this approach is expected in the future, but at the present it remains primarily a forecasting option of large organizations.

The Pro Forma Organization Structure

After human resource requirements have been determined, the next logical step in the forecasting process is to develop an organization structure or series of structures that reflect the form the enterprise will assume in the future. The strategic business plan may necessitate creation of new departments, additional geographical units, elimination of existing offices, or a variety of other changes. The purpose of the pro forma structure is to show not only these changes, but also the personnel needs required to accommodate them. While the organization structure of the future may resemble the traditional organization chart, effective human resource planning carries the chart one step further: it identifies function by function, department by department, and unit by unit the number and kinds of jobs made necessary by the future structure. To accomplish this task, staffing tables such as the one presented in Figure 6.6 are often created for each anticipated organizational unit.

Even though the staffing table shown is a simplistic one, close examination of it will reveal its usefulness in identifying the points at which jobs will be created or additional employees will be needed for existing jobs. Knowledge of this kind permits the organization to begin its requisite staffing activities well in advance of actual need, thereby ensuring that sufficient qualified people are available when they are needed.

AVAILABILITY FORECASTING

The requirements phase of the human resource planning process provides the organization with knowledge of how many and what kinds of employees will be needed and when they will be needed. But the organization must also determine if it will be able to obtain employees with the necessary skills and from what sources these individuals may be secured. This is the task of availability forecasting. The demand for employees may be met by obtaining people from inside the company or resorting to external sources of supply or both.

Internal Sources

Many of the employees who will be needed for future positions are already employed by the institution. Through transfer and promotion these

Figure 6.6
Staffing Table

WORK CENTER: FINAL ASSEMBLY	PRODUCTION VOLUME									
DEPARTMENT: PRODUCTION	NUMBER OF UNITS ASSEMBLED (IN THOUSANDS)									
STAFFING REQUIREMENTS	2.0	2.1	2.2	2.3	2.4	2.5	2.6	2.7	2.8	2.9
SUPERVISOR	1	1	1	1	1	1	1	1	1	1
ASSISTANT SUPERVISOR	–	–	–	–	–	–	–	1	1	1
LEADPERSON	–	–	–	–	1	1	1	1	1	1
CLERICAL ASSISTANT	–	–	–	–	1	1	1	1	1	1
EXPEDITOR	–	–	–	–	–	1	1	2	2	2
INVENTORY CONTROL CLERK	1	1	1	1	1	1	1	1	1	2
ASSEMBLER "A"	9	9	9	10	10	11	11	12	12	13
ASSEMBLER "B"	4	4	4	4	4	4	4	4	5	5
ASSEMBLER TRAINEE	–	1	2	2	2	3	3	3	4	4
TOTAL STAFF	15	16	17	18	20	23	23	26	28	30

individuals can be shifted laterally to other jobs or elevated to positions of greater responsibility. The major problem for large firms is being able to identify the internal talent that is available so that this talent can be matched with the company's needs. Two approaches that are valuable in the identification and matching process are skills inventories and management inventories.

Skills Inventories. Information maintained on nonmanagerial employees as to their availability and preparedness to move into higher level or lateral positions is referred to as a skills inventory. The purpose of the inventory is to enable the organization to determine readily which employees may be shifted from one job to another to meet the changing employment needs of the firm. Essential data maintained in such a record would include, but not be limited to, the following:

• Educational background
• Work experience in the organization or elsewhere
• Specific work skills such as the ability to operate particular pieces of equipment

- Licenses or certifications held
- Biographical data, including protected class status
- Previous performance appraisal evaluations
- In-house training programs completed
- Career goals and aspirations

Essential information on employee skills can easily be maintained and updated today on computerized systems; it can also be maintained on manual systems in smaller organizations. Regardless of how the information is kept, it seems important to do so in order not to overlook the best source of employees for future positions—those already employed by the enterprise.

Management Inventories. Managerial talent is a critical resource for every organization, thus it is more common for firms to maintain data on managers than it is for them to keep the same kind of detailed records of employee skills. A management inventory, defined very simply, is a collection of data that is used in determining the potential of present managers to progress to positions of even greater responsibility.[10] Essentially, this type of inventory provides information for replacement and promotion decisions. It differs from a skills inventory primarily in terms of the amount of information maintained and the detailed nature of that information. Typically included in a management inventory would be data pertaining to:

- Work history and experience
- Educational background
- Assessment of strengths and weaknesses
- Developmental needs
- Promotional potential at present and with further development
- Current job performance
- Field of specialization
- Job preferences
- Geographical preferences
- Career goals and aspirations
- Anticipated retirement date
- Personal history including psychological assessments

As with the employee skills inventory, this kind of information can be maintained in either computerized or manual fashion.

Both skills and management inventories are valuable tools that assist a company in making the best possible use of its present human resources. Effectively utilized, inventories can also have a positive effect on morale because they signify an organization's interest in and commitment to a promotion from within policy. Inventories help ensure that talented employees will not be overlooked when promotional opportunities become available. For these tools to function properly, however, the informational database must be kept current through frequent updating.

External Sources

Since not all demands for human resources can be met internally, the organization will from time to time have to resort to external sources for the skilled people it needs. Anticipating the number and kinds of skilled people who will be available is no easy task for human resource planners. Many environmental factors influence the potential availability of employees. Planners must carefully analyze each factor and assess its likely impact on the supply of workers the firm may need. Among the items that must be considered are:

- Population changes
- Population shifts from one part of the country to another
- Changes in the total work force
- Composition of the work force
- Increasing educational levels
- Societal attitudes toward particular careers, industries, and institutions
- Economic conditions
- Technological changes
- Political conditions
- Governmental regulations[11]

Much of the needed information is available from federal agencies such as the U.S. Bureau of Labor Statistics, which publishes monthly, quarterly, and annual reports on current and expected conditions in various labor markets, or the U.S. Census Bureau, which issues periodic reports and projections on population changes. Many trade associations also publish data on trends in specific industries. The task of the human resource planner is to sift through the tremendous amount of information that is available and determine how the future availability of personnel for a particular organization is likely to be affected by changes in the overall environment. Of necessity, forecasting availability of employees is a continuous function of human resource planning. Rapid employment of new employees is difficult; consequently, a firm must be capable of determining not only the number of employees required but also where and when they can be obtained.

Specific external sources of supply are discussed in detail in the following chapter.

Requirements and Availability Comparison

Although a rather simple step in the planning process, the requirements-availability comparison is nevertheless quite important because it reveals the staffing situation that will confront the enterprise in the future. Knowledge of the impending situation then sets the stage for taking appropriate action to ensure that the organization will have the right numbers and kinds of individuals in the right jobs at the right time.

The comparison may reveal that: (1) the demand for employees will be equal to the supply, (2) the demand for personnel will be less than the supply, or (3) the demand for human resources will be greater than the anticipated supply. Since the basic purpose of human resource planning is to equate labor demand to labor supply, each of these three situations calls for developing different courses of action. Specific actions that may be taken are described in the following section.

EQUATING HUMAN RESOURCE DEMAND TO SUPPLY

The first two phases of human resource planning are analytical and conceptual in nature. The third phase is action oriented; it is here that steps are formulated and then implemented to obtain a balance between the number and kinds of employees needed and the number and kinds available.

Demand Equals Supply

Should labor demand equal labor supply—a situation that could occur in very small firms operating in a stable environment but is not likely to happen in large organizations facing dynamic conditions—no action need be taken. The company can simply continue doing what it is doing; nothing else is required, at least in the short run. No intensification of recruiting is needed; no layoffs are necessary; no additional training programs have to be implemented; no early retirements have to be encouraged. Maintenance of the status quo is all that is called for.

Demand Is Less Than Supply

As more and more large organizations downsize, restructure, and streamline to cut costs, increase efficiency, improve productivity, and remain competitive,[12] the likelihood of demand for employees being less than the available supply is a distinct possibility with which firms will have to deal. In such a situation, attention must be focused on maintaining sufficient people in the organization to produce the firm's goods or services while simultaneously reducing the total number of employees. Several means are available for equating demand and supply when faced with this condition.

Restricted Hiring. A simple way of reducing the number of employees, provided the surplus is not too great, is to let normal attrition take its course and not replace employees who leave the company. Knowledge of the attrition rate would indicate how long it would take to achieve the desired reduction in force by this method. Exceptions will, of course, have to be made to a no-hiring policy. The criticality of the position is the deciding factor in determining which departing employees will be replaced. For example, the loss of one production worker would pose no problem because the slack could be picked up by other workers. But the departure of a tool and die maker might cause disruptions in the production process. Workers essential to maintaining company operations would be replaced under a hiring freeze, others would not. Where the surplus of personnel is large, other measures will have to be taken in addition to restricted hiring to reduce the firm's employment level.

Reduced Hours. Reductions in hourly workers can be accomplished effectively without cutting the force by simply reducing the number of hours worked. Instead of continuing a standard work week of forty hours, a work week of thirty-five hours may be instituted. A cut in working hours of this magnitude is tantamount to a 12.5 percent decrease in the total number of employees. This method cannot be used to reduce the effective number of salaried employees inasmuch as they are paid on a weekly or monthly basis.

Early Retirement. Reductions in the total number of employees can also be accomplished through the use of incentives that encourage employees to retire at an earlier than normal age. An additional advantage to this approach is that employees who are eligible to retire early are generally higher paid employees; consequently, the organization not only reduces the number of workers through this means, but also reduces its personnel expenses.

Layoffs. When faced with an acute surplus of personnel, an organization may have no choice other than a layoff. Layoffs may be used in an across-the-board fashion—in which case a stipulated percentage of employees in each department is laid off—or used only to reduce the number of workers in specific departments where excess personnel can be readily identified. In nonunionized firms, layoffs can be used at the discretion of the employer; in unionized companies, strict procedures must be followed.

Personnel reductions are extremely sensitive matters that may affect an organization's future staffing efforts. They should always be approached carefully and deliberately so as to minimize the potential impact of unsought consequences.

Demand Is Greater Than Supply

Faced with a shortage of personnel, an organizaton must intensify its efforts to obtain the necessary supply of people to meet the needs of the firm. Several actions may be in order.

Creative Recruiting. A shortage of personnel may mean that new approaches to recruiting will have to be tried. The organization may have to recruit in different geographical areas than in the past, explore new methods, and seek different kinds of candidates. Creative recruiting may take many forms. For example, a relatively large builder of single family homes, faced with a serious shortage of construction workers, experimented with several approaches. This company broadened its recruiting area for skilled workers from its normal local area to locales across the country where there were surpluses of workers. The company advertised its hiring needs on radio stations and billboards. These efforts, unusual for a local construction company, secured employees who otherwise might not have applied for jobs with the organization.[13]

Compensation Incentives. With other firms competing for skilled workers in a short supply, high demand situation, various forms of compensation incentives may have to be used to attract individuals to a particular company. Premium pay is one obvious method, but is an approach that may trigger a bidding war that the organization cannot sustain for an extended period. More subtle forms of compensatory rewards may be required to attract employees to a firm: four-day work weeks, flexible working hours, part-time employment, child care centers, and so forth. The number of incentives that could be offered is limited only by the imagination of human resource specialists.

Training Programs. Acute shortages of personnel may necessitate the implementation of special training programs to prepare previously unemployable individuals for positions with a firm. Remedial education and skills training are two types of programs that may help attract individuals to a particular company. The construction company mentioned above, in addition to its creative recruiting efforts, also implemented its own ten-week training program to satisfy the need for bricklayers to build its tract homes. This unique effort, reported in the media and spread by word of mouth, resulted in additional applicants seeking employment with the company in order to take advantage of its skills-training program.

Different Selection Standards. Another approach to dealing with shortages of required human resources is lowering of employment standards. Various selection criteria that eliminate workers may have to be altered to ensure that sufficient numbers of people are available to fill jobs. This means of coping with a personnel shortage may be coupled with training programs to ensure that employees are qualified to perform the jobs for which they are hired.

SUMMARY

Human resource planning is a complex endeavor, but an essential one for organizations in today's uncertain environment. Admittedly, this chapter has only scratched the surface of what is involved with anticipating personnel requirements and ensuring that those requirements are met. The pivotal point of what has been presented is that requirements must be anticipated and actions taken to ensure that an organization will have the requisite human resources on hand when they are needed. All other staffing activities depend upon the accuracy of this information.

NOTES

1. Charles F. Russ, Jr., "Manpower Planning Systems: Part II," *Personnel Journal*, February 1982, p. 123.

2. Guvenc G. Alpander, *Human Resources Management Planning* (New York: AMACOM, 1982), p. 2.

3. James W. Walker, *Human Resource Planning* (New York: McGraw-Hill Book Company, 1980), p. 5.

4. Alpander, *Human Resources*, p. 2.

5. R. Wayne Mondy and Robert M. Noe III, *Personnel: the Management of Human Resources*, 2nd ed. (Boston: Allyn and Bacon, 1984), p. 106.

6. Ibid., p. 100.

7. R. Wayne Mondy and Robert M. Noe III, *Personnel: The Management of Human Resources*, 3rd ed. (Boston: Allyn and Bacon, 1987), p. 136.

8. Ibid., p. 137.

9. Ibid., p. 135.

10. Ibid., p. 139.

11. Walker, *Human Resource Planning*, pp. 24-46.

12. George Russell, "Rebuilding to Survive," *Time*, February 16, 1987, p. 44.

13. Based on one of the author's experiences as a manager with this firm.

7

The Recruiting Process

Recruiting involves locating individuals, with appropriate qualifications and in sufficient numbers, and encouraging them to apply for jobs with a particular organization. The basic purpose of recruiting is to ensure a sufficient pool of applicants from which the most qualified individual may be selected. Recruiting is an essential activity for any firm regardless of its size. In most medium and large organizations, the human resource department is responsible for all recruiting activities. In small companies, individual managers often conduct their own recruiting efforts. Whether conducted by operating managers or staffing specialists, effective recruiting is crucial because sufficient qualified applicants are needed to ensure that selection can be accomplished successfully.

A GENERALIZED RECRUITING MODEL

Figure 7-1 depicts a basic model of the recruiting process. The need to recruit is triggered by either the human resource planning function or the human resource administration function. The former provides information on the number and kinds of new positions to be filled, while the latter identifies existing positions that must be filled due to terminations, promotions, retirements, and the like. New or open positions may be filled from within the organization, from outside the organization, or by using alternative methods such as overtime, subcontracting, or temporary employees secured from outside agencies. If positions cannot be filled from within or if the use of alternative methods is not feasible, the organization must look to the labor market for the people it needs. Sources of employees must be identified, methods to reach these sources must be selected, and qualified individuals must be encouraged to apply for job openings in order to create a sufficient pool of applicants.

Typically, the first step in filling a position is for a department manager to initiate an employee requisition. This document specifies various details such as job title, department, date employee is needed, and justification for filling the

Figure 7.1
A Model of the Recruiting Process

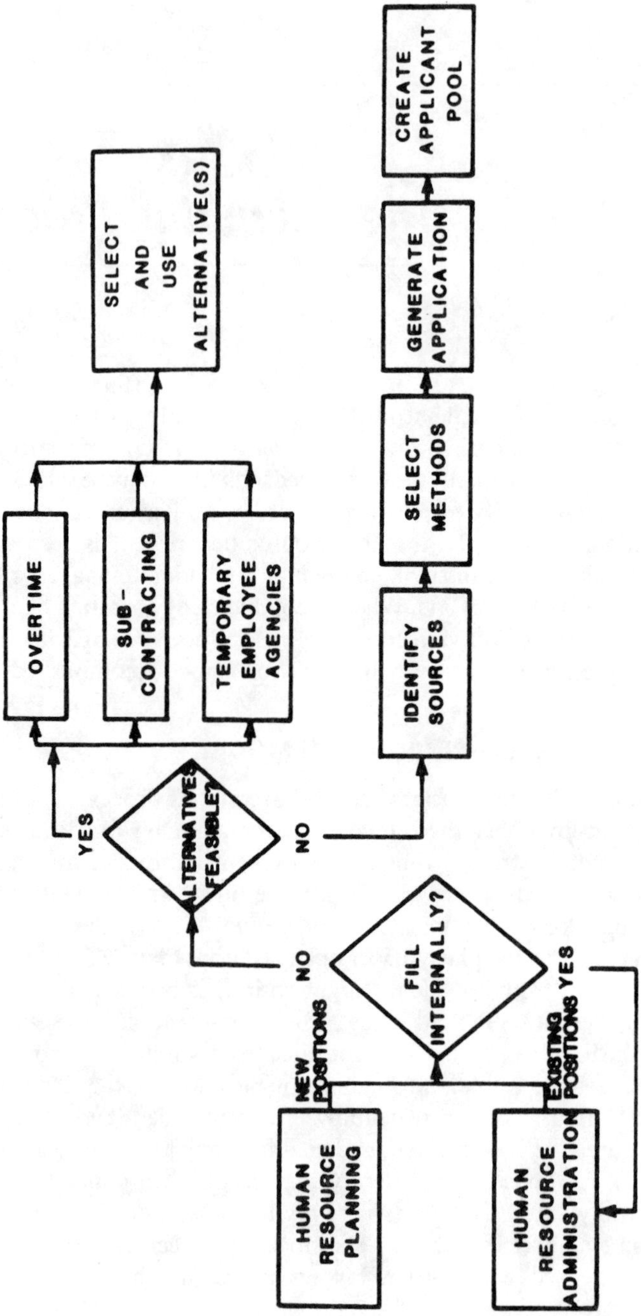

position. A copy of the job description and job specifications is often attached to the requisition, particularly if the position is a new one. This information then sets in motion the series of actions leading to filling the job.

ALTERNATIVES TO RECRUITING

When there is a need for additional or replacement employees, a firm may choose to explore alternatives to recruiting. Recruitment costs can be high. Moreover, once employees are placed on the payroll, they may be difficult to remove even if their performance is marginal. Consequently, an organization is well advised to consider alternatives to adding full-time staff members. Three viable options are: increasing the use of overtime, subcontracting work to other organizations, and utilizing temporary employees provided by firms specializing in this service.

Overtime

The most common approach to meeting requirements for additional personnel, especially when the need is generated by short-term increases in work volume, is overtime. Both employer and employee may benefit from overtime: the employer voids the cost of recruiting, selecting, and training while the employee gains an increase in compensation.

Overtime, however, is not without its disadvantages. Many managers feel, and justifiably so, that when employees are required to work extra hours over an extended length of time, the organization pays more and receives less per hour in return. This situation may become worse if excessive overtime is required; employees may become fatigued and lack the energy to perform at normal levels.

Two other potential problems are related to prolonged overtime. First, employees may, consciously or unconsciously, pace themselves during normal hours so that overtime is ensured. Second, employees tend to become accustomed to the added income resulting from overtime pay and may even elevate their standard of living to the level permitted by this additional income. When overtime is no longer required and the paycheck shrinks to its normal level, employees may become disgruntled at what they perceive as a cut in pay.

An interesting problem with overtime in contemporary organizations is that many employees, particularly younger ones, do not want to work more than the required forty hours a week. Due to a change in values, leisure time is more important to a growing number of workers than is the prospect of earning additional income by working longer hours.

Despite its potential drawbacks and problems, the use of overtime does offer an alternative to increasing an organization's permanent staff and should be evaluated carefully when the need for additional employees arises.

Subcontracting

When faced with an increased demand for its goods and services, an organization may decide against expanding its work force and elect to subcontract work to another company. This alternative may be particularly attractive when the increased demand is expected to be short run in nature. Even in the long run, though, subcontracting can be beneficial as a means of avoiding increases in a company's employment level.

Two essential considerations in the use of subcontracting are the costs involved and the maintenance of quality standards in the firm's goods or services. To be a feasible alternative, subcontracting should be cost effective; that is, the subcontractor should be able to perform the necessary work at a lower cost than if the contracting organization increased the size of its work force to handle increased production demands. The subcontractor must also be capable of maintaining quality levels specified by the contractor. It would be self-defeating to attempt to save staffing costs if the result was a product or service of an inferior nature.

Many organizations use subcontracting not only for major products or services but also for ancillary activities such as in-house cafeteria operations, security work, and janitorial services—functions that are frequently performed more efficiently and inexpensively by outside firms.

Temporary Employees

Another alternative to work force expansion, especially in the short run, is the use of temporary help. It is estimated that as many as nine out of ten companies in this country have used temporary help firms as sources of employees.[1] Temporary help companies usually assist their client organizations by assigning their own employees (technically, the employee works for the temporary help firm but does not get paid unless he or she is given an assignment with a client) to handle excess or special workloads of the client. The temporary help firm fulfills all the obligations associated with being an employer. The user organization avoids the expense of recruitment and the cost of employee benefits as well as absenteeism and turnover. Firms specializing in providing temporary employees now comprise a $2 billion industry—a strong indication of the usefulness of this alternative to recruiting.[2]

Not all aspects of using temporary help are positive. Temporary employees may lack required specialized training. Providing this training my take more time than can be justified and, at the same time, cause feelings of resentment among regular employees who have to conduct the training. Also, since temporaries are not on the client's payroll, their loyalty or commitment to the organization may not be as strong as that of permanent employees.

One very positive benefit of using temporaries is that it gives the company an opportunity to preview and evaluate the performance of individuals. Many companies end up hiring temporaries as permanent employees.

A variation of the temporary help firm is the "job shopper—an independent worker who takes assignments with organizations on a contractual basis. The job shopper is usually a skilled professional such as an engineer, draftsman, or systems analyst who is willing to work on a non-permanent basis because of the high rate of pay involved. Job shoppers are very prevalent in the aerospace and defense industries, where companies often face the need for additional skilled employees on a short-run basis to meet project deadlines or demands.

INTERNAL ENVIRONMENTAL RECRUITMENT FACTORS

An organization's own internal practices and policies affect the recruiting process. A major factor that can influence the success of a recruiting program is whether the firm engages in human resource planning. In most instances, an organization cannot attract prospective employees with the required skills in sufficient numbers overnight. It takes time to examine the options concerning the appropriate sources of applicants and the most productive methods for encouraging individuals to apply for open positions. Once the best alternatives have been identified, recruiting plans may be made. Thus, effective human resource planning that indicates in advance when employees will be needed and what kinds of skills they must possess greatly facilitates recruiting efforts.

An organization's promotion policy can also have a significant impact on its recruiting program. Basically, there are two approaches an organization can follow. It can stress a policy of promotion from within or it can follow a policy of filling the majority of positions with individuals from outside the company. There is a logical rationale for each approach.

When an organization emphasizes promotion from within, its employees have increased incentive to strive for advancement. As they witness promotions occurring within the company, employees become increasingly aware of their own opportunities. Consequently, a promotion from within policy enhances motivation and leads to a relatively high level of morale. However, a strictly applied promotion from within policy is not always possible or practicable because a firm may need fresh ideas or new skills that can only be obtained from outsiders. In any event, a promotion policy that first considers insiders before looking at outsiders boosts morale and motivation.

A distinct advantage of filling positions internally is that the organization is already aware of its employees' capabilities. While a person's past performance in a given job may not, by itself, be a reliable criterion for promotion, nevertheless, many personal and job-related qualities are known since the person has established a track record with the company. An outsider is always an "unknown quantity" to some extent.

Yet it is unlikely that any firm can or would desire to adhere rigidly to a practice of promotion from within because such a practice eventually leads to in-breeding, a lack of new ideas, and a lack of creativity. Management may believe that new blood is badly needed to provide new ideas and innovation. In such cases, even organizations that emphasize internal promotion periodically have to look outside for new talent.

Another problem of promotion from within is that it may trigger a series of promotions, thus necessitating additional efforts to fill other positions vacated by promoted individuals. If so, the organization is faced with the need of identifying not just one, but two or more candidates for vacant positions. And, too, there is the matter of training. Every time a person is promoted, he or she has to be trained in the new job. Promotion from within may create the need for training several individuals in their new job duties.

METHODS USED IN INTERNAL RECRUITING

Management must be able to identify current employees who are capable of filling higher level positions as these positions become available. Helpful tools used for internal recruitment include management and skills inventories and job posting and bidding procedures. As mentioned in Chapter 6, management and skills inventories permit organizations to determine whether needed qualifications are possessed by current employees. As an internal recruitment device, these inventories have proven to be extremely valuable to organizations in locating talent; provided, of course, that the inventories are maintained on an up-to-date basis. Also, their use strongly supports the concept of promotion from within.

Another excellent internal recruiting approach is a job posting and bidding system. The purpose of job posting is to communicate to employees the fact that job openings exist. Job bidding permits individuals in the organization to apply for any job they believe they have the qualifications for. Some firms provide their employees with a weekly list of jobs available within the organization. Other firms post lists of job openings on bulletin boards. Job posting and bidding minimizes the complaint commonly heard in many companies that insiders never hear of an opening until it has been filled with an outsider. Numerous organizations actually have a policy that requires a job to be posted for a specified length of time before any effort is made to fill the vacancy from outside.

When properly administered, a job posting and bidding system reflects a management philosophy of openness and genuine interest in the advancement of its employees. Additionally, such a system can often assist in outside recruitment efforts because it demonstrates a firm's interest in career advancement and individual growth.

EXTERNAL SOURCES OF JOB APPLICANTS

Inevitably, an organization must look to outside sources for additional employees. This is especially true when a company is expanding its work force on a permanent basis. The following circumstances generally necessitate external recruiting: (1) creation of new entry level jobs, (2) vacancies in entry level jobs created by internal promotions, (3) need to acquire skills not possessed by current employees, (4) need for new ideas, (5) opening of new facilities, (6) expansion into new product or service lines, and (7) expansion into new geographic areas.

Some of the most common sources of new employees are high schools, community colleges and vocational schools, colleges and universities, competitors and other organizations, and unsolicited applicants.

High Schools

High schools are one of the major sources of applicants for entry level or unskilled positions. Many schools now sponsor career days where local area employers visit the school and explain career opportunities in their organizations. Cooperative education programs, where a student goes to school part of the day and works the remainder of the day, also afford employers the opportunity to tap this source of employees. Some companies find it advantageous to familiarize high school counselors with job opportunities so that the counselors can refer students to the prospective employer.

Community Colleges and Vocational Schools

Typically, community colleges serve two functions: they prepare students for completion of a four-year degree program, or they prepare students for a specific occupation such as auto mechanic, draftsman, secretary, or computer programmer. A number of these colleges have done an outstanding job of defining the employment needs in their areas and have designed programs that produce students to fill these needs. Often, these colleges work in conjunction with local employers so that the courses students take fit the needs of specific occupations. Employers frequently offer internship programs to enable students to gain practical work experience. For many entry level jobs, community colleges are an excellent source of potential employees.

Vocational schools train individuals for specific occupations. Because they normally offer placement assistance to their students, vocational schools maintain working relationships with employers in their local areas, thus functioning as a good source of trained applicants for entry level positions.

Colleges and Universities

Colleges and universities represent a major source of recruitment for organizations. A substantial number of entry level professional, technical, and management employees are found in these institutions. College recruiters who visit campuses on an annual or semiannual basis are commonly used as the vehicle for reaching this source of potential employees. Because schools differ widely in terms of their curriculi and specifications, the key to using this recruiting source effectively is to determine which colleges or universities provide the proper training or educational experiences to fulfill the organization's employment needs.

Placement directors, faculty, and administrators are potentially helpful to organizations as they attempt to take advantage of this source of applicants. For instance, the large retailer, Bloomingdale's, has improved its credibility on college campuses by making personal contacts with business professors and providing grants for studies and offering internships. The company has also used alumni to establish relationships with college placement offices and recruit students.[3]

Since college recruitment is mutually beneficial, both employers and universities should take steps to develop and maintain close working relationships. Once a company has established a college recruiting program, it is important that contacts and visits be continued year after year to ensure an effective relationship.

Competitors and Other Organizations

Competitors and other organizations in the industry or in the area are the most important sources of applicants for positions requiring experience. It is estimated that at any given time about 5 percent of the working population is actively seeking or is receptive to a change in employment. Furthermore, one out of every three people—especially managers and professionals—

change jobs every five years.[4] These facts underscore the importance of other employers as a potential source of applicants.

Even where promotion from within is the rule, organizations are sometimes forced to "raid" other organizations to fill important positions or acquire expertise that is not available internally. This practice is not a rare occurrence nor is it an unethical one, per se.

Small firms in particular look for employees who have been trained by larger organizations that have the resources needed to support extensive training and development programs.[5]

It is not uncommon for organizations to recruit professionals and managers from the public accounting and management consulting firms that provide services to the organizations. As one executive with a Big Eight accounting firm once confided to one of the authors, "We run the world's largest employment agency. We didn't plan it that way. It just happened." Accountants or consultants familiar with an organization are, obviously, potential employees.

Unsolicited Applicants

If an organization is well known, has high visibility, or a reputation for being a good place to work, it will usually be able to attract prospective employees without engaging in extensive recruiting efforts. High quality individuals may seek out a specific company on their own initiative to apply for a job. Unsolicited applicants often prove to be a valuable source of potential employees for positions ranging from entry level to top level managers. However, it is not advisable for an organization to rely on this source exclusively. Unsolicited applicants are likely to be an intermittent source—they may not appear when employees are needed or they may appear in great numbers when an organization has no openings.

RECRUITING METHODS

An analysis of recruitment sources enables organizations to determine where potential job applicants are likely to be found. Recruiting methods are then used to encourage potential candidates to seek employment with the company. Recruiting methods such as advertising, employment agencies, and employee referrals may be effective in attracting virtually any type of candidate. College recruiters, job fairs, and internships are designed basically to attract entry level professionals, although job fairs may be used for high level professionals, too. Executive search firms and professional associations are helpful in the recruiting of managerial and professional employees.

Advertising

One of the most widely used recruiting methods is advertising, primarily in newspapers. The answers to several questions provide the basis for successful employment advertising planning. These questions include:

- Who does the organization want to hire?
- How many applicants must be attracted to ensure a sufficient applicant pool?
- When will the new employee(s) be needed?
- What message should the advertising convey?
- What specific journals or publications should be used?
- What has been the organization's previous experience with advertising?
- What is the anticipated cost effectiveness of advertising?

Job descriptions and specifications answer the first question. The organization's past experience, based on the typical ratio of hires to qualified applicants generated, assists in determining the number of responses needed to achieve an adequate applicant pool. While advertising produces a number of applicants, not all of these applicants will be qualified; thus, previous experience relative to the number of qualified applicants is more important than simply the total number of responses produced.

When employees will be needed is contingent upon human resource planning or the existence of vacancies within the organization. Recruitment through advertising should be planned well in advance of anticipated openings, where possible, to avoid the crisis situation of needing employees "yesterday." Selections made under the pressure of time often result in poor employment decisions.

In determining the content of the advertising message, an organization has to decide upon the image it wants to project. Obviously, the prospective applicants should be given a clear and honest picture of the job and the organization—something that may be difficult to achieve in a short piece of advertising copy. At the same time, an attempt should be made to determine what appeals to the self-interest of potential applicants. The advertisement must communicate to the prospect why he or she should be interested in the job and the organization. The message should also clearly indicate how the applicant is to respond; that is, in person, by submitting a resume, by telephone, or by letter.

The advertising medium to be used is purely an individual organizational decision. The firm's previous experience with various media should suggest what publications or approaches should be taken for specific kinds of jobs.

As far as cost effectiveness is concerned, the most inexpensive form of advertising that typically generates the greatest number of responses is newspaper advertising. The biggest problem with this approach, however, is the number of responses from individuals who are not qualified for the position—although each response will have to be evaluated, an organization will not have to respond to each individual if it uses a blind box number in its advertisement. But if a blind box number is used the organization does not have the advantage that accrues from using its name in the advertisement.

An effective employment advertisement should avoid generalities and provide concise information about the job, the organization, and possibilities for career mobility. It is not enough to simply say that the organization has a position open; thus, advertisements must be written with a great deal of careful thought if they are to be effective in producing sufficient responses from qualified applicants.

Advertisements placed in publications such as *The Wall Street Journal* are reserved for managerial, professional, and high level technical positions. The reading audience of this periodical is largely composed of individuals who are likely to be qualified for these kinds of positions. Consequently, there is less likelihood of receiving responses from marginally or even totally unqualified applicants when this publication is used for the aforementioned types of job openings.

Virtually every professional group publishes a journal or newsletter that is widely read by its members. When advertising for personnel executives, for example, *Personnel Administrator* or *Resource*, both publications of the American Society for Personnel Administration, would be an excellent medium for reaching the desired target audience.

Trade journals are widely used for employment advertising, but this medium is not without problems.[6] For example, since regional editions are not offered, these journals may not be very useful to employers desiring to avoid relocation expenses. Also, journals lack scheduling flexibility: deadlines for black and white copy are usually thirty days prior to the issue date and may be even further in advance for four-color copy. Since staffing needs cannot always be anticipated far in advance nor can long delays be tolerated in filling positions, the use of trade journals for recruiting may be inappropriate at times.

Recruiting advertisers assume that qualified employment prospects read newspapers and trade journals and that they are dissatisfied to the extent that they peruse employment ads. This is not always the case, particularly for those individuals who are not currently considering a job change. Therefore, in high demand situations, a firm should consider all available media, not just newspapers and journals.[7]

Other advertising media that can be used for recruiting purposes include radio, billboards, and television. While normally more expensive than newspapers or journals, these media have been used quite successfully in specific situations.[8] A regional medical center, for instance, was able to attract registered nurses by using billboards. A large manufacturing firm was successful in attracting production trainees with radio spot advertisements. An electronics firm used television advertising to attract experienced engineers when the company opened a new facility and needed a number of engineers immediately. In situations where hiring needs are urgent, radio and television can provide much faster results than print media. However, broadcasting used alone may not be sufficient. It can alert people to the fact that an organization is seeking recruits, but it is limited in its ability to provide data such as company address, telephone number, and person to contact. For this reason, broadcasting and print are often used in conjunction with each other.

While most organizations use advertising in their recruiting efforts, evidence suggests that it may be somewhat ineffective. It is estimated that less than 40 percent of all job openings are filled though recruitment advertising.[9]

Private Employment Agencies

A private employment agency is a company that assists firms in recruiting employees and, at the same time, aids individuals in their attempts to locate jobs. Agencies perform many recruiting and selecting activities for employers such as advertising job openings, reviewing resumés, obtaining application blank data, conducting screening interviews, and testing.

Private agencies are used by companies for filling virtually every type of job opening, although they are best known for their role in recruiting white collar personnel. Although the private employment agency industry has a bad reputation in some areas, there are a number of highly reputable agencies that have been in operation for decades. One difficulty that poses problems for agencies is that there are few industry standards. The quality of a particular agency is dependent upon the professionalism of its management and employment counselors.

Regardless of problems, private agencies are an important method for bringing qualified applicants and job openings together. Because of the recruiting and selecting functions it performs, an agency can save an employer a great deal of time in finding potential employees.

Agencies work on a fee basis, charging either the company or the individual a certain percentage of annual gross salary of the position being filled. In the past, this fee was normally paid by the employee, but increasingly today employers are paying the fee.

In using private agencies, organizations may list job openings with several agencies or they may use one agency exclusively. Using several agencies tends to broaden the scope of recruiting efforts. However, working with a single agency allows an organization the opportunity to develop a relationship that may lead to better referrals from the agency since the agency comes to know more about the company and the kinds of employees it needs.

Public Employment Agencies

While public employment agencies are operated by each state under guidelines set by that state, they receive overall policy direction from the U.S. Employment Service. Historically, public employment agencies have been best known for their efforts in recruiting and placing individuals in blue collar jobs. Recently they have become increasingly involved with filling technical, professional, and managerial positions. Thus, public agencies now represent a good source of applicants for all types of positions—a source that should not be overlooked by employers in their recruiting efforts.

Public agencies perform many of the same recruiting and selecting activities for employers as are performed by private agencies. In some instances computerized job matching systems are used to facilitate the recruiting process. The services provided by public agencies are supported by payroll taxes levied on employers. The employer pays no additional charge for listing job openings and securing employees through this source. The services are provided free of charge to job seekers.

Company Recruiters

The most common use of company recruiters is with vocational schools, community colleges, and colleges and universities. The key contact for the recruiter is usually the director of student placement at the school. The placement director assists the recruiter by identifying qualified candidates, scheduling interviews, providing interviewing facilities, and, in some cases, maintaining student files that include resumés, references, and other types of information.

The company recruiter obviously plays a vital role in attracting applicants for an organization. The recruiter's actions may be viewed by students as reflecting the attitudes, philosophy, and character of the company the recruiter represents. If the recruiter is dull, the company represented may be considered dull; if he or she is apathetic, discourteous, or vulgar, all of these negative characteristics may well be attributed to the firm doing the recruiting. It is imperative that both company and recruiter be cognizant of the potential impact that may be made when recruiting on school campuses.

Recruiters determine which individuals possess the required qualifications and encourage them to continue exploring job opportunities with the organization. In achieving this purpose, the recruiter becomes involved in a two-way communication process by providing information about the company, its products or services, its general organizational structure, its policies, the duties and responsibilities of the job to be filled, compensation and benefits, and so forth.

Considering the importance of the occasion, the campus interview is often extremely short, averaging about thirty minutes. Thus, it is important that:

- The interview begin on time
- The recruiter be well prepared
- The interview take place in an area free from disturbance

By 1980, thirty college placement offices, in an effort to facilitate the process of campus recruiting, had installed the visual equivalent of a juke box to handle recruiting messages from companies. With the proliferation of video equipment, it has been suggested that organizations in need of critical skills utilize video tapes and VCRs to expedite the recruiting process. Because of the high cost of recruiting on campuses, it has even been suggested that cable and satellite communications systems be used.[10]

Special Events

The two most commonly used special events in recruiting are job fairs and open houses. Job fairs are normally sponsored by a group of organizations that pool their efforts to bring together a large number of applicants at the same time and place in a convention type of atmosphere. The advantage to the job seeker is obvious: he or she can visit with a variety of organizations in a limited amount of time. The advantage to the employers is that a greater number of applicants are generated than could be generated by any one employer alone. Newspaper ads and radio spots are the normal vehicles for announcing a job fair.

An open house is a special event conducted by a single company. Customarily, an open house is held on a Saturday to ensure maximum turnout of applicants. Company representatives from different departments are available to explain various job opportunities. Newspaper ads and radio spots are also used to alert applicants to an open house.

Special events are best suited for use as recruiting methods when a company needs to employ substantial numbers of people in relatively short periods of time.

Internships

Internships are a recruiting method that has value not only to the firm involved, but also to students and schools. Internships may involve temporary jobs during the summer, part-time jobs during the school year, or alternating periods of employment and school attendance. During the period of working with a company, students are given the opportunity to learn something about a particular business as well as make a contribution to the company by performing needed tasks. Through this relationship, the student can then determine whether the organization would likely be a suitable employer after graduation. Likewise, the organization can make better judgments about the qualifications of the individual because it has the opportunity to evaluate the person in the work situation.[11] This method of recruiting is limited in scope since any one organization can utilize only a limited number of interns at one time. Moreover, it is not feasible for many types of jobs. It can, though, be highly effective where it is practicable.

Executive Search Firms

Executive search firms are used by organizations to locate experienced professionals and top level executives. These firms "are retained to search for the most qualified executive available for specific positions, only on assignment from the company seeking a specific type of individual."[12]

Over the past fifteen years or so, the executive search industry has evolved from a basic recruitment service to a highly sophisticated profession filling a greatly expanded role. Search firms are now serving as sounding boards to assist organizations in determining their human resource needs, establish compensation ranges, and provide advice concerning organizational structures.[13]

Executive search firms differ from employment agencies in that they do not work for individuals; they are retained and compensated by the client organizations they serve.

Firms in this business often visit their clients' offices to interview company management. This enables them to gain a clear understanding of the company's goals, the requirements of the position, and the qualifications needed by a candidate. After this information is obtained, the search firm seeks out potential candidates, reviews their resumés, conducts interviews, and performs background checks. As a general rule, the best three or four candidates will be referred to the client organization for the actual selection decision.

The search firm's fee is usually a stipulated percentage of the individual's annual income. However, the manner in which the fee is earned may differ from firm to firm. Some firms operate on a contingency basis, receiving their fee only if the organization hires one of the referred candidates. Other firms agree to furnish three or four well-qualified candidates and the organization agrees to pay the fee regardless of whether it actually hires one of the candidates. Expenses incurred in the search are customarily added to any agreed upon fees.

Perhaps the key problem in executive searches is poor communication between the client and the search firm. Reaching agreement on specifications and qualifications is absolutely essential if the search firm is to do its job effectively.

Professional Associations

Associations in business professions such as finance, marketing, data processing, and personnel frequently provide placement services on a national, regional, or local basis for their members. Acting as a clearing house, these associations maintain lists of positions that member companies are attempting to fill and lists of individual members seeking new jobs. The association's role is limited to one of simply providing information. Where an opening needs to be filled in a specific profession, organizations may want to consider this method.

Employee Referrals

Many organizations have found that their employees can assist in the recruitment process by actively soliciting applications from their friends and associates. In fact, although more research is needed to substantiate it fully, some studies indicate that employee referrals are among the best sources of long-tenure employees.[14]

Some organizations emphasize referrals by paying the referring employee a bonus if the applicant is hired and stays on the job for a stated length of time.

One potential problem with referrals that an organization should be aware of is that referrals tend to perpetuate the current composition of the work force; that is, if the present work force is largely composed of white males, the majority of referred applicants will be white males. Relying solely on referrals could possibly result in a situation that has discriminatory impact even though there is no intention to discriminate.[15]

MATCHING METHODS TO SOURCES

Organizations differ widely and, because they do, the types and qualifications of workers needed to fill various positions is also different.

Recruitment efforts, if they are to be successful, must then be tailored to meet the specific needs of an organization. Realistically, each job may require identifying different sources of potential employees and using different methods of recruiting to secure personnel from these sources.

A staffing specialist must first identify the source—where people are likely to be found—before the methods—how to attract people to the organization—can be chosen. Suppose, for example, that a large firm has an immediate need for a data processing manager with a minimum of five years experience managing a substantial computer operation. Studying the sources, it is clear that this individual must come from competitors or other companies. Once the source of recruiting has been identified, the staffing specialist must next choose the method or methods of recruiting that will have the best chance of encouraging qualified candidates to apply for the job. Several choices are available in this example: (1) an advertisement in the employment section of *The Wall Street Journal*, (2) an ad in *Computerworld*, (3) attending meetings of the Data Processing Management Association, (4) an executive search firm, or (5) employment agencies that specialize in data processing personnel. Some methods would not be appropriate at all for trying to fill this position—public employment agencies, college recruiters, special events, internships, and employee referrals.

On the other hand, suppose that a firm has a need for a twenty-year-old entry level machine operator and the firm is willing to train the person to operate the equipment. High schools, vocational schools, and unsolicited applicants are likely recruiting sources. Effective recruiting methods might include newspaper advertisements, public employment agencies, employee referrals, and recruiter contact with schools.

The specific methods used in recruiting also depend upon external environmental factors, such as labor supply and demand. Because of the differences in companies, some methods may prove satisfactory for one organization but be virtually useless for another. To match methods to sources effectively, each organization should maintain records on recruiting efforts and conduct research to determine the best methods to use for specific job categories.

RECRUITMENT RESEARCH

If a company has information revealing where its employees were recruited, statistics on present and past employees may be used to indicate the best sources of recruiting. For instance, a firm may discover that graduates from a particular college or university adapt well to the firm's environment. One large farming equipment manufacturer has achieved excellent success in recruiting from schools located in rural areas. Managers in this firm believe that since many of the students in these schools come from a farming environment, they can adapt more quickly to the firm's type of operations.

Other organizations have identified sources of employees by determining where their current employees live. This type of research, however, is likely to be more revealing where entry level production or clerical workers are concerned. If a firm discovers that the majority of its lower level employees reside within twenty miles of the workplace, recruiting efforts for these kinds of employees should be concentrated within that geographical area.

Recruiting research can assist not only in identifying sources of employees but also in predicting what types of individuals are more apt to succeed in the organization. When a regional medical center, located a fairly good distance from a large metropolitan area, reviewed its personnel records, it discovered that registered nurses who were born and raised in smaller towns adapted better to the small town environment in which the center was located than did those who grew up in large metropolitan areas. Based on this study, the hospital modified its recruiting efforts.[16]

Examples of improper recruiting are numerous. Managers of a large convenience store, for example, were disturbed that their employee turnover was high. Upon analyzing their recruiting efforts, they learned that the majority of short-term employees had merely seen a sign in the store window advertising a job opening. The individuals hired in this manner were often unemployed and highly transient. The source of supply and the recruiting method used practically ensured a high turnover rate. Once these facts were discovered, new sources of supply and new methods were used and employee turnover decreased significantly.

Because recruiting is expensive—in terms of both direct and indirect costs—it is essential that organizations conduct research in this area to ensure that recruiting efforts are as effective as possible.

EQUAL EMPLOYMENT OPPORTUNITY AND RECRUITING

Although recruiting is not expressly mentioned in Title VII of the Civil Rights Act of 1964, as Amended, the manner in which recruiting is carried out can potentially lead to discrimination or to the perpetuation of historical patterns of discrimination. When an organization operates under an affirmative action plan, the recruiting effort must not only be free from discrimination, but also take actions above those normally employed to ensure that sufficient utilization of minorities and women in the workforce is attained.

Analysis of Recruiting Procedures

To ensure that its recruiting program is non-discriminatory, a firm must thoroughly analyze its recruiting procedures and practices. It might, for example, be unwise to use employee referral as a primary method and unsolicited applicants as a main recruitment source. These actions tend to perpetuate the traditional composition of an organization's work force. Particularly where minorities and women are not well represented at all organizational levels, the courts have ruled that reliance on these practices is discriminatory.

In identifying sources of continuing discrimination, it is helpful to develop a record of applicant flow. (Such a record, of course, may be a requirement if an organization has to file an EEO-1 Report, has been found guilty of discrimination, or operates under an affirmative action plan). This record should include minority status and job-related data concerning each applicant; it should indicate whether a job offer was extended. If no job offer was made, a written explanation must be provided. Records including this kind of information facilitate the analysis of recruiting practices relative to protected classes and enable an organization to modify the ways it recruits.

Utilization of Minorities and Women

Each individual who engages in recruiting must be trained to use objective, job-related standards. Two objective measures pertaining to job relatedness are specific skills and work experience. Recruiting based on these kinds of standards goes a long way toward eliminating discrimination.

Recruiters themselves play a critical role in either encouraging or discouraging protected class members to apply for employment with an organization. In this regard, qualified minorities and women should be utilized as much as possible in key recruiting activities. Using minorities as college recruiters or in job fairs and open houses is a way of suggesting to other minority group members that they, too, are potential candidates for employment with the organization.

Pictures of minority and women employees in employment advertisements and recruiting brochures also help an organization establish credibility as an equal employment opportunity employer.

All of these things must, however, be underscored by a genuine commitment on the part of management to increase minority participation.

Advertising

With few exeptions, jobs must be open to all individuals. Consequently, all advertisements must be free from discriminatory preferences unless the reason for preferring a particular type of individual over another has been firmly established as a bona fide occupational qualification. Some of the terms that must be avoided in employment advertising are:

- Young
- Boy
- Girl
- Age 25 to 35
- Age over 50
- Attractive lady
- Real sharp girl
- Career minded men
- College student
- Recent college graduate
- Retired person

The courts have ruled that each of the preceding terms is discriminatory either on the basis of sex or age.[17]

To ensure that advertisements reach an adequate number of minorities, organizations must do more than simply place a help wanted ad in the major local newspaper; they must advertise in places and through media that will reach the target group. Potentially effective media include ethnic newspapers, urban contemporary radio broadcasts, and Hispanic radio broadcasts.

All advertising copy used in print media should also contain the phrase "Equal Opportunity Employer, M/F" to convey the idea that job opportunities are available not only to traditional minorities but also to women. Many people have the mistaken impression that "EEO Employer" suggests only racial non-discrimination.

Employment Agencies

An organization should emphasize its non-discriminatory recruitment practices when placing job orders with employment agencies. Inasmuch as employment agencies are covered under Title VII, the potential employer cannot go so far as to say, "We want a black . . . an Hispanic . . . a woman . . . someone over 50 . . . for this position." By specifying minority status desired for a job opening, the organization is open to discrimination charges. Likewise, the agency that screens individuals on this basis is engaging in discriminatory practices. Complete non-discrimination must be the rule.

Jobs at all levels should also be listed with the local state employment agency. Often, these agencies can provide valuable assistance to organizations seeking to fulfill affirmative action goals.

Other Affirmative Action Recruiting Approaches

Personal contacts should be made with counselors and administrators at high schools, vocational schools, and colleges with large minority or female enrollments to indicate that an organization is actively seeking minorities and females for job openings. The possibilities of internships and summer employment for students of these schools should be carefully explored and provided wherever possible.

Organizations engaged in affirmative recruitment should develop positive working relationships with minority, women's, ethnic, and other community organizations. While the most productive sources may vary in each locality, some helpful organizations to contact include: National Association for the Advancement of Colored People, National Urban League, League of United Latin American Citizens, American Business Women's Association, American Association of University Women, Federation of Professional Women's Talent Bank, National Council of Negro Women, and the local Veterans Administration. Regional offices of the Equal Employment Opportunity Commission will assist employers in locating appropriate agencies.

NOTES

1. Charles J. Sigrist, "Nine Out of Ten Firms Use Temporary Help," *The Office*, January 1978, p. 90.

2. Howard Rudnitsky, "A Cushion for Business," *Forbes*, February 5, 1979. p. 78.

3. "Combing Colleges for Execs," *Chain Store Age Executive*, July 1977, p. 27.

4. Dan Lionel, "Dow Jones Tests Recruitment Weekly," *Editor & Publisher*, May 24, 1980, p. 29.

5. Patrick Crow, "Industry Scrambling to Get Adequate Manpower," *The Oil and Gas Journal*, December 11, 1978, p. 33.

6. Dan Lionel, "Trade Journals 'Inefficient' for Recruiting," *Editor & Publisher*, May 2, 1981, p. 18.

7. Jo Bredwell, "The Use of Broadcast Advertising for Recruitment," *Personnel Administrator*, February 1981, pp. 45–49.

8. Ibid.

9. James W. Schreier, "Deciphering Messages in Recruitment Ads," *Personnel Administrator*, March 1983, pp. 35–39.

10. Roy G. Foltz, "Recruiting Communications," *Personnel Administrator*, February 1981, p. 12.

11. H. Felix Kloman, "The Student Intern," *Risk Management*, February 1979, p. 10.

12. Richard J. Cronin, "Executive Recruiters: Are They Necessary?" *Personnel Administrator*, February 1981, p. 32.

13. Thomas C. Amory, "Searching for a Search Firm," *Personnel Journal*, February 1983, pp. 114–116.

14. James A. Breaugh, "Relationships between Recruiting Sources and Employee Performance, Absenteeism, and Work Attitudes," *Academy of Management Journal*, March 1981, pp. 142–147.

15. S. Prakash Sethi, *Up Against the Corporate Wall* (Englewood Cliffs, N.J.: Prentice-Hall, 1971), pp. 84–106.

16. Van M. Evans, "Recruitment Advertising in the '80s," *The Personnel Administrator*, December 1978, p. 23.

17. Barbara Lindemann Schlei and Paul Grossman, *Employment Discrimination Law* (Washington, D.C.: Bureau of National Affairs, 1983), p. 486.

8

The Selecting Process

Selecting is the process of choosing from a group of applicants that individual deemed to be best qualified for a particular job opening. An organization's success in its recruiting activities significantly affects the efficiency and effectiveness of selection. An adequate pool of applicants provides an organization greater latitude in choosing employees; an inadequate pool reduces the amount of latitude and may result in the employment of marginally qualified candidates.

Selecting is, at best, a difficult process because it involves making judgments about people. Three essential questions must be answered if the most qualified person is to be selected. These questions are: What is the applicant's "can do" ability? What is the applicant's "will do" ability? How well will the applicant "fit" into the organization? "Can do" ability refers to experience and education required to perform a specific job; "will do" ability refers to the level of motivation the person will actually exert in performing the job; "fit" refers to how well the individual will conform to the socio-psychological environment of the organization. Making these determinations requires skill, effort, and time. Moreover, they must be made carefully if selection is to be achieved effectively.

Mistakes made in selecting can be costly. Hiring individuals who cannot or will not do their jobs leads to output and quality problems, and ultimately to employee turnover. Hiring individuals who do not fit into the organization leads not only to the same problems, but may also adversely affect the morale of other employees. Consequently, selecting must be done carefully in order to minimize potential negative impacts on the organization.

As emphasized throughout this book, the entire human resource management function operates in an increasingly legalistic environment. Nowhere is it more open to discrimination charges and lawsuits than in selection. The challenge to an organization, then, in selecting employees is twofold: one, to select the best qualified individual and, two, to make the selection decision in accordance with the letter and spirit of the law.

Selecting is such an important activity that three chapters of this book are devoted to it. This chapter presents an overview of the entire selecting process. The following two chapters examine crucial elements of the process: testing and interviewing, respectively.

A GENERALIZED SELECTING MODEL

A generalized model of the selecting process is depicted in Figure 8-1. Selection begins where recruiting ends—with the applicant pool—and proceeds through five stages: initial screening, secondary screening, candidacy, verification, and final decision. Before examining the model more closely, it is important to remember that selection procedures vary from organization to organization; consequently, the steps outlined may not be followed in the described sequence by a specific firm. Also, an applicant may be rejected at any point during the first four stages. The purpose of the model is to illustrate the basic steps, in a logical sequence, that are typically followed in evaluating and ultimately hiring a person who applies for a job with a particular organization.

Once individuals are interested in applying for employment, they may do so by submitting a resumé (a common procedure for technical, professional, or managerial positions) or by completing an employment application (standard procedure for entry level, operative, clerical, or other non-exempt positions). The majority of applicants will be screened out at this point based on an individual evaluation of the resumé or the employment application. Applicants who submitted a resumé may be asked to complete an employment application if their credentials survive the initial review.

The two components of Stage II are the screening interview and testing. The purpose of the screening interview is to eliminate from further consideration those individuals whose qualifications, although passing preliminary inspection, do not really measure up to the standards of the position. Based on the screening interview, applicants for certain types of positions may be asked to take employment tests. Applicants passing the screening interview who have not yet completed an employment application will be asked to do so at this stage. On occasion, applicants may move from the completion of the employment application in Stage I directly into employment testing before the screening interview takes place—a common procedure for typists or machine operators. If the test results are favorable, the screening interview then takes place.

Since the vast majority of applicants are eliminated in Stages I and II, only genuinely qualified candidates, assuming that the previous selection

Figure 8.1
A Model of the Selecting Process

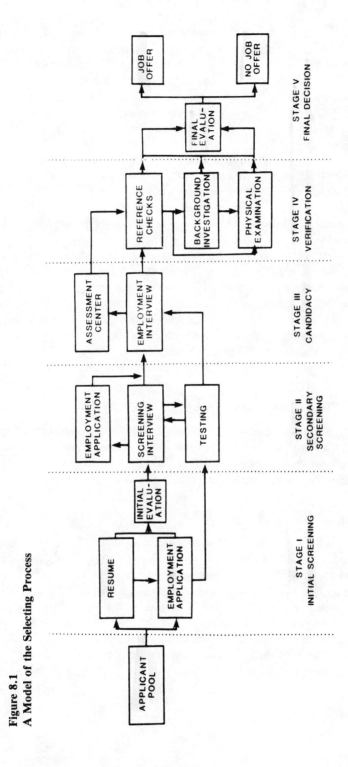

procedures are working effectively, enter Stage III. The basic component of this stage is the employment interview or series of employment interviews designed to ascertain an in-depth evaluation of the applicant's qualifications. In some organizations, individuals successfully completing their employment interviews are sent to an assessment center where they may complete batteries of tests and engage in simulations of various kinds to further assess their capabilities. Applicants completing Stage III are potential employees.

Stage IV is concerned with verifying information furnished by applicants, ensuring that there is nothing in the individual's background that would preclude employment (an absolute necessity where governmental security clearances are required), and determining if the individual is physically fit to perform the job (where physical requirements are a bona fide occupational qualification).

Stage V is the decision-making stage. All information that can be collected has been collected. The organization must evaluate this information and decide which of two or more candidates is most qualified or best suited for the job opening.

In reviewing the generalized selecting model, note that the least time consuming, least expensive selection activities are performed first. The most time consuming, most expensive activities are performed later in the process. This is done to ensure the cost effectiveness of selection.

FACTORS AFFECTING THE SELECTING PROCESS

While a generalized selection model is helpful in showing the series of logical steps that are usually taken in choosing employees, specific procedures do vary from firm to firm. Additionally, there are other organizational variables and influences that may affect the process.

Organizational Hierarchy

The selection process would be greatly simplified if a single standardized procedure could be developed—and that would be followed—for all applicants. Deviations from any predetermined steps, however, are often necessary to accommodate the needs of specific situations. In particular, variations are appropriate, even required, when filling positions at different levels in the organizational hierarchy. For instance, consider the differences that exist in hiring a top level executive as opposed to a secretary. Exhaustive interviewing of the potential executive followed by extensive background checks to verify experience, education, and personal impeccability are essential for a senior level position. On the other hand, an applicant for a secretarial position may only take a typing test and be subjected to a short employment interview.

As a general rule, the higher the position in the organization or the more sensitive the position is, the more involved and complicated the selection process will be. The lower the position, the less likely the full series of steps specified by the model will be followed.

Speed of Decision Making

The time available for making a selection decision can also exert a major influence on the selecting process. Suppose, for instance, that a firm's only two quality control inspectors terminate without advance notice. Filling these positions immediately is a matter of critical importance. Consequently, the algorithmic steps in the selection process are likely to be heuristically short circuited. Since speed is of the essence, a few telephone calls and two short interviews may comprise the entire selection process. Conversely, when the need for filling a position is known well in advance, more time can be spent rigidly following the normal selection procedure steps.

Applicant Pool

The number of applicants for a particular job also affects the selecting process. An organization can be highly selective if there are many applicants for a specific position. It cannot be as selective or uncompromising in its requirements if few applicants are available. In the latter case, selection becomes largely a matter of choosing whomever is available.

The number of persons hired for a particular job compared to the number of qualified individuals in the applicant pool is known as the selection ratio. This ratio is determined as follows:

$$\frac{\text{Number of individuals hired for a particular job}}{\text{Number of qualified applicants available}} = \text{Selection Ratio}$$

A selection ratio below 1.0 indicates that there are more qualified applicants than there are jobs; a selection ratio above 1.0 indicates that there are more jobs than there are applicants. Obviously, the lower the ratio, the more choice an organization has; the higher the ratio, the less choice it has. Thus, the applicant pool generated by recruiting has a significant impact on selection.

Type of Organization

The specific kind of enterprise where individuals are to be employed—

private, not-for-profit, or governmental—can also affect the selection process. A business in the private sector is profit oriented and prospective employees are likely to be screened with regard to the potential contributions they can make toward helping the organization achieve its profit objectives—especially professionals and managers. Profit-making enterprises are apt to be more stringent in their selection criteria.

Governments—federal, state, and local, but especially federal—typically identify qualified applicants through competitive examinations. Often, the hiring manager is permitted to select only from the three top qualifying applicants for a given position. A manager in the governmental sector may not have the prerogative to interview candidates other than the top scorers on the competitive examination.

In not-for-profit organizations such as the American Heart Association, the Boy Scouts of America, or the YWCA, the situation is even more different. Because salary levels in these types of organizations are not normally competitive with those in industry or government, selection must center on not only the applicant's qualifications for job performance, but also on an assessment of the applicant's dedication to the kind of work involved.

Clearly, the type of organization involved affects both the sorts of individuals who will be attracted as well as the selection criteria that will be used in making a hiring decision.

Probationary Period

Many organizations use a probationary period that provides for evaluation of an employee's ability to perform before permanent employment is assured. The probationary period may be a substitute for, or supplement to, the use of other selection procedures. The rationale for using a probationary period in lieu of other selection measures is that if a person can successfuly perform the job during the trial period, tests or other predictors of success are not needed.

Even though a firm may be unionized, a new employee typically is not protected by the labor-management agreement until after completing a probationary period—usually thirty days. During this time, the employee may be terminated with minimum justification. However, once the probationary period is over, it may prove to be quite difficult to terminate even a marginal employee who belongs to a union. Selection under these conditions requires careful identification of qualified workers and realistic evaluation of their performance during the probationary period.

EMPLOYMENT APPLICATIONS

For the majority of positions, the selecting process begins with the prospective employee completing an application form. The application is then reviewed (either by someone in the personnel department or by the hiring manager, depending upon how selection is carried out in a particular organization) to determine if there appears to be a possible match between the applicant and the open position.

The specific types of information requested in employment applications vary from company to company, and even by job types within a given organization. Sections of an application typically include personal data such as name, address, and telephone number; educational background; work experience; military service; and specific job qualifications.

The employment application must reflect not only the firm's informational needs, but also adhere to federal legislation and Equal Employment Opportunity Commission Guidelines. An illustration of a properly designed application is provided in Figure 8-2. Note that many traditional informational requests that are potentially discriminatory have been eliminated from the form. Among the missing items are such things as sex, race, age, number of children living at home, and credit references. Questions relating to a person's arrest record are illegal and, if they appear on an application, they may be regarded as a prima facie violation by EEOC. While there are no other questions that are illegal per se, there are numerous questions that may expose an organization to discrimination charges. Some of the items that should be viewed as inappropriate for an employment application are:

- Date of birth
- Height
- Weight
- Number of children
- Dependents other than children
- List any physical defects
- Have you ever been injured?
- Do you have any defects in hearing?
- Do you have any defects in vision?
- Do you have any defects in speech?
- What is your general physical condition?
- Spouse's name
- Spouse's place of employment
- Spouse's position
- Length of time on job for spouse
- Marital Status
- Credit references

Figure 8.2
Employment Application

Position _____   Date _____

Referred By _____   Date Available to Work _____

Monthly Salary Expected $ _____

PERSONAL DATA

Name _____ Social Security No. _____

Street Address _____ City _____ State _____ Zip _____

Telephone No. (_____)_____   Are you over 18 years old ☐ Yes ☐ No

Do you have any physical limitations that restrict or limit ability to work? ____Yes ____No   If yes please describe _____

_____

Last Date of Physical Exam _____List acquaintances or relatives who work for the credit union _____

_____

Are you or any member of your family a member of this credit union?   ☐ Yes   ☐ No

Have you been employed by any other credit union? ____Yes ____No If yes please name_____

In case of emergency, notify (Name) _____ Telephone # _____

Address _____

EDUCATION

| | Name and Address | Dates Attended | | Course of Study | Diploma |
		From	To	General Major	or Degree
High School					
College/ University					
Trade/ Business					
Other					

SPECIAL SKILLS   List all skills, abilities, training, etc. that you feel would assist in qualifying you for the position. Include any machines or special equipment you have operated.

_____ is an equal opportunity employer dedicated to a policy of non-discrimination on any basis including race, creed, color age, sex, religion, or national origin.

Figure 8.2 (continued)

EMPLOYMENT HISTORY (List Most Recent Employment First)

Company	From ___ Mo. ___ Yr.	Starting Sal. $ Mo.	REFERENCE	
Address	To ___ Mo ___ Yr.	Final Sal. $ Mo.	Tel. No.	May Be Contacted? ☐ Yes ☐ No
Dept.	Position Held:		Duties:	
Reason for Leaving				
Company	From ___ Mo. ___ Yr.	Starting Sal. $ Mo.	REFERENCE	
Address	To ___ Mo ___ Yr.	Final Sal. $ Mo.	Tel. No.	May Be Contacted? ☐ Yes ☐ No
Dept.	Position Held:		Duties:	
Reason for Leaving				
Company	From ___ Mo. ___ Yr.	Starting Sal. $ Mo.	REFERENCE	
Address	To ___ Mo ___ Yr.	Final Sal. $ Mo.	Tel. No.	May Be Contacted? ☐ Yes ☐ No
Dept.	Position Held:		Duties:	
Reason for Leaving				

PROFESSIONAL REFERENCES   (List 3 most recent supervisors who can be contacted for work reference, excluding relatives.)

Name	Company	Job Title	Phone

PERSONAL REFERENCE   (Give the names and addresses of 3 persons who can be contacted for personal references, excluding relatives & former employers.)

Name	Address	Occupation	Phone No.

I authorize investigation of all statements contained in this application. I understand that misrepresentation or omission of facts called for is cause for termination. Further, I understand and agree that my employment is for no definite period and may be terminated by the credit union at any time.

_____   _____
Signature of Applicant   Date

FOR CREDIT UNION USE:

Interviewed By: _____	New Hire ☐ Declined ☐
Position: _____	Job Grade: _____ Reason: _____
Salary Information: _____	Review Schedule: _____
Approval: _____	Effective: _____
Vice President	

- Nature of military discharge
- Native language
- Date graduated from high school
- Date graduated from college

The information contained in a completed employment application should be compared with the job description and the job specifications to determine the degree to which a match exists between the applicant and the job. This is often a difficult task. Applicants may exaggerate their qualifications in order to present themselves in a more favorable light. Also, it is hard to compare duties and responsibilities of previously held positions with those of the position the applicant is seeking. Job titles, too, can be misleading. A person who has the title of vice president in one organization, for example, may actually perform few managerial tasks while a person with the same title in another organization may have extensive managerial responsibility.

The purpose of reviewing the application is not, however, to make a selection decision. The purpose is to eliminate from further consideration those applicants who do not possess the minimum qualifications.

RESUMÉ ANALYSIS

Resumés are documents that often play a significant role in the selection process. For managerial, professional, and technical positions they are commonly the first information received from a job applicant. A resumé is a relatively short, detailed account of the candidate's work history, educational background, and other qualifications.

A common mistake in reviewing a resumé is to assume that all of the data shown are factual.[1] In fact, it is estimated that as many as four out of every five resumés contains false job history information and about 30 percent of all resumés provide inaccurate educational data. Consequently, resumé reviewers are well advised not to accept a resumé at face value. They should peruse it carefully, noting any inconsistencies and referencing any items that may warrant later verification.

The initial thrust in reviewing a resumé is the same as for an employment application: does the applicant seemingly possess the necessary qualifications for the job at hand? Again, job descriptions and job specifications are used to compare the person's experience and background with the requirements of the position for which he or she is applying.

Additionally, there are some other general considerations the reviewer should pay attention to in order to determine if the resumé is worthy of in-depth review.[2] These are:

- *Positive image conveyed.* Does the applicant present positive factors first? Is the overall tone positive or is it negative? What is the general appearance of the resumé?

- *Evidence of contributions.* Does the applicant emphasize the contributions he or she has made to previous organizations? Or does the applicant simply list job duties?

- *Logical presentation.* Are the data presented in a logical, easy to follow manner? Is work history listed in reverse chronological order so that most recent experience can be seen first?

- *Carefully written.* Is the resumé carefully written so that it is free of grammatical mistakes and typographical errors? Or does it appear to be hastily compiled with little thought given to writing style?

- *Specifics rather than generalities.* Does the resumé deal with previous experience in terms of specifics or does it deal with experience in terms of vague generalities that could be interpreted several ways?

THE SCREENING INTERVIEW

The purpose of the screening interview is to tentatively identify viable employment candidates. A review of the employment application or the resumé eliminates many applicants; those not eliminated by this review process are then screened to see if they do in fact, possess the necessary qualifications. The screening interview reduces the number of applicants to a more manageable number.

The typical screening interview is relatively short. (In fact, one of the authors once witnessed a screening interview that could not have lasted over fifteen seconds. At the end of the interview, the applicant was referred to the hiring supervisor for a final interview and employment decision.) A few straightforward questions are asked: "Do you know how to . . . ? Have you ever operated a . . . ? What is your experience with . . . ? What is your knowledge relative to . . . ? Have you ever set up a . . . ? Do you have a . . . ?" If the applicant does not have the required experience, know-how, or background, any further consideration in the employment process would benefit neither the individual nor the organization.

In addition to quickly eliminating the obviously unqualified job applicants for specific positions, screening interviews may produce other positive benefits for an organization. It is likely that the position for which the individual is applying is not the only one available. A skilled interviewer who has knowledge of other vacancies in the firm may be able, in the process of screening for one position, to identify prospective employees for other open positions. The fact that the applicant does not qualify for one job does not mean that he or she could not qualify for other jobs. For example, an applicant may be obviously unqualified to fill the position of senior programming analyst, but may well possess the necessary skills to work as a computer operator. It is important that the person doing the screening remember that his or her responsibility is not only to eliminate candidates for one position, but also to identify candidates for other positions. Recognizing this dual responsibility, the interviewer can build goodwill for the employer as well as maximize recruiting and selecting efforts.

EVALUATING BACKGROUND AND BIOGRAPHICAL DATA

Over the years considerable effort has been devoted to using application form data to assist in differentiating between individuals who will be successful and unsuccessful in particular jobs. Research during the past fifty years has suggested that the employment application can be a valuable predictive device in selection for certain types of positions. Personal factors such as number of dependents, hobbies (if not related to sex, race, religion, national origin, or age), years of education, and work experience have been found to be predictive of length of service and success on a job. One large firm, for example, discovered that the single most reliable indicator of a college graduate's success in the organization was the person's rank in his or her graduating class. Additionally, this firm found that class ranking was even more important as a predictor than the actual college attended.[3] The weighted application blank and regression analysis, two specific approaches to evaluating background and biographical data, are discussed below.

Weighted Application Blank

The oldest and perhaps best known technique for identifying factors that differentiate between successful and less successful employees is the weighted application blank (WAB). When the WAB is used, an attempt is made to identify factors on the application form that differentiate between long- and short-term employees, productive and less productive employees, or satisfied and less satisfied employees. One such variable, "years on last job," is shown in Figure 8-3.

Although any of several techniques can be used for calculating the weights to be used, the simplest approach is the horizontal percent method.[4] In using this method, however, the sample size must be fairly large. Examining Figure 8-3, we can see how the calculations are done. The number of employees in the sample is first divided into two groups: short term and long term. Short-term employees are those who left the current organization after a limited tenure, usually within the first year of employment, or possibly the first two years. Long-term employees are those who

Figure 8.3
Example of a Weighted Application Blank Question

Number of Responses

Item	Short-term Employees	Long-term Employees	Total Employees	% Long-term Employees	Weight
Years on Last Job					
Less than 1	18	3	21	14%	1
1 to 1½	42	12	54	22%	2
1½ to 2½	46	23	69	33%	3
2½ to 3	17	13	30	43%	4
More than 3	10	11	21	52%	5
Totals	133	62	195		

stayed on the job longer than one or two years. The two groups of employees are classified as to the length of time spent with their previous employer. The percentage of long-term employees is then determined by years spent on last job. In this example, we see that only 14 percent of the long-term employees were with their last employer less than one year, whereas 52 percent had three or more years job service with their last employer. The weight for each category of years on last job is determined by moving the decimal point one place to the right; thus, less than one year on the previous job has an actual weight of 1.4. To simplify the matter of weighting, the number is customarily rounded off to the nearest whole number.

Once weights for all variables on the application blank have been computed, applicants can be screened based on the point total they receive on the WAB. Applicants with the highest point totals are considered to have the highest potential for success on a particular job or with the organization.

In specific instances, the WAB has been proved to be very accurate; at other times, its usefulness has been only marginal. Consequently, the vast majority of companies continue to use the traditional application.

Regression Analysis

Regression analysis, mentioned in Chapter 4 as a human resources planning technique, has also been used successfully for evaluating employment application data. The purpose of regression analysis is to establish the relationship between two or more variables so that one variable can be predicted from the other variables.[5]

In some instances organizations need to determine whether employee productivity can be estimated from information available on the employment application. In regression analysis terminology, the productivity level, in this example, is referred to as the dependent variable. Any item or items on the application used to predict or estimate the productivity level are called independent variables. Commonly used independent variables that are predictive of productivity are work experience and education.

Although the potential for successful use of regression analysis in the selection process appears to be significant, it is used by few organizations. One limitation on its use is the fact that a substantial data base is required for any degree of statistical significance to be established. Moreover, since regression analysis should be conducted on specific jobs or job categories, only very large companies are able to accumulate sufficient numbers with which to work.

Other problems with the use of regression analysis are that a model developed for one company cannot be used by another company; the model must be tailored to fit each organization. When utilized in different geographical areas, a regression model becomes less accurate because of cultural or labor market factors. The regression model must also be continually updated with current employment application data or its accuracy is likely to diminish over time. Despite the problems associated with this analytical tool, it can be of assistance in making selection decisions.

TESTING

Testing is frequently used early in the selecting process to determine if the applicant is qualified for a particular job. Typing or other work sample tests are commonly used for lower level positions. Because of the complex issues involved in testing, the following chapter is devoted to an examination of this area. As a step in the selection process, testing may be advantageous as a means of verifying specific skills.

THE EMPLOYMENT INTERVIEW

One of the most critical steps in the selection process is the employment interview. Applicants reaching this step are those considered to be most qualified for a position inasmuch as unqualified or marginally qualified applicants have already been eliminated from serious consideration prior to this step. The employment interview is essentially an in-depth probing of the candidate's background that provides substantial evidence upon which the hiring decision will be made. Employment interviewing is the subject of Chapter 10.

ASSESSMENT CENTERS

An assessment center is a technique that can be used in selection to identify management potential in candidates. Although primarily used as an internal selection and development device, it is sometimes used in the selection of external candidates.

The popularity of assessment centers is reflected in the growing usage of this device—from just over 100 companies in 1973 to over 2,000 less than a decade later. AT&T pioneered the use of assessment centers in the business world. Today, they are used not only by business organizations, but also governmental units, including the Equal Employment Oportunity Commission itself.[6] One reason for their popularity is the degree to which the approach lends itself to test validation studies.

In assessment centers, candidates are subject to a variety of exercises contructed to simulate the job for which they are applying. These exercises, or test batteries on occasion, are developed through thorough job analyses of positions.

The assessment center method requires candidates to participate in a series of activities similar to those they may be expected to encounter in the actual job itself. Commonly used activities include in-basket exercises, management games, leaderless discussion groups, mock interviews, and other simulations. A team of assessors is used to observe and evaluate the participants.

Because of the time and costs involved, assessment centers are not widely used as a device for selecting new employees.

REFERENCE CHECKS

As suggested earlier, prospective employees sometimes record inaccurate information on employment applications and resumés in order to present a more positive image. The purpose of the reference check is to verify the accuracy of the data furnished. Typically, job applicants are required to furnish names of previous supervisors or names of several business references. Checks on these references are then made by letter or telephone. Because of the possible legalities involved, reference information provided by one organization to another organization is usually limited to job title, dates of employment, and eligibility for rehire. When conducted by telephone, other information may be furnished: for example, absentee record, promotions and demotions, compensation, and stated reasons for termination.

Since the passage of the Federal Privacy Act of 1974, a person who has been employed by the federal government has the legal right to review reference checks that have been made concerning his or her employment unless the person has waived his right. There have been instances where applicants have sued and won court cases when it was proven that the reference information given out was biased or incorrect. Because of the possible extension of the Privacy Act to the private sector, many firms and individuals are now reluctant to provide any kind of negative reference information on former employees or business associates.

Another difficulty related to references is that the job applicant normally provides them. Applicants may selectively choose their references to ensure that positive information only is furnished. It is unlikely, except where the names of previous supervisors are requested, that an applicant would list anyone who might give an unfavorable report. Thus, references tend to be biased in a positive manner.

Because some individuals are reluctant to state their opinions about former employees or colleagues in writing, many organizations prefer to use the telephone when checking references. Since there is no written record of the conversation, greater amounts of information may be secured in this fashion. However, there is still a potential problem with bias—the reference may offer a negatively biased opinion just as easily as a positively biased one.

Some suggestions for improving the reference checking process are:

- *Train employment specialists.* Telephone interviewing techniques, how to ask questions, and how to probe for information are some of the topics that should be covered.

- *Communicate preferences to applicants.* Indicate the kinds of references preferred, whether former supervisors or business colleagues. Inform the applicant as to how references will be contacted.

- *Communicate preferences to recruiting sources.* Outside parties used in employment agencies can often obtain additional reference information on applicants if they know the kinds of information the organization is seeking.

- *Provide feedback to references.* Thank you letters build goodwill for the company and help ensure cooperation from those who may be regular suppliers of reference information.[7]

BACKGROUND INVESTIGATIONS

Although a reference check often provides information to verify certain statements on an employment application or resumé, there are times when it does not. Often, it is necessary to perform a background investigation of the applicant's past employment history. This investigation may be helpful in determining if past work experience is related to the qualifications needed for the new job. As noted previously, job titles are quite deceptive when attempting to evaluate past work experience.

In the defense industry background investigations are required if the individual must have a security clearance to perform job duties. This type of investigation is quite thorough and includes checking into the personal life and habits of the person.

Background investigations have become more important in recent years because there has been an increase in the number of incidents of credential fraud.[8] It is estimated that between 7 and 10 percent of job applicants are not what they present themselves to be, claiming degrees, certifications, and other credentials that they do not possess.[9] Background investigations are useful in combating this kind of misrepresentation.

PHYSICAL EXAMINATIONS

One of the final steps in the selecting process is the physical examination. This examination serves three purposes. First, it screens out individuals who have contagious or communicable diseases that make them unfit for the work to be performed; for example, an applicant for the position of salad chef who has hepatitis or tuberculosis. Second, the examination assists in determining if an applicant is physically capable of performing the work. In the construction industry, where some jobs involve considerable bending, stooping, lifting, and carrying, spinal x-rays are customarily taken to see if the applicant's back is free of defects that might be aggravated while performing the job. Third, physical examination information can be used to determine if there are certain physical capabilities that differentiate between successful and less successful performers. Because of the requirements of Title VII, if a physical quality is specified in the job description, it must be shown to be job related. The examination is a means of collecting data to make this sort of determination.

Physical examinations are increasingly being used for purposes of drug screening, particularly in the federal government and the defense industry. Applicants for positions that involve the operation of public vehicles—taxis, buses, trains, ships, and airplanes—are also commonly screened for drug usage. The intent of drug testing is to eliminate applicants who potentially pose a risk to themselves or to others or who pose a risk to security. Drug screening has become an issue of major national importance. It is likely that in the near future the majority of organizations in this country will require drug testing for all applicants.

THE SELECTION DECISION

After all information has been obtained from appropriate selection devices, the most critical step in the entire process—the decision to hire or not to hire—takes place. The other stages in the selecting process have been used to continuously narrow the number of candidates. The final decision is made from among those individuals who are still being actively considered after reference checks, background investigations, and physical examinations have been completed.

The human resource department is normally involved in all phases leading up to the final employment decision. The selection decision is usually the prerogative of the operating manager, who may or may not seek the advice of the personnel group. The rationale for permitting the manager or supervisor to make the final selection decision is simple: this is the individual who will be responsible for the new employee. Yet there are times when the decision is a collective one, notably in those instances where an employee will have to interface with others across organizational lines.

In some cases, the human resource manager may have strong influence on the decision. If the organization is attempting to meet minority hiring goals under an affirmative action plan, a recommendation from the personnel manager may have considerable bearing on the candidate hired. It is important that the personnel manager refrain from exerting too much pressure on the decision since such action may undermine the operating manager's authority.

Making the Job Offer

Once the decision to hire a particular individual has been made, the candidate is customarily notified by telephone and then sent a letter confirming in writing all of the aspects of the job offer—starting date, rate of pay, and so forth. If the individual is currently employed by another firm, it is necessary to set the reporting date far enough in advance so that the person can give his or her current employer sufficient notice of termination—two weeks in most cases, but possibly much longer for high level professional or managerial positions. Even after this notice, the individual may need some personal time to prepare for the new job, especially if the job requires moving to another city.

The firm itself may also want to delay the date of employment. If the new employee's first assignment upon joining the firm is to attend a particular training school, the organization may request that the person delay joining the firm until perhaps a week before the school begins. This prevents having idle, non-productive, and possibly bored employees on the payroll.

Because there is no guarantee that the person offered the job will accept, the organization should make sure that it has placed candidates in rank order. If the first candidate declines the offer, the offer can then be extended to the second-ranked applicant.

Rejecting Candidates

Applicants may, of course, be rejected at any stage of the selection process. If the process is functioning properly, only a few candidates—possibly three to six—will reach the selection decision stage.

When an individual makes application for employment, he or she is essentially saying, "I think I am qualified for this job. Will you hire me?" Tension increases as the applicant progresses through the selection process. If the person is eliminated early in the process, there is likely to be only a minimum amount of ego lost. The company, in fact, may even be able to inform the individual of other jobs in the organization that better match his or her qualifications.

For many people, the employment interview is not a pleasant experience. Taking tests that affect a person's career can be a period of high anxiety, too. Suffering through all of these experiences only to be told at the end, "There does not appear to be a proper match between your qualifications and our needs," may be extremely painful for the individual involved. Many firms recognize these facts and take deliberate action to protect the applicant's ego. Still, it is quite difficult to tell people that they are not going to be hired.

All organizations should recognize that both firm and candidate have invested considerable time in the selection process. Candidates who are rejected are entitled to a reasonable explanation as to why they were rejected. Form letters or callous expressions such as "Don't call us. We will call you," must be avoided. The treatment afforded a rejected applicant can have an impact on company goodwill as well as future recruiting efforts. Organizations should remember that today's rejected candidate may be tomorrow's employee.

Rejections can be handled effectively in one of three ways: personal conference with the applicant, telephone conversation, or personalized letter. The most effective practice is the personal conference. It is also the most time consuming and expensive. At times, it may not even be practicable because of the geographical separation between applicant and company. Where it can be used, it offers the opportunity to explain carefully why the applicant was not hired. It provides information to the applicant that may be useful in further job searches and it suggests the organization's genuine interest in people. Unfortunately, this approach is the exception rather than the rule.

Personal telephone calls serve essentially the same purposes as the conference approach, offering an opportunity for explanation and building goodwill for the company.

If for some reason applicants must be rejected by letter, the letter should be a personalized one that reduces the stigma of rejection and lessens the chance that the applicant will resent the firm's actions.

No matter which method of rejection is used, rejected candidates should be notified as quickly as possible so that they may pursue other employment opportunities. All too often, organizations keep candidates in a state of suspended animation before informing them they will not be hired.

REALISTIC JOB PREVIEWS

Many candidates have unrealistic expectations about a prospective job or employer.[10] These inaccurate perceptions can have negative consequences for an organization if such candidates are hired: job dissatisfaction, absenteeism, and turnover are examples. Unrealistic expectations are often created by the hiring organizations themselves as they attempt to portray the organization and the job in the most favorable light possible. To correct this situation, it is suggested that at some point in the selecting process applicants be given a realistic preview of both job and company. This preview may be provided either before or during the employment interview. It is crucial, however, that it occur before a job offer is made.

A realistic job preview conveys important job and organizational information to an applicant in an unbiased manner so that both positive and negative aspects of the job and company are presented objectively. Describing negative and positive features assists applicants in developing a more accurate perception of the job and the firm. Research studies indicate that newly hired employees who receive realistic job previews have greater job survival and higher job satisfaction. At the same time, use of this approach does not reduce the flow of qualified applicants. A comparison of the results of traditional job preview procedures with those of realistic job preview procedures is shown in Figure 8-4. Certainly, every organization desires to present itself in a positive manner. But it should not overemphasize positive aspects nor should it downplay negative features. Realism in describing the employment situation should be the objective.

Figure 8.4
Comparison of Results: Typical Versus Realistic Job Previews

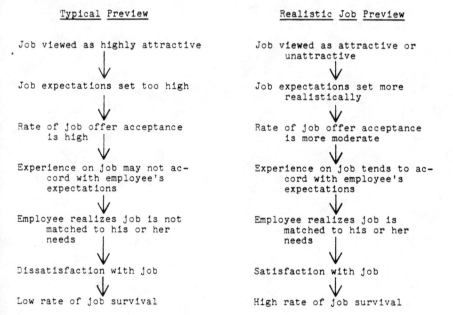

Adapted from: John P. Wanous, "Tell It Like It Is at Realistic Job Previews," Personnel, July-August, 1975, p. 54

NOTES

1. Karen E. Debats, "Resume Fraud," *Personnel Journal*, December 1981, p. 914.

2. Adapted from Robert Half, "How to Write (or Read) a Resume," *Practical Accountant*, May 1981, pp. 63-64.

3. Wayne F. Cascio, *Applied Psychology in Personnel Management*, 2nd ed. (Reston, Va., Reston Publishing Company, 1982), pp. 192-193.

4. Daniel G. Lawrence, Barbara L. Salsburg, John Dawson, and Zachary D. Fashman, "Design and Use of Weighted Application Blanks," *Personnel Administrator*, March 1982, p. 47.

5. John Nettler and William Wassterman, *Applied Linear Statistics* (Homewood, Ill., Richard D. Irwin, 1974), p. 21.

6. Cabot L. Jaffee and Joseph T. Sefcik, Jr., "What Is an Assessment Center?" *Personnel Administrator*, February 1980, pp. 40-43.

7. Adapted from Bruce D. Wonder and Kenneth S. Deleman, "Increasing the Value of Reference Information," *Personnel Administrator*, March 1984, pp. 102-103.

8. Kenneth C. Cooper, "Those 'Qualified' Applicants and Their Phony Credentials," *Administrative Management*, August 1977, p. 44.

9. Scott T. Rickard, "Effective Staff Selection," *Personnel Journal*, June 1981, p. 477.

10. John P. Wanous, "Tell It Like It Is at Realistic Job Previews," in Kendrith M. Rowland, Manual London, Gerald R. Ferris, and Jay L. Sherman, eds., *Current Issues in Personnel Management* (Boston: Allyn & Bacon, 1980), pp. 41-50.

9

Selection Tests

Psychological tests are objective, standardized measures of samples of behavior. The types of behavior measured may range from general intelligence to interests, from aptitudes to levels of achievement, from personality to eye-hand coordination. When used in the selection process, they measure behavior that indicates which individuals possess the needed skills or qualifications for specific jobs. The extent to which psychological tests are used in the private sector as selection aids is not known; however, it is known that the use of such devices has been declining and that rigid government standards concerning tests have created a situation in which potentially useful instruments have been discarded along with the poor ones.[1]

Passage of the Civil Rights Act of 1964 and subsequent court interpretations of its provisions produced a sharp decline in the use of employment tests. In the landmark *Griggs* v. *Duke Power Company* decision, as discussed earlier, the Supreme Court ruled that selection tests must show a relationship to job performance. In *Albermarle* v. *Moody*, the Court again ruled that any test used in selection or promotion decisions must be validated if its use has had an adverse impact on protected classes. Additionally, the *Uniform Guidelines* promulgated standards to which tests must adhere if they are to be considered non-discriminatory. Rather than conduct validation studies, many employers dropped selection testing altogether, while others cut back on test usage.

By curtailing use of what are commonly considered tests, some employers apparently felt that their selection procedures would be immune from validation studies or legal challenge. However, as the *Uniform Guidelines* make abundantly clear, *any* selection device, not just psychological instruments, are tests subject to the same validation requirements as paper-and-pencil tests. While many staffing specialists distrust tests and many organizations are fearful of potential legal implications in their use, tests may well be one of the most valid predictors of job success available to managers. Recognition of this fact, coupled with increased awareness of the interview's fallibility, has recently produced a resurgence of test usage in the selection process.[2]

Research suggests several things about test usage: (1) tests are more widely used in the public sector than they are in the private sector, (2) large to medium size companies are more likely to use tests than small companies, (3) larger firms are more likely to have trained specialists running their testing programs than other companies, and (4) tests are more apt to be used to fill office positions than other types of jobs—more than 80 percent of the companies in one survey use them for office jobs, 20 percent for production jobs, and 10 percent for sales and service jobs.[3]

ADVANTAGES OF SELECTION TESTS

Selection tests, used as one of several and not the sole criterion for hiring individuals, are valuable in the overall selection process because their judicious use can assist an employer in making better hiring and placement decisions. Among the advantages claimed for tests are:

- *Objectivity*. The results produced by or the score received by the person taking the test is not influenced by those evaluating the results or the scores. Thus, tests are not prone to subjective interpretation as are other parts of the selection process, for example, the interview. The test scores speak for themselves.

- *Cost effectiveness*. Tests used to select the right workers for jobs can be an inexpensive way not only to choose workers but also to improve organizational productivity. Cognitive ability tests used by the Philadelphia Police Department to select officers are reported to have saved the department some $18 million in labor costs annually.[4] Another study suggested that if all computer programmers employed by the federal government had been selected by use of a specific test, there would have been a gain in productivity of about $1.2 billion.[5]

- *Quality of information*. Tests can provide information about individuals that cannot be adequately acquired through other selection devices. Possession of aptitudes, abilities, and skills are not always uncovered by resumés, application blanks, or interviews. In fact, they can be misrepresented, faked, or even omitted. Tests offer a method of determining what an individual can really do and whether the person has the necessary qualifications to perform the job successfully.

- *Validity*. Because tests provide quantitative data, they lend themselves more readily to objective statistical validation in terms of job performance than do other selection approaches.

- *Legally defensible*. Where validation studies that establish a demonstrable relationship between test scores and job performance have been conducted, the organization has a solid basis for defending any legal challenge to its use of tests. The same cannot be said as easily for other selection methods.

It is important to remember that tests can serve a useful purpose in selection decisions. Their use should not be avoided simply because of certain limitations placed on their role in selection by the courts or federal agencies.

DISADVANTAGES OF SELECTION TESTS

If selection tests were perfect indicators of job performance, there would be little or no need for interviews, reference checks, and the like. There are definite disadvantages to using selection tests. These include:

- *Tests do not measure motivational levels.* Successful performance on any job is basically dependent on two variables: "can do" ability and "will do" ability. The first ability refers to the skills necessary to perform the job, while the second ability refers to the person's willingness to exert the motivation required to get the job done. Tests are more accurate in measuring "can do" than they are at ascertaining "will do." There are numerous examples in almost every organization of individuals who have the ability and potential to succeed in a job, but for some reason never do. Lack of motivation, poor relationships on the job, personal problems, and other factors that are not readily measurable through testing, not lack of ability, account for unwillingness to perform the job at the expected level.

- *Tests are more accurate at predicating failures than successes.* Studies can establish the minimum level of ability needed to perform a job and indicate that people with less than this level of ability are apt to fail in the job. But, as mentioned above, tests may be inadequate measures of who will actually succeed in the job.

- *Tests are more predictive for groups than they are for specific individuals.* Again, this is primarily related to the motivational level of individuals. Of a total group of people taking a test, the test can reveal with some certainty which subgroup is likely to perform well, but it cannot identify which individuals are most likely to perform well.

- *Some tests are susceptible to dishonesty.* Personality tests or interest inventories, for example, may not be responded to truthfully. The individual may answer the questions in such a manner as to convey the impression he or she wants to create or in accordance with the answers he or she believes the organization desires. Although some tests have built-in lie detection scales, the problem of faking answers still exists.

- *Tests often create anxiety on the part of the test taker.* Individuals seeking employment may become nervous or tense when confronting another hurdle that could eliminate them from further employment consideration. Consequently, the results may not accurately reflect the actual abilities of certain individuals.

- *Tests are subject to legal challenge.* Perhaps because they are highly visible or because many applicants are suspicious of them, tests are often open to charges of discrimination

In deciding whether to use selection tests as part of the overall selection process, organizations should carefully weigh the advantages of tests against the disadvantages. Even with the best tests available, errors in predicating job success will be made. Nevertheless, they may provide additional information that can be used along with other criteria.

CHARACTERISTICS OF PROPERLY DESIGNED TESTS

A well-designed selection test is one that is standardized, objective, based on sufficient normative data, and valid. Tests that do not possess these five characteristics should not be used in the selection process.

Standardization

Standardization refers to the uniformity of the procedures and conditions involved in administering and scoring tests. For the results to be useful, the test should be given to all individuals under conditions that are as similar as possible. Even the physical environment of the testing room should be the same for all test takers. If some individuals take the test in a noisy, drafty, or poorly lit room, while others take it in a quiet, pleasant atmosphere, test results are likely to be distorted. Standardization also means that the same materials must be used each time, the same time limits employed, identical instructions given to the individuals, and so forth. Even the way oral instructions are given and preliminary questions are answered should be identical.[6] Ensuring standardized conditions is the responsibility of the test administrator—a responsibility that requires detailed advance preparation.[7]

Objectivity

Objectivity refers to the scoring of test results. If all individuals scoring a given test obtain the same results, the test is said to be objective. The most objective of all employment tests are those that use multiple-choice or true-false answers since the test taker either chooses the correct answer or does not. Scoring, in this instance, is then largely a clerical process that can be performed by an individual with little training. Often, tests of this nature are machine scored.

There are some tests—not widely used in the selection process—that are highly subjective as far as their scoring is concerned. The Rorschach "inkblot" test and the Thematic Apperception Test (TAT) are two such subjective instruments open to different interpretations by different scorers. With the Rorschach, the applicant is shown a series of cards containing inkblots of varying sizes, shapes, and colors and asked to offer an explanation of what he or she perceives in the inkblot. Obviously, there can be no uniform scoring here because there are no uniform answers. The scorer has to interpret the applicant's answers. In the TAT, applicants are shown pictures of real-life situations and asked to provide their interpretations of each picture. Again, there are no standardized answers. The scorer utilizes a great deal of judgment in deciphering the responses. The highly subjective nature of these tests require trained psychologists as scorers or interpreters, and, even so, the psychologists often differ from each other in interpreting the results.

Normative Data

Normative data provide a frame of reference for comparing an applicant's performance on a test with that of a representative group of similar individuals who have previously taken the test. The test performance of the representative or sample group thus becomes the standard or norm by which the scores of future test takers will be evaluated or interpreted. Norms, more specifically, reflect the distribution of many scores obtained from the sample group.

Typically, the scores from the sample group will be distributed according to a normal probability (bell-shaped) curve with approximately 68.3 percent of the scores falling within one standard deviation of the mean (arithmetic average). Applicants scoring within one standard deviation—a measurement of the dispursion of the data from the sample group—would be considered average relative to the sample population. Applicants scoring outside the range of 2 standard deviations would be considered to be unlikely performers if the 2 standard deviations were less than the mean or to be likely high performers if the standard deviations were more than the mean.[8]

Normative data may also be developed by using percentile scores. Percentile scores are expressed in terms of the percentage of the sample group who fall below a specified raw score on the test. A percentile ranking thus indicates the test taker's relative position in terms of the sample group taking the test. Percentile standings are calculated from the bottom up so that the lower the individual's percentile, the lower the person's standing as compared to the sample population; the higher the individual's percentile, the higher the person's standing relative to the group.

Developers of commercially distributed employment tests usually provide employers with detailed normative data since this adds to the usefulness of the instrument as a selection device. Organizations that have sufficient numbers of employees performing similar work may elect to develop their own norms, although this is not usually the case. Where the developers of the test have computed statistically sound norms, these are generally used. In any event, the test must have sufficient normative data for it to be considered a usable selection tool.

Reliability

The reliability of a selection test is the extent to which it provides consistent results. If a person takes the same test several times, his or her actual scores will vary; this variance is referred to as the standard error, and is a measurement of the extent to which differences in scores are due to chance error. The closer the scores are to each other, the more reliability the test has; the farther apart the scores are, the less reliability the instrument has. If a test has low reliability, its usefulness as a predicator of job success will probably be low inasmuch as the applicant takes the test only once and his or her actual score may not be reflective of actual ability—it may be due entirely to chance error. Reliability of a test is expressed as a coefficient of correlation. Ideally, this coefficient should exceed +0.801 for a test to be considered reliable enough to be used as a selection instrument.[9]

The actual reliability of a particular instrument can be determined three ways: test-retest, equivalent forms, or split-halves.

Test-retest. This method of reliability determination requires giving the test twice to the same group of people and correlating the scores from the two testing instances. A perfect positive correlation would be +1.0, indicating that the instrument is as reliable as possible, statistically speaking. The closer the reliability coefficient is to +1.0, the more consistent the test results are and, therefore, the more useful the test is as a method of selection.

There are several problems associated with the test-retest method: the costs of administering the test twice, the necessity of ensuring that group composition is identical on both occasions, the possibility that test takers may recall test questions if the retest is given too soon after the original test, and the learning that may have taken place between test administrations that could affect the results. Despite these problems, the method is a sound one for ascertaining reliability.

Equivalent Forms. A second method of determining reliability involves using two tests that are similar but not identical. The scores on each test are then correlated to establish the reliability of the first instrument. While this method overcomes some of the difficulties associated with test-retest, there is a definite problem of finding or developing two tests that are essentially the same, yet not the same.

Split-Halves. This method examines the reliability of a test by dividing it into two parts and then correlating the results from each half. In its simplest form, odd-numbered items from the test constitute the first half and even-numbered items constitute the second half. The two scores for each person taking the test are then correlated to arrive at a reliability coefficient.

Unmistakably, such an approach can eliminate the problems entailed with either test-retest or equivalent forms. The biggest difficulty, admittedly, is ensuring that the two halves are equal in content, difficulty, and nature.

Validity

The *sine qua non* of any test, psychological or otherwise, is that it actually measures what it purports to measure. This is what is referred to as validity. If a selection test does not actually measure ability to perform a job, it is useless as a selection tool and, as stated in earlier chapters and sections, vulnerable to successful legal challenge in the courts under existing federal statutes and the *Uniform Guidelines*. Test validity is, has been, and probably always will be a proper concern of organizations using selection tests. In recent years, because of the emphasis given to employment of women and minorities, greater emphasis has been placed on establishing test validity.

Validity is usually expressed as a correlation coefficient that indicates the relationship between two variables: test scores and actual job performance. A coefficient of 0 would indicate no relationship between the variables while a coefficient of $+1.0$ or -1.0 would indicate a perfect relationship—the former a completely positive one and the latter a completely negative one. Certainly, no selection test will ever be 100 percent valid; but organizations that use tests should strive for the highest possible coefficient of validity. If a test is designed to be a predictor of job success and validity studies show a high correlation coefficient, an organization can be reasonably assured that applicants who score high on the test are likely to be successful on the job. Valid tests enable an employer to select better qualified, potentially more productive workers.

Employers are not automatically required to validate the selection tests they use. Generally speaking, validation is required only when the instrument used or the selection process as a whole results in adverse impact on a protected class.[10] While validation of selection tests is expensive, it is something that should be done. Otherwise, an organization cannot know whether a test is actually measuring the qualities and abilities that it is supposed to measure.

VALIDATION STUDIES

The *Uniform Guidelines* identified three methods that may be used to validate selection tests: criterion-related validity studies, content validity studies, or construct validity studies.

Criterion-related Validity

Criterion-related validity indicates the efficacy of a test in predicting an individual's performance in specified situations. Performance on the test is compared with a criterion—an independent measure of what the test is designed to predict.[11] If, for example, a typing test is used, the criterion might be subsequent job performance as a typist in producing quantity or quality of work. A high correlation between the test score and work volume would suggest that the test is valid.

The two basic forms of criterion-related validity are concurrent validity and predictive validity. With concurrent validity, the test scores and the criterion information are collected at basically the same time. Assume, for the sake of illustration, that a company wants to validate a mechanical aptitude test for use in selecting machine operators. The concurrent methodology would entail giving the test to all currently employed machine operators while at the same time collecting information about each operator's job performance. The test scores and job performance criterion would then be correlated to determine the relationship between the two items. If the correlation coefficient is high (that is, workers who score high on the test are the most productive and workers who score low on the test are the least productive), the test would be a valid predictor of job success or performance. If there was little or no relationship between test scores and job performance, the test would not be valid.

A potential problem that could affect the results obtained from this validation procedure comes from changes that may have occurred within the work group before the study was conducted. The less productive employees may already have been terminated because of poor performance while the most productive workers may have been promoted out of the group.[12]

The major difference between concurrent and predictive validity studies is the time interval between administering the test and collecting the criterion data.[13] For example, a particular test might be given to all computer programmers hired, but the test results would not be used in making selection decisions. At a later time, performance data would be collected and correlated with test scores to ascertain whether the employer could predict success on the job from the test scores.

Predictive validity is considered by some to be the soundest method for assessing the validity of a test,[14] but there are problems associated with this approach. First, many organizations do not have the time or the resources to conduct a study that extends over a long period. Second, if legally challenged on the use of a test, a company may have to establish the test's validity very quickly. The longitudinal nature of the predictive validity method precludes obtaining results in a short time span.

Content Validity

Content validation involves the systematic examination and analysis of test content to determine whether the test contains a representative sample of the behaviors, skills, and knowledge required for job performance. The classic example of content validity is a typing test in which an applicant would be required to type samples of the same kinds of items that would be typed on the job.

A content validity study normally involves three steps.[15] First, a thorough job analysis is conducted to identify basic tasks, responsibilities, and skills involved in the job. The relevancy, importance, and frequency of task performance and skill usage is also determined. Second, test items are written or representative "work samples" of the job are developed. Third, the test items or work samples are reviewed by individuals familiar with the job to determine if the test items are accurate reflections of job content.

Although content validity is far less statistically oriented than the other two approaches to validity, many human resource practitioners believe it to be a more sensible approach to validation.[16]

Construct Validity

Construct validity is a method used to determine the extent to which a test measures some theoretical construct or trait such as intelligence, mechanical comprehension, or verbal ability.[17] Because it deals with fairly abstract behaviors, "construct validity requires the gradual accumulation of information from a variety of sources."[18] While several different techniques may be used to validate a construct, the complexity of this approach, its time-consuming nature, and the degree of psychometric expertise required render it an infrequently used procedure in the validation of employment tests.[19]

ESTABLISHING CUT-OFF SCORES

Once a test has been validated, it is necessary to set an appropriate cut-off score. The cut-off score is that test score below which an applicant will not be accepted. The actual cut-off score used on a particular test may be altered from time to time, depending upon the organization's selection ratio. During periods when there are a great number of applicants applying for jobs, higher cut-off scores will be used because the firm can afford to be more selective in the employees it hires. When there are fewer applicants, the cut-off score may be lowered so that job vacancies can be filled. Regardless of where they may be set, cut-off scores should reflect a reasonable expectation of success on the job.

Establishing cut-off scores is not as easy a matter as it may seem. Validation studies will typically show that some employees who scored low on a test are actually successful on the job while some employees who scored high were unsuccessful in job performance. Figure 9-1 illustrates the nature

Figure 9.1
Cut-off Score for a Validated Test

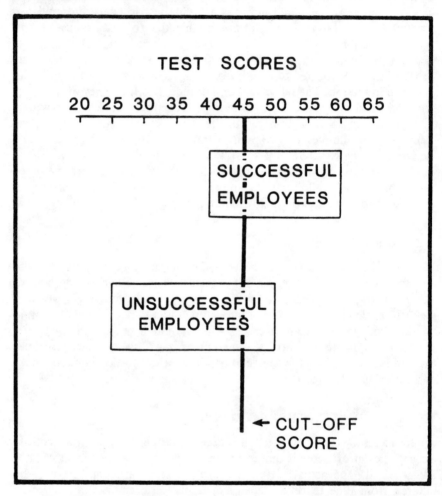

of this problem. In examining the data presented, it can be seen that successful employees scored between 40 and 60 on the test and unsuccessful employees scored between 25 and 50. It is the area of overlapping scores that produces the difficulty in setting a cut-off score. In this example, several possibilities exist. One, the organization could set the cut-off score at 50, thereby assuring itself that it would be hiring only employees who would be good performers. But, setting the score at this point would also eliminate a sizeable percentage of other applicants who are likely to be successful. Two, the organization could set the cut-off at 40—the lower limit for successful employees—but if it did so it would hire many applicants who would be poor performers. Third, the organization could compromise and set the score somewhere between 40 and 50, recognizing that some successful performers will be eliminated by the test and some unsuccessful performers will not. In the illustration it is this third option that has been exercised. With a cut-off score of 45 the majority of unsuccessful employees will be eliminated by the test along with a few successful ones.

Obviously, since no test is a perfect predicator, establshing a cut-off score is a grey area. When tests are used, therefore, they should be used as only one of several selection criteria and not as a sole basis for the selection decision.

TECHNICAL STANDARDS FOR VALIDITY STUDIES

The bulk of the *Uniform Guidelines* consists of the federal government's interpretation of standards for conducting validation studies. According to the *Guidelines*, there are certain minimum standards that should be met in performing a validity study. The standards established cover all three accepted procedures: criterion-related, content, and construct validity.[20]

Criterion-related Validity Studies

The following factors apply in conducting criterion-related validation studies.

Technical Feasibility. Employers electing to validate a test by criterion-related procedures should determine if it is technically feasible to do so. For a meaningful study to be conducted there should be: (1) an adequate sample of individuals available so that findings of statistical significance can be achieved, (2) availability of a sufficient range of test scores and job performance measures to produce results that are representative, and (3) availability of unbiased, reliable, and relevant measures of job performance or employee success.

Criterion Measures. Whatever criteria are used should represent important work outcomes or behaviors. Among the items that might be used are production rates, error rates, tardiness, absenteeism, and length of service. Other measures may be used where appropriate, including performance in a training program.

Representativeness of the Sample. Whether the validity study is a predictive or concurrent one, the sample of individuals used should be as representative as possible of the candidates normally available in the relevant labor market for the job or jobs in question. To the extent feasible, the sample should approximate the mix of races, sexes, and ethnic groups normally found in the relevant labor market.

Statistical Relationships. Professionally acceptable statistical procedures should be used to determine the degree of relationship between test scores and criterion measures. A statistically significant relationship is said to exist at the 0.05 level of significance; in other words, the relationship is sufficiently high enough to have occurred by chance only once in twenty times.

Operational Use of Selection Procedures. Generally, the greater the correlation between performance on a test and one or more job performance factors, and the greater the number and importance of job performance factors covered by the criteria, the more likely it is that the test will be appropriate for use in the selection process. While there are no minimum correlation coefficients applicable in all employment situations, low correlations that result in a large adverse impact will be subject to close review by EEOC. Likewise, reliance on a single test that is related to only one of many job factors will be subject to close scrutiny.

Overstatement of Validity Findings. Reliance upon a few selection procedures or criteria of acceptable job performance when many selection procedures or criteria have been studied may tend to inflate validity findings that result from chance error. To safeguard against this possibility, large samples should be used and cross validation studies should be conducted.

Fairness. When members of a protected class score lower on a test than members of another group, and the difference in scores is not reflected in job performance, use of the instrument is questionable, since protected class members are denied job opportunities. When a test results in adverse impact and the group affected is significantly represented in the relevant labor market, the employer should investigate the situation further if it is technically feasible to do so. If unfairness is demonstrated through showing that members of a particular group perform better or poorer on the job than their scores on the selection test would indicate through comparisons with members of other groups, the employer may either revise or replace the test or continue to use it with appropriate revisions in its use to ensure greater compatibility between the probability of successful job performance and the probability of being selected.

Content Validity Studies

The eight factors that should be applied in conducting content validity studies are described below.

Appropriateness. A test can be supported by a content validity procedure to the extent that the test if a representative sample of job content. The content validity approach is not appropriate for validating tests that measure traits or constructs such as personality, intelligence, aptitude, and the like. Nor is it a proper procedure when the test involves skills, abilities, or knowledge that the employee will be expected to acquire on the job.

Job Analysis. A job analysis should be conducted to idenfify important work behaviors and their relative importance to the job; if the behavior results in a work product, the analysis should include this product. Any behaviors selected for measurement should be critical behaviors that constitute the bulk of the job.

Development of Selection Procedures. A test designed to measure work behavior may be developed from job analysis or may have previously been developed by the employer, other users, or by a test publisher.

Standards for Demonstrating Content Validity. To establish the content validity of a test, the employer should show that the behaviors of the job in question or the test itself provides a representative sample of actual job behaviors or work products. When a test measures knowledge, skill, or ability, the item being measured should be operationally defined. Knowledge is that body of learned information that is used in and a necessary prerequisite for job performance. Skill or ability relates to observable aspects of work behavior or job performance. Any test that measures knowledge, skill, or ability should be a representative sample of what is used in the job and is a necessary prerequisite to performance of the work entailed in the job.

Reliability. Wherever possible, statistical estimates of the reliability of the job content test should be made.

Prior Training or Experience. Requirements for prior training or experience should be justified on the basis of the relationship between the content of the training and experience and the actual content of the job for which such training or experience is required.

Operational Use. A selection test that is supported on the basis of content validity may be used if it represents critical work behaviors that constitute most of the important parts of a job.

Ranking Based on Content Validity Studies. If an employer can show that a higher score on a content-valid test is likely to result in better job performance, the results of the test may be used to rank individuals who score above minimally acceptable levels. Where a test supported solely or primarily by content validity is used to rank job applicants, the test should measure those aspects of performance that differentiate among the various levels of job performance.

Construct Validity Studies

When a test is validated by construct validity procedures the following factors should apply.

Appropriateness. Construct validity is a more complex method than the other two forms of validation. Moreover, it is a relatively new and emerging procedure in the employment field. Efforts to obtain sufficient empirical support for such studies is an extensive and arduous task involving a series of research studies that may utilize both criterion-related and content validity studies. Particular care should be taken in utilizing this method because of the lack of research supporting its use in the selection process.

Job Analysis. Job analysis is essential when construct validity is used. The analysis should show the work behavior required for successful job performance, the critical or important work behaviors in the job, and an identification of the construct or constructs believed to underlie these critical or important work behaviors. Each construct should be named and clearly defined.

Relationship to the Job. A selection test should be identified or developed that measures the construct believed to be crucial to successful performance of the job. The relationship between the construct and job performance should be supported by empirical evidence.

Use of Construct Validity Study without New Criterion-related Evidence. Federal agencies will accept a claim of construct validity without a criterion-related study only when the selection test has been used elsewhere in a situation where a criterion-related study has been conducted and its use lends itself to the test and situation at hand. If construct validity is to be generalized to other jobs or groups of jobs not included in the original criterion-related study, additional empirical research evidence is expected.

As the preceding standards for test validation indicate, the *Uniform Guidelines* require rather stringent, methodical procedures for validating tests. While these requirements may seem burdensome, time-consuming, and expensive, they are necessary to ensure the fair, non-discriminatory usage of selection instruments.

TYPES OF PSYCHOLOGICAL TESTS

Psychological testing is basically concerned with identifying and measuring differences among individuals. Five differences that are important in the employment setting, because they relate to success or failure on the job, are cognitive abilities, psychomotor abilities, job knowledge, interests, and personality. Over the years, various tests have been developed to measure these differences.[21]

Cognitive Aptitude Tests

Cognitive aptitude or ability is a person's capacity to learn or to perform a job that has been previously learned. Tests that measure this characteristic are most often used in the selection of employees who have had little or no job experience. Aptitudes or abilities may be broken down into many factors, but the ones that are most often job related are verbal, numerical, perceptual speed, spatial, and reasoning.

Verbal Ability. Verbal aptitude refers to an individual's ability to use words in thinking and communication. Managerial, technical, and sales positions are jobs for which verbal ability is crucial. Conversely, it is relatively unimportant for manual or operative level production jobs. Measurement of a person's ability in this area is usually accomplished by a vocabulary test.

Numerical Ability. Numerical aptitude is the ability to perform basic arithmetic functions: adding, subtracting, multiplying, and dividing. These abilities are essential in engineering, accounting, and related jobs.

Perceptual Speed. This is the ability to identify rapidly, accurately, and in detail similarities and differences. Tests that measure this aptitude typically utilize pairs of numbers and names. The individual must make a quick comparison and indicate if a pair is identical or not. Perceptual speed is most likely to be used to ascertain clerical aptitude.

Spatial Ability. This ability is concerned with visualizing objects in space and determining their relationship to each other. Jobs that may require this aptitute include design engineer, tool and die maker, aviation mechanic, and assembler.

Reasoning Ability. Reasoning is the ability to analyze items or facts and make correct judgments based on the logical implications of the items or facts given. Reasoning ability may be measured relative to very concrete things or it may be measured relative to abstract concepts. Because of its relationship to decision making and conceptualization, this aptitude is critical for executive, managerial, or sales jobs.

General Intelligence. Intelligence refers to an individual's overall mental abilities. Tests used in this area attempt to arrive at some global estimate of a person's intellectual performance or aptitude. Normally, they provide a single score such as an IQ. Although general intelligence tests have been in existence for many years and have been widely used in selection, their use as employment devices is highly questionable today. In the first place, intelligence consists of a number of separate abilities that do not lend themselves to the development of a single composite score.[22] Second, EEOC regards intelligence tests with great disfavor since they tend to adversely impact blacks and other minorities. Third, intelligence tests often contain items that are unrelated to successful job performance. If an organization chooses to use an intelligence test, it should proceed with caution, making absolutely certain that the test has been validated in terms of job relatedness and performance.

Psychomotor Abilities

Psychomotor abilities refer to strength, dexterity, coordination, and other aspects of muscular performance. Tests that measure these abilities are very important for selecting the right kinds of employees for some jobs. In the electronics industry, for example, workers may assemble components so small that the operation has to be performed under a high-powered magnifying glass using very delicate instruments. Particular psychomotor abilities are crucial to performance of this type of work.

There are a number of abilities that may be measured in the psychomotor area. *Finger dexterity* is the ability to make precise, skillful, coordinated manipulations of small objects by using one's fingers. *Manual dexterity* refers to the ability to make skillful, coordinated, well-directed movements of the hands and arms. *Wrist-finger speed* is the ability to make rapid movements such as the ones involved in tapping. *Aiming* is the ability to move the hands and fingers rapidly, accurately, and successfully from one location to another. *Arm-hand steadiness* is the ability to make precise positioning movements where strength and speed are minimized. *Reaction time* is the speed with which an individual can respond to a stimulus when it appears.

Job Knowledge Tests

Job knowledge tests measure an applicant's level of understanding of the duties and responsibilities of the position for which he or she is applying. While there are commercially available tests, a test for any specific organizational job can be designed based on the data gathered from an in-depth job analysis. These tests may require written responses or they may be administered orally. Normally, these tests are short, consisting of a limited number of key questions that readily distinguish experienced applicants from less experienced ones. A primary advantage of the job knowledge test is that it is by definition job related.

Work Sample Tests

A work sample test is one in which the applicant completes a task or series of tasks that are representative of or actually a part of the job the person is applying for. Mentioned earlier in this chapter was the example of a typing test, probably the most commonly used of all work samples.

Evidence suggests that work sample tests can produce high predictive validities and reduce adverse impact.[23] Moreover, they tend to be more acceptable to applicants than other forms of testing. There are, however, some problems associated with work samples. One, it may not be feasible, if operation of a large piece of equipment is involved, to have the machine available in the human resource department so that the applicant can demonstrate his or her proficiency in operating it. Second, assuming that the person is taken to the shop floor to demonstrate ability to operate a machine, there is the potential risk of damage to the equipment or injury to the individual if the applicant, in fact, does not know how to perform on it. Third, work sample tests do not lend themselves readily to group administration. Rather, they have to be given individually and are thus more expensive than tests that can be given to a group.

Vocational Interest Tests

Interest tests are designed to measure the degree of interest a person has in various occupations. Theoretically, the higher the level of interest, the more likely the individual would be to succeed in that field of endeavor. Most of these tests determine occupational interest by comparing the test taker's scores with those of a representative sample of people already in particular jobs.

Interests should not be confused with aptitudes or abilities. It is very possible that a person may have a high interest in a given career field, yet lack the basic abilities to perform well in that field. Consequently, interest measures should always be used in conjunction with aptitude and ability tests.

Test dishonesty can be a major problem in using interest tests in selection because answers can be faked to display a high degree of affinity for whatever position may be under consideration. While it is possible that interest tests may have some application in employee selection, their primary use has been in career counseling and vocational guidance.

Personality Tests

Personality tests have limited use as selection devices. Such tests are often low in both reliability and validity. Inasmuch as some personality instruments require a subjective interpretation, when they are used the services of a trained psychologist are needed. There are questions, too, about the job relatedness of personality tests. Considerably more research on these instruments is needed before they can be used with confidence as selection criteria.

ESTABLISHING A TESTING PROGRAM

The first step in establishing a selection testing program is, of course, job analysis. Through analyzing, examining, and carefully studying the jobs in an organization, data can be developed that indicate the behaviors and abilities needed for successful performance on a specific job or a group of similar jobs. After this has been accomplished, the proper test or tests can either be developed by the organization or selected from those already commercially available.

There are advantages and disadvantages to developing organization-specific tests as well as to using tests that have already been developed. Perhaps the biggest advantage of using an available test is cost. Test development is expensive; thus, from a cost standpoint, an organization may find it more economically feasible to buy a test than to attempt to develop one. Also, if a firm has an immediate need to begin testing applicants, there may simply be insufficient time to develop a test because development is usually a lengthy process. On the other hand, it is possible that an existing test that has been demonstrated to be valid for one organization may not be valid for another. Several factors may account for this phenomenon: the jobs in one company may be subtly different from those in another firm; jobs that have the same title in two organizations may be entirely different; or applicants from different regions of the country may possess different characteristics and motivations.

While historically it has been held that test validity must be established on a situation-specific basis and that a test validated for one location may not be valid in another, a new concept is emerging. This development stems from the *Uniform Guidelines*, wherein methods necessary to generalize validity results from one set of jobs to other similar jobs are explained. Recent court decisions have further embraced the concept of validity transportability. For example, in *Pegues* v. *Mississippi State Employment Service* (31 FEP 257), the plaintiff questioned the use of aptitude tests that had not been validated for the particular set of tasks, location, and applicant population involved. The court found in favor of the organization and held that generalized validity evidence was acceptable.

Developing Selection Tests

In preparing a new selection test, a personnel specialist—normally a psychologist trained in tests and measurements—must develop appropriate items (questions) from job analysis data. Once the test has been prepared, its validity for a specific purpose must be determined. In validating the instrument, the designer conducts an item-by-item analysis to determine how well each item distinguishes between those individuals who scored high on the overall test and those who scored low. A test question that is perfectly valid is one that was answered correctly by all those scoring high on the total test and was incorrectly answered by all those scoring low. Only items that have a high validity correlation coefficient would be included in the final version of the test.

Another question that must be addressed by the test designer is the difficulty level of each question. If test questions are too easy, most individuals taking the test will score high; if the questions are too difficult, most test takers will score low. In either case, it would be difficult to distinguish between extreme and moderate ability levels on the basis of the test results. Thus, establishing the appropriate level of difficulty is a major challenge for the designer.

In continuing the validation study, the previously discussed procedures for ascertaining reliability and validity would be used.

Selecting an Existing Test

Thousands of tests are commercially available for use in selecting employees. In fact, about 300 publishers in the United States distribute printed tests of various kinds.[24] Needless to say, not all of the tests offered for sale have been properly developed or validated. Some are probably worthless at best.

In searching for appropriate selection tests one of the most important sources of information is the series of *Mental Measurements Yearbooks* edited by Oscar Buros. Each of the periodically published *Yearbooks* describes tests published during a specific span of time, thus supplementing each of the earlier volumes. Almost all of the commercially available psychological, educational, and vocational tests printed in English are included in this series.[25] Information on publisher, price, usage, and critical reviews by test specialists are included for each test.

Because all tests are not reliable or valid, caution must be exercised in choosing proper instruments. Staffing specialists play an important role in the human resource management function by assisting organizations in finding tests that provide a better basis for making selection decisions.

NOTES

1. "Ability Tests: They Can Provide Useful Information About the Probability of an Applicant's Performing Successfully on the Job," *Across the Board*, July/August 1982, p. 31.

2. "Employee Selection Tests: Upping the Odds for Success," *Personnel*, November-December 1980, p. 48.

3. "Ability Tests," p. 27.

4. John E. Hunter and Frank L. Schmidt, "Ability Tests: Economic Benefits versus the Issue of Fairness," *Industrial Relations*, Fall 1982, p. 293.

5. Frank L. Schmidt, John E. Hunter, Robert C. McKenzie, and Tressie W. Muldrown, "Impact of Valid Selection Procedures on Work-Force Productivity," *Journal of Applied Psychology*, vol. 64, 1979, p. 624.

6. Anne Anastasi, *Psychological Testing*, 5th ed. (New York: Macmillan Publishing Co., 1982), p. 24.

7. Ibid., pp. 32-36.

8. R. Wayne Mondy and Robert M. Noe III, *Personnel: The Management of Human Resources*, 3rd ed. (Boston: Allyn and Bacon, 1987), p. 214.

9. Duane P. Schultz, *Psychology and Industry Today*, 2nd ed. (New York: Macmillan Publishing Co., 1978), p. 122.

10. Charles F. Schanie and William L. Holley, "An Interpretive Review of Federal Uniform Guidelines on Employee Selection Procedures," *Personnel Administrator*, June 1980, p. 45.

11. Anastasi, *Psychological Testing*, p. 137.

12. Mondy and Noe, *Personnel*, p. 216.

13. Anastasi, *Psychological Testing*, p. 137.

14. Richard D. Arvey, *Fairness in Selecting Employees* (Reading, Mass.: Addison-Wesley Publishing Company, 1979), p. 31.

15. Ibid., p. 34.

16. Mondy and Noe, *Personnel*, p. 217.

17. Anastasi, *Psychological Testing*, p. 144.

18. Ibid.

19. Benjamin Schneider and Neal Schmitt, *Staffing Organizations*, 2nd ed. (Glenview, Ill.: Scott, Foresman and Company, 1986), p. 249.

20. *Uniform Guidelines on Employee Selection Procedures*, sections 1607.5–1607.14.

21. C. Harold Stone and Floyd L. Ruch, "Selection Interviewing and Testing," in Dale Yoder and Herbert G. Heneman, eds., *Staffing Policies and Strategies, ASPA Handbook of Personnel and Industrial Relations*, Vol. 1 (Washington, D.C.: Bureau of National Affairs, 1974), pp. 4-138–4-142.

22. Joseph Tiffin and Ernest J. McCormick, *Industrial Psychology*, 5th ed. (Englewood Cliffs, N.J., Prentice-Hall, 1965), p. 153.

23. I. T. Robertson and R. S. Kandola, "Work Sample Tests: Validity, Adverse Impact, and Applicant Reaction," *Journal of Occupational Psychology*, Vol. 55, 1982, p. 180.

24. B. von Haller Gilmer and Edward L. Deci, *Industrial and Organizational Psychology*, 4th ed. (New York: McGraw-Hill Book Company, 1977), p. 281.

25. Anastasi, *Psychological Testing*, p. 19.

10

Employment Interviewing

The most basic selection tool, used by virtually every organization for filling every job opening, is the employment interview. The interview is a significant step in the selection process because it is the point at which a decision will be made concerning an applicant's suitability for a particular position. Applicants who reach this state are obvious viable candidates; they have survived the screening interview, scored satisfactorily on selection tests, and fared well on reference or background checks. Consequently, candidates reaching the employment interview appear to be qualified, at least on paper. Every experienced manager knows, however, that appearances can be deceiving. It is by means of the interview that additional information is gathered to determine if the candidate can actually perform the work of the job, is willing to exert the effort necessary for successful performance, and can adapt to the environment of the job and the company.

THE EMPLOYMENT INTERVIEW DEFINED

The employment interview is a directed, goal-oriented discussion in which the interviewer and the applicant exchange relevant information so that both parties can make an intelligent decision about a job opening. The interviewer's purpose in this interactive process is to determine if the applicant is right for the position and the company. The applicant's purpose is essentially the same except that it is highly personal.

The employment interview has three general objectives. The first is to obtain additional, specific information from applicants so that their suitability for a particular position can be meaningfully evaluated. Resumés, employment applications, test results, and other similar devices provide, at best, only a sketchy profile of an applicant. The interview extracts more detailed information, clarifies certain points, and educes additional facts about the applicant.

191

The second general objective of the interview is to give the applicant information about the job, the company, coworkers, benefits, and other relevant matters. This information should be conveyed in a truthful manner wherein both positive and negative aspects are shared with the candidate.

The third objective of the interview is to create a positive feeling toward the prospective employer, regardless of the outcome of the interview. If the applicant leaves the interview with a negative impression of the organization, he or she is unlikely to consider the company for any future employment opportunities. Moreover, the individual may be adversely influenced as a consumer of the firm's products or services or may be totally unwilling to refer other applicants to the organization.

Clearly, the interview must be carefully planned and conducted if it is to fulfill its objectives effectively.

RESPONSIBILITY FOR THE EMPLOYMENT INTERVIEW

The employment interview is typically conducted by the supervisor or manager for whom the applicant will be working. Other managers may also participate depending upon the level of the position to be filled. For some types of clerical or entry level production jobs, it is not unusual for the human resource manager or a staffing specialist to handle the interview and actually make the hiring decision.

For professional and managerial positions, multiple interviews are generally the rule. These interviews would include the immediate supervisor, the next higher manager, and possibly other managers as well. Because professionals and managers frequently interface across departmental or organizational lines, the viewpoints of several managers may be desired to ensure a more objective decision about the candidate. While the opinions of all interviewers involved are important, the judgment of the manager for whom the applicant is to work will likely carry the greatest weight in making the final selection decision.

Although the immediate supervisor may have primary responsibility for the employment interview, the human resource department is typically responsible for developing and monitoring the interview process. A key concern in this area is that interviews be conducted in a consistent manner throughout the organization and that they adhere to the legal requirements imposed on interviewing.

LEGAL IMPLICATIONS OF INTERVIEWING

Following the 1971 Supreme Court decision in *Griggs* v. *Duke Power Company*, many employers abandoned the use of selection tests altogether and relied almost exclusively upon employment interviews as selection tools. This abrupt switch in personnel practices occurred primarily because of the false assumption that the Court decision requiring validation of tests applied only to paper-and-pencil tests and not to other selection devices.[1] But, as pointed out in Chapter 4, under the *Uniform Guidelines on Employee Selection Procedures*, a test encompasses "any measure, combination of measures, or procedure used as a basis for any employment decision." Hence, the interview is definitely a test and is subject to the same validation requirements as any other test or step in the selection process should adverse impact on a protected class be shown. For the interview, the matter of validation presents special difficulties. Few firms are willing to pay the cost or put forth the effort necessary for validating their interviews. Interviews can only be validated by a follow-up method that requires collecting data over a fairly long period of time. For any test to withstand legal challenge, it must also be reliable; that is, it must measure what it purports to measure. This is also a problem area for employment interviews inasmuch as significant evidence exists to indicate that if two managers in a firm interview the same applicant at different times, the outcomes will differ.[2]

The interview is perhaps more vulnerable to potential charges of discrimination than any other tool used in selection. In the majority of instances, there is little or no documentation of the questions asked or the answers received. There is, since most interviews take place in a private one-on-one setting, little or no organizational control over the type of questions the interviewer may pose to an applicant. Some interviewers may ask totally irrelevant questions; others may ask blatantly discriminatory ones. Some interviewers are inclined to ask questions that are not job related but that reflect their personal biases, believing that this practice will remain free of criticism or challenge since there is no documentation of what occurred in the interview.

The legal risks associated with employment interviewing are real; consequently, it is imperative that anyone conducting interviews knows what can and cannot be asked in an interview. Table 10-1 at the end of this chapter shows the types of questions that should be avoided in conducting a nondiscriminatory employment interview.

PLANNING FOR THE INTERVIEW

Planning is absolutely essential for conducting effective employment interviews. As a prerequisite to planning the interview, the interviewer must have a basic understanding of the job for which an applicant is applying, a knowledge of the company and the environment in which the candidate may be working, and an insight into human behavior.

Assuming the interviewer has the necessary background information, the first step in planning is to develop a set of specific objectives to be accomplished during the interview. These objectives involve the information that must be obtained from the applicant and the information that must be provided to the applicant. Because of the time constraints typically imposed on an interview, the interviewer must have a specific idea of what questions to ask and what information to furnish. By clarifying in his or her own mind the objectives of the interview, the interviewer is more likely to conduct an effective interview and make efficient use of the time available.

During the interview, the interviewer becomes the personification of his or her organization. The impression conveyed by the person conducting the interview may far outweigh any other factors such as physical facilities, impressive brochures, or annual reports of the company's operations. It is important that interviewers recognize their role as company representatives and prepare themselves to conduct the interview in a highly professional manner that will convey the proper impression to the candidate.[3]

Inasmuch as questions asked in the interview must be job related, each interview should be structured to some extent and tailored to the specific job to be filled. The interviewer must be familiar with the major duties of the job and the human qualifications necessary for successful job performance. To accomplish this, the interviewer should obtain a copy of the job description and the accompanying job specifications and familiarize himself or herself with both duties and qualifications. The interviewer should understand thoroughly such items as job content, education and experience requirements, and personal characteristics required.

Additionally, the interviewer must review the applicant's resumé (if one has been provided), employment application, test scores, reference checks, and so on in order to have a general indication of the individual's qualifications and background. This review frequently provides an indication of the candidate's potential interest in the position as well as areas to be probed in determining the person's potential for satisfactorily performing the job.

Another planning concern is the physical location in which the interview will take place. Ideally, the interview should be conducted in a place that ensures privacy, is relatively quiet, and is free from disruptions of any kind. (The primary disrupting factor in many interviews is the telephone; thus, the interviewer should make sure that he or she will not be required to answer any telephone calls during the interview.) While the physical environment need not be plush—an impossibility in many organizations—it should at least be comfortable enough to alleviate as much anxiety as possible on the part of the interviewee.

The importance of sound planning cannot be overemphasized. The interview must be a well-planned event, not just a casual happening.

INTERVIEW TYPES

Interviews may be classified by the degree to which they are structured.

At one end of the spectrum are those that are highly structured, with practically every question and the precise order in which it is to be asked specified in advance. At the other end of the spectrum is the completely non-structured interview where questions are posed as they occur to the interviewer. In actual practice, most interviews fall somewhere between these two extremes, but with tendencies toward one side or the other. Regardless of which approach is used, the interview must always gather three basic types of information from the applicant: ability to perform the job, motivation to stay on the job, and adaptability to the job situation and organizational environment.[4] Obviously, the structured interview is much more likely to secure this information than the non-structured interview.

Some interviewers may oppose the structured interview because they feel it restricts their freedom to ask questions or explore areas that might be of personal, although not job related, interest. The non-structured interview, on the other hand, poses a risk for the organization: where there is no structure the wrong questions may be asked, including those that expose the organization to discrimination charges. Consequently, a total lack of structure in the interview is not recommended. There is, however, a middle ground between structure and non-structure that allows the interviewer some freedom as to the types of questions that may be asked and the order in which they may be posed—the non-directive interview. In the following paragraphs this type of interview will be described as will the structured interview.

The Non-directive Interview

This type of interview is comprehensive in nature and may cover a broad range of topics. Probing, open-ended questions are one of its main features. The responsibility of the interviewer is to keep the applicant talking as much as possible. The assumption is that as the applicant responds to open-ended questions, he or she is likely to reveal information that might not otherwise be elicited. Typical questions used in this interview format include:

- Tell me something about yourself.
- Why do you want to leave your present job?
- What do you consider to be some of your most important accomplishments?
- What are your primary strengths?
- What are your primary weaknesses?
- What contribution do you feel you can make to this organization?
- Describe the best boss you ever worked for. What do you think made this person such a good boss?
- Describe the worst boss you ever had. What do you think made this person a bad boss?

- What do you consider to be your most significant contribution to your last employer?
- Where do you see yourself in five years from now?
- What are some other things I should know about you?

As these questions indicate, the intent of the non-directive is to get applicants to reveal as much about themselves as possible. Often, the answers to the questions are not as important to the interviewer as the way in which the questions are answered and the thought processes utilized in formulating responses.

Because of the nature of the questions used, the non-directive interview is generally much more time consuming than a more structured approach. Yet, some interviewers believe it is extremely effective in obtaining significant information. For this type of interview to be really effective, however, a highly trained and skilled interviewer is required.

The results of the non-directive interview may be difficult to summarize objectively. Different candidates respond in different ways to the questions asked. The appraisal of candidates may, therefore, be highly subjective in nature. The verbally facile candidate is likely to receive a higher evaluation that the candidate who has trouble expressing himself well, even though the latter may be more qualified for the job than the former.

Research conducted on traditional selection interviews, such as the non-directive, indicates that they have low reliability and little or no validity.

The Structured Interview

The structured interview consists of a series of job-related questions—with predetermined acceptable answers—that are consistently asked of each applicant for a particular job.[5] It is believed that this kind of interview increases reliability and accuracy by reducing the subjectivity and inconsistency present in more traditional interview approaches. The advantages of structure are diminished, however, if the interviewer asks each of the questions in a perfunctory manner. The structured interview, too, may easily result in an overly formal or cold atmosphere that severely impedes the candidate's ability or desire to respond.

A structured interview typically contains four types of questions: situational, job knowledge, job simulation, and worker requirements.[6]

Situational questions pose a hypothetical job situation to determine what the applicant would do in such a situation. For example, "If the main valve on the hydro-impulse regulator malfunctioned, what action would you take to correct the problem?" Theoretically, questions of this kind provide information on the applicant's ability to recognize and deal with problems that might actually occur on the job.

Job knowledge questions assess the applicant's grasp of requisite background knowledge for performing a job. These questions may be related to basic educational skills or complex scientific or managerial skills. For instance, "How do you determine the radius of a circle?"

Job simulation questions may require the applicant to actually perform a sample task from the job such as demonstrating how to operate a machine or typing samples of letters. When physical performance of activities is not feasible, some other kind of simulation of critical job aspects may be used.

Worker requirements questions seek to determine the applicant's willingness to conform to the requirements of the job. The applicant may be asked, for example, about his or her willingness to perform repetitive work, travel extensively, relocate, work weekends, and so forth. These questions, centering as they often do on the negative aspects of the job, are attempts to ascertain some idea of the applicant's motivational level and tolerance for adverse job aspects. They also serve as realistic previews of the job and afford the candidate the opportunity to evaluate whether he or she really wants the job.

A properly designed structured interview contains only those questions that are job related. Each question is asked for a specific purpose.

INTERVIEW METHODS

Several different methods may be used for conducting employment interviews. These range from the traditional one-on-one method to the controversial stress method. As explained below, each interview method has certain advantages and disadvantages. The choice of method is usually contingent upon the specific job to be filled, its level in the organization, and the preferences of those conducting the interviews.

One-on-One Interviews

By far the most widely used interview method is the one-on-one approach where applicant and interviewer meet in private. Since the interview itself is often a highly emotional experience for the job applicant, this interview method is probably the least threatening one that can be used. The disadvantage of this method, unless a series of interviews is incorporated in the selection procedure, is that evaluation of the candidate is the responsibility of a single interviewer.

Group Interviews

Unlike one-on-one interviews, a group interview consists of several applicants interacting in the presence of one or more company representatives.

This method may provide useful insights into the candidates' interpersonal competence as they engage in group discussion. An advantage of this approach is that it saves time for the interviewer since several applicants can be evaluated at once. Two major disadvantages are: (1) the interview is hard to control (the candidates may, in fact, take charge of the interview and prevent the interviewer from getting to really pertinent questions and issues) and (2) the situation may be highly threatening to the candidates since they know they are competing with each other for a job opening. The group interview is best used in conjunction with, and not to the exclusion of, other methods. Also, it is normally suited only for those jobs where a great deal of interpersonal actions are involved.

Panel Interviews

In a panel interview, one candidate is questioned by several interviewers sitting as a board. This approach allows for a thorough examination of the applicant in that several interviewers are more likely to cover all significant areas than is a single interviewer. On the other hand, the panel may be very intimidating or threatening to the interviewee. Also, this type of interview may be time consuming and costly since several company representatives are tied up at the same time. In actual practice, the panel method is usually reserved for higher level positions or for positions where the applicant would have to interact frequently on the job with the members of the panel.

Stress Interviews

While most interviews attempt to alleviate discomfort and threat for the applicant, the stress interview intentionally creates a relatively stressful—even hostile—environment for the candidate. The purpose is, of course, to see how the applicant reacts to and deals with the pressure of the situation.

Advocates of this method point to the fact that many jobs involve dealing with stressful situations and that it is better to discover how a person will react to an unfavorable environment before that person is placed in the job. For example, some companies subject applicants for sales positions to stress interviews that attempt to simulate actual job conditions. In the first interview the exchange of information may progress very smoothly. The candidate is led to believe that practically all he or she has to do is come back for the second interview and a job offer will be made. However, on the second interview the candidate might be kept waiting in an outer office for a considerable period of time before the interview begins—a tactic that may cause the individual's anxiety level to increase. Once the interview begins, the interviewer may open the conversation by very curtly stating, "Mr.

Hargett, I appreciate your time and interest, but I don't feel there is any need for further discussion. It's obvious that your qualifications just don't match our current needs." The purpose of this approach is to test the applicant's reaction to a totally unexpected situation. Some interviewers believe that candidates who are able to turn such a situation around are likely to become good sales representatives inasmuch as this is a common situation in sales work.

Does the stress interview actually achieve what it is supposed to achieve? Research suggests that it does not. The information exchanged in a stress situation is often distorted and misinterpreted—hardly the type of information upon which to base a selection decision.[7] Moreover, the stress interview is apt to create ill will on the part of job applicants, even those who may be hired. Bad feelings about the company and the way it treats applicants may impede recruiting efforts as candidates share this information with outsiders. Consequently, it seems clear that the stress interview is completely inappropriate for the vast majority of situations.

CONTENT OF THE INTERVIEW

Specific content of an employment interview varies greatly by organization and level of the job concerned. However, the following general topics are the ones most commonly covered: work experience, educational background, interpersonal skills, career orientation, and personal qualities. Because of the potentiality of discrimination the interviewer should deal only with information in these categories that is job related.

Work Experience

Exploring an individual's previous work experience provides an indication of the applicant's skills, abilities, and willingness to handle the duties and responsibilities of the position for which the person is applying. Although good performance in one job does not guarantee good performance in another job, it is an indication of the applicant's capabilities. Areas of work experience that should be explored in the interview encompass the following:

- The degree to which previous work experiences are similar to the requirements of the open position.
- Any qualifications or skills acquired in previous jobs that will be important to successful performance in the new job.
- Level of performance and significant accomplishments in previous positions.
- The situation and organizational context in which experience was gained and the relevance of this background to the organization and work climate of the prospective employer.

- Ability of the candidate to transfer, generalize, and capitalize on earlier work experiences as the individual has progressed through his or her career.[8]

Questions relative to previous work experience are the most important ones to be asked in an interview. In hiring a person an organization is, in reality, buying skills, abilities, talents, and knowledge; consequently, a complete, probing investigation of previous experience is essential to determine if the applicant possesses what the organization actually needs. Moreover, questions relating to work experience are the safest questions (that is, non-discriminatory) that can be asked.

Educational Background

Although an applicant's education record is usually shown on the employment application, a mere listing of schools attended or courses taken does not provide much assistance in making effective hiring decisions. It is the interviewer's responsibility to pursue a line of questioning that will uncover the relevance of the candidate's educational background to the position under consideration. Some useful questions to ask would include the following:

- Summarize your educational background for me.
- How has this background prepared you for the position for which you are applying?
- In college, what were your favorite courses? Why did you like these courses best?
- In college, what courses did you dislike? Why did you dislike these courses?
- What was your major course of study? Why did you choose that field?
- How would you compare your academic performance with other students at your school?
- Since graduating from college, what other education or training have you been involved in? How does this education or training relate to the job you are seeking?
- What are your future educational or training plans?

Note that the general thrust of the preceeding questions is toward obtaining the applicant's assessment of the relevance of education and training to the position under consideration. A secondary thrust is toward identifying the applicant's interests and motivation. Having a degree in business, engineering, or computer science does not mean that that is the area of the applicant's real interests. Nor does a degree in a particular field mean that the applicant has acquired the skills and knowledge necessary for successful job performance.

Interpersonal Skills

The major reason for job failure is not lack of technical competence, it is inability to work effectively with other people. Thus, the interviewer should attempt to determine how well the applicant can relate to and work with others. Questions aimed at making this determination include:

- How well do you feel you get along with other people?
- How well do you feel other people get along with you?
- What are some of the major factors that influence your ability to get along with others?
- What is your usual way of interacting with others?
- Describe the kinds of people you get along with best.
- Describe the kinds of people that irritate you the most.
- Do you feel that you work best in group or one-on-one situations? Why?
- What was your relationship with the people on your last job?

The interviewer may also want to pose questions concerning the applicant's interpersonal relations with family, friends, or in social or civic situations. This line of questioning should be pursued carefully, however, because it may lead into areas where charges of discrimination could arise.

Career Orientation

Questions about a candidate's career objectives may aid the interviewer in determining the degree to which an applicant's aspirations are realistic. Hiring an applicant with unrealistic expectations usually results in fairly rapid dissatisfaction with the organization and employee turnover. Some useful questions in this area are:

- Where do you see yourself in this company in the next two years? Five years?
- What do you consider to be your ultimate career objective?
- What kinds of things might you like to do in future jobs?
- What kinds of things might you like to avoid in future jobs?
- What are you doing now to prepare yourself for future positions?
- Assuming that your progress in this organization is not as rapid as you might desire, what would you be most likely to do?

In addition to determining the applicant's career goals, the interviewer should present an honest, accurate description of advancement and career prospects in the organization. Complete honesty is essential on this point. The candidate should not be led to believe that opportunities exist where they, in fact, do not. Deception is counterproductive in that when the truth unfolds the applicant is certain to become dissatisfied with the organization and likely to leave. If so, the firm has lost a substantial investment in the individual's recruitment, selection, and training.

Personal Qualities

Personal qualities that are normally observed during the interview encompass such factors as physical appearance, speaking ability, vocabulary, poise, attitude, motivation, and assertiveness. Some of these qualities may be job related, many may not be. Because all interviewers have personal biases and prejudices, care must be exercised to prevent the interviewer's biases from interfering with a factual assessment of the applicant. Unless a particular personal quality can be substantiated as a bona fide occupational qualification, it should not be a major influencing factor in the selection decision.

Questions, too, may be used to gather information about an applicant's personal qualities. These include the following:

- What sort of things seem to motivate you the best?
- What is your usual reaction when you encounter setbacks on a job?
- What do you consider to be three of your best personal qualities?
- What work-related professional groups do you belong to? What is the extent of your participation in these groups?

CONDUCTING THE INTERVIEW

A job interview is, for most individuals, a stressful situation. The interviewee is apt to be tense and anxious. Thus, the first requirement for the interviewer is to alleviate the tension and create an atmosphere conducive to discussion. A warm, natural, friendly, and sincere welcome for the candidate helps. Also helpful is the use of an "ice breaker," a brief discussion or question about something non-threatening to the candidate, for example, the weather, some event on television the previous night, or the candidate's flight from Chicago to visit the company. The ice breaker usually requires no more than a minute or so, but accomplishes three purposes: it relaxes the applicant, it eases the interviewer into the interview, and it creates an environment for a more pleasant exchange of information.[9]

Since much surface data on the candidate are already available on the employment application or resumé, the interviewer's task is to seek additional information, gather explanations of experience and background, and fill in gaps. A critical mistake that some interviewers make is to ask questions that have already been answered on the application or resumé. For example, "I see you attended Elon College" or "Your last job was with Henson and Bedges, wasn't it?" or "You have a degree in horticulture, don't you?" Spending time on such matters does not generate any new information helpful to the interviewer in making an assessment of the candidate and should be avoided. Moreover, it may be annoying to the interviewee.

During the interview, questions should initially be general in nature. Then, as the interview progresses, the questions should become more specific. Using the previously suggested interview content as a basis, it is appropriate for an interview to proceed along the following lines:

1. Discussion of work experience
2. Exploration of educational background
3. Examination of interpersonal skills
4. Discussion of career orientation
5. Examination of personal qualities
6. Description of the company and job
7. Answering of questions from applicant

While it is not absolutely essential that strict adherence to this sequence be observed, all of the topics should be covered in the interview. Observing the suggested progression will introduce structure into the interview and keep it from going off on tangents.

When the necessary information has been obtained and the applicant's questions have been answered, the interview should be brought to a conclusion. At this point, the applicant should be told when and how he or she will receive notification of the company's decision. An inconclusive response such as, "We will be contacting you at a later date," should definitely be avoided. It is far more preferable to say, "We are interviewing two other candidates for this position. We will call you next Tuesday to let you know of our decision." The organization should not keep the candidate hanging nor should it run the risk of hurting its reputation by being ambiguous about when an employment decision will be made.

After each interview, the interviewer should prepare a written assessment of the candidate. This assessment need not be elaborate but should reflect the interviewer's evaluation of the applicant's work experience, educational background, interpersonal skills, career orientation, personal qualities, and overall impression. Many organizations use an evaluation form similar to the one shown in Figure 10-1. Use of an appraisal form helps ensure that all

Figure 10.1
Applicant Evaluation Form

APPLICANT _____   INTERVIEWER _____

POSITION _____   DATE _____

FACTOR	COMMENTS		RATING
	FAVORABLE	UNFAVORABLE	
EXPERIENCE			1 2 3 4 5
EDUCATION			1 2 3 4 5
INTERPERSONAL SKILLS			1 2 3 4 5
CAREER ORIENTATION			1 2 3 4 5
PERSONAL QUALITIES			1 2 3 4 5
OVERALL EVALUATION			1 2 3 4 5

interviewers are evaluating on the basis of the same criteria. Furthermore, it documents the reasons for making employment decisions—a practice that is important should claims of discrimination arise.

POTENTIAL PROBLEMS IN INTERVIEWING

As one of the most imperfect processes in human resource management, employment interviewing contains a number of potential problems or pitfalls, especially for the untrained interviewer. It is critically important, therefore, for any interviewer to be fully aware of these potential problems so that they can be satisfactorily dealt with.

Lack of Goals

It is an axiom in management that clearly stated goals are essential if meaningful activity is to take place. The requirement for goals or objectives is no less essential for the interviewing process. Goals for the selection interview are tied to both the job to be filled and the qualifications of the applicants being considered. It is unfortunate, but often true, that individuals are selected on the basis of whim, with less consideration for specifications (skills, abilities, and knowledge) than is typically given for the acquisition of a typewriter or other type of non-human asset.

In order to conduct an interview effectively, the interviewer must have a good understanding of the duties and responsibilities of the job to be filled and the human qualifications necessary for satisfactory job performance. The goal of the interview is, quite simply, to find the best qualified person to perform the job. But unless the interviewer understands the job and the qualifications needed, it is unlikely that an effective match between job and individual will be made. The information needed to establish clear-cut goals for the interview can be obtained from the job description and the job specifications for the position to be filled.

Premature Judgments

One of the easiest traps to fall into when interviewing is to make a premature judgment of the applicant in the first minute or less of the interview.[10] Physical appearance, speaking voice, height, weight, and similar factors may lead the interviewer to immediately form an opinion about the applicant and spend the remainder of the interview attempting to validate this first impression. The interviewer must remember that first impressions are likely to be wrong. Thus, a more appropriate approach is to deliberately suppress one's first impression, objectively collect the needed information, analyze this information, and then make a final evaluation.

Interviewer Domination

When interviewers dominate the conservation, the collection of job-related information about the candidate is severely hindered. In an effective employment interview, the applicant should be permitted to talk about 75 percent of the time. This probably does not happen in the great majority of interviews. Since the objective of the employment interview is to acquire sufficient information for making an informed selection decision, if the interviewer dominates the conversation this objective cannot be met. The interviewer's primary responsibilities are to pose questions and gather information from the applicant, not to do all of the talking.

Inconsequential or Trivial Questions

Without a somewhat structured approach or specific goals for an interview, the interviewer is likely to succumb to asking questions that have little or no bearing on the position to be filled. These questions may be asked because the interviewer does not know what to ask or they may be asked simply to kill time. Inconsequential or trivial questions can be risky because they frequently lead into discussions of areas where the potential for discrimination exists. For example, "Tell me about your family," is inconsequential because it is not job related; it is potentially discriminatory because it may lead to a discussion of national origin, religious preference, or a subset of sex such as number of children or marital status.

Halo/Horns Error

This is a type of bias that is manifested when an interviewer is overly impressed (halo effect) or overly repulsed (horns effect) by one or more personal characteristics of the applicant and allows this bias to unduly affect his or her opinion of the candidate. An interviewer who places high value on neatness and conservatism in dress, for example, may automatically favor candidates who rate high in this area and just as automatically underrate those who do not meet his or her standards of dress—regardless of skills, abilities, or other job-related factors. As with other forms of bias, the interviewer must recognize its existence and make a conscious effort to withhold judgment on the applicant until hard data has been collected.

Contrast Effects

A contrast effect is an error in judgment that occurs when an interviewer meets with one or more poor or marginally qualified candidates and then interviews a candidate who, without benefit of comparison with the previous applicants, would be considered only fair in skills and abilities. By comparison, the last applicant may appear to the interviewer as a "superstar" because previous applicants have been so poorly qualified. Realistic, objective, written evaluations of candidates are crucial to combating this kind of error.

Stereotyping

Stereotyping is another form of interviewer bias. It usually occurs when the interviewer has a preconceived notion of the ideal candidate. Some interviewers may believe, for example, that women or blacks are not qualified to handle executive or professional positions because such individuals do not fit the interviewer's preconceived idea of the ideal candidate—a white male. Some interviewers still think of women or minorities as being more suited for secretarial, clerical, or menial jobs. While actions taken on stereotyped views are illogical and clearly illegal, they do occur, and as a result interfere with the selection of qualified candidates.

Lack of Interviewer Training

Lack of training is both an interviewing problem and a cause of interviewing problems. Many organizations do not provide any training in interviewing for their managers. Without training, there is a tendency for interviewers to emulate the approaches used by others who have interviewed them—a practice that might be acceptable if there were more well-trained interviewers around to serve as role models. Because of the lack of training, goals are not set for the interview, the wrong questions are asked, the right information is not secured, discriminatory areas are explored, biases are not controlled, and poor selections are made.

Behavior Sample

At best, an employment interview is a very small sample of an applicant's behavior. Moreover, the candidate's behavior during the interview is seldom typical or natural due to the stress or anxiety of the situation. Unfortunately, this problem will always exist in interviews. It is incumbent upon the interviewer to recognize that he or she is dealing with behavior samples. Emphasis should be placed on gathering factual information; even then the sample may be too small to make a totally accurate evaluation.

Interpretation of Behavior

An extension of the previous problem is that of assessing the behavior that is observed in the interview. If the applicant fidgets constantly or continually shifts his position in the chair during the interview, how should this behavior be interpreted? As a sign of anxiety? As simply tension? Or as an indication that the applicant is afraid that something will slip out that he doesn't want known? If the applicant slouches in a chair and casually answers questions without much elaboration, should this be viewed as a sign of disinterest? No one, including the experts in interviewing, has satisfactorily solved this problem of interpretation. Because the interview is an unnatural situation for the applicant, it is probably best for the interviewer to withhold judgment on these kinds of behavior and concentrate on evaluating the candidate's qualifications.

Inappropriate Questions

A basic requirement in employee selection is that all information requested be job related. This is as true for the interview as it is for any other selection device or procedure. Employers must be extremely cautious in asking questions that are risky from a legal point of view. Unfortunately, illegal questions are still being asked in interviews today. Table 10-1 shows the kinds of questions that should be avoided.[11] Careful examination of the table will show that each of these questions is not job related.

Table 10.1
Selected Questions to Avoid in Interviewing

Question	Discriminatory Potential
Have you ever been arrested?	Race
Did you receive an honorable discharge from the armed services?	Race
Have your wages ever been garnished?	Race; national origin
What is your credit rating?	Race; national origin
Do you own a car?	Race; national origin
Do you have a telephone?	Race; national origin
Do you have a high school diploma?	Race; national origin
Do you have a current driver's license?	Race; national origin
Do you own your own home?	Race; national origin
Have you ever been refused a surety bond?	Race; national origin
To what social organizations, clubs, or societies do you belong?	Race; national origin; religion
Do you have relatives from a foreign country?	National origin
How did you learn to speak Spanish, Polish, etc.?	National origin
Where were you born?	National origin
What is your native language?	National origin
What is the nationality of your parents?	National origin
Do you attend religious services on Saturday or Sunday?	Religion
Do you attend church regularly?	Religion
Are you married?	Sex
How many children do you have?	Sex
What are the ages of your children?	Sex
Do you plan to have any more children?	Sex
How reliable are your arrangements for child care?	Sex
Are you pregnant?	Sex
Do you prefer to be addressed as Ms. or Mrs.?	Sex
Where does your spouse work?	Sex
What is your maiden name?	Sex
How does your husband feel about your being away from home?	Sex
How old are you?	Age
What is your date of birth?	Age
When did you graduate from high school? From college?	Age
Are you handicapped in any way?	Handicap
Do you have any physical defects?	Handicap
What is the general status of your health?	Handicap

THE IMPORTANCE OF LISTENING

A large part of the interviewer's job is to listen effectively. To accomplish this the interviewer must learn to listen empathetically, to attempt to put himself or herself in the applicant's place so that what is being said can be more readily understood. Empathetic listening requires that the listener put aside his own biases and frames of reference. While all transmission from the applicant must ultimately be evaluated, the evaluation should not be made prematurely but should be delayed until the entire message has been received and a sincere effort has been made to fully comprehend what the applicant has said. Some helpful guidelines for the interviewer to follow are:

- *Listen with patience.* Allow the applicant ample time to present his or her thoughts without interruption. Do not feel that it is necessary to maintain a continuous flow of conversation. Silence frequently encourages the applicant to keep talking.
- *Listen with objectivity.* Recognize biases and not allow those biases to interfere with what the applicant is saying. Concentrate on the communication and not the communicator.
- *Listen with the proper attitude.* Don't overreact to what is said. Pay close attention to what the applicant is saying.
- *Listen actively.* Ask questions that help the applicant clarify what he or she is trying to say. Restate what has been said to make sure that it has been completely understood.

Effective listening is crucial to interviewing. It is also hard work. But it is a task at which every interviewer must become proficient.

MAKING THE HIRING DECISION

Once the candidates for a position have all been interviewed, a decision must be made as to which candidate is the best for the job and the organization. At best, any hiring decision is a trade-off because there is no such thing as an ideal candidate. Experience, education, and the other selection factors must be weighed carefully. Certainly, any applicant hired must possess the skills and knowledge to perform the job—"can do" ability. The applicant, at the same time, must possess sufficient motivation to want to perform the job—"will do" ability. Additionally, the person hired should be one that will reasonably fit into the work unit and the organization. Assessing all of these factors is difficult, but the task is somewhat easier if the interviewers have completed applicant evaluation forms for each person interviewed. The one cardinal rule in making a hiring decision is this: if there is *any* doubt about the candidate's ability to perform or if there is *any* doubt about the candidate's motivation to perform, do not hire that person.[12] Doubts about a candidate too often become self-fulfilling prophesies.

THE NEED FOR INTERVIEWER TRAINING

Because of the importance of interviewing in the selection process as well as the potential legal ramifications involved, it is imperative that organizations provide sufficient training in interviewing for those managers who must perform this vital task. For small organizations, training can be provided through various public seminars that are available. Large organizations may wish to consider offering their own in-house programs due to the numbers of people who need to be trained. The following list shows the kinds of topics that are typically included in an employment interviewing training program:

- Overview of the Interviewing Process
- Definition and Purpose of the Employment Interview
- Preparing for the Interview: Establishing Objectives
- Establishing and Maintaining Rapport
- Structuring and Controlling the Interview
- Methods for Obtaining Information: Questioning Techniques
- Methods for Obtaining Information: Listening Techniques
- Note Taking
- Closing the Interview
- Interpretation of Interview Data
- Problems to Avoid in Interviewing
- Practice Exercises in Interviewing
- Legal Issues in Interviewing

NOTES

1. James G. Goodale, *The Fine Art of Interviewing*, (Englewood Cliffs, New Jersey: Prentice-Hall, 1982), p. 41.

2. James G. Goodale, "The Neglected Art of Interviewing," *Supervisory Management*, July 1981, p. 27.

3. Ibid., p. 51.

4. Barbara Felton and Sue Ries Lamb, "A Model for Systematic Selection Interviewing," *Personnel*, January-February 1982, p. 43.

5. Elliott D. Pursell, Michael A. Campion, and Sarah R. Gaylord, "Structured Interviewing: Avoiding Selection Problems," *Personnel Journal*, November 1980, p. 908.

6. Ibid., p. 909.

7. Susan Gribbem, "A Guide to the Hiring Process," *CA Magazine*, September 1982, p. 85.

8. Charles G. Tharp, "A Manager's Guide to Selection Interviewing," *Personnel Journal*, August 1983, pp. 636–637.

9. Henry H. Morgan and John W. Cogger, *The Interviewer's Manual*, 2nd ed. (New York: Drake-Beam & Associates, 1980), p. 28.

10. Dr. Joyce Brothers, "How to Get the Job You Want," *Parade Magazine*, November 16, 1986, p. 4.

11. Adapted from Don Caruth, Frank Rachel, and Bill Middlebrook, *Management Dynamics II*, (Carrollton, Tex.: Spinnaker Publications, 1983), pp. 44–47.

12. Ibid., p. 41.

11

Performance Appraisal

Individuals working in an organization perform at varying levels of proficiency. Some use their skills, energy, and time effectively and efficiently. Others do not. Some display an abundance of initiative and seek opportunities for additional responsibilities. Others do not. Decision making in many areas of human resource management depends upon management's ability not only to recognize such differences in individual performance but also to measure them accurately. This is the task of performance appraisal.

Performance appraisal is by no means a simple task, yet it is a crucial one. Decisions made in this area affect other parts of the human resource management system as well as the organization itself. Compensation, promotion, career development, job design, selection criteria, and training are some of the areas directly influenced by the appraisal process. Consequently, a sound, effective approach to determining how well employees are performing their jobs is essential to organizations of all types and sizes.

PERFORMANCE APPRAISAL DEFINED

Performance appraisal may be defined as "an on-going, systematic evaluation of how well an individual is carrying out the duties and responsibilities of his or her current job. Additionally, it typically includes an assessment of the individual's need or potential for further development."[1]

Four key terms in this definition merit further consideration because they indicate the nature of an effective approach to assessing employee performance. These terms are: (1) ongoing, (2) systematic, (3) evaluation, and (4) development.

Performance appraisal is an *ongoing* activity, not something that is done once a year when a supervisor or manager completes an employee evaluation form.[2] Monitoring and assessing the efforts expended and results

213

produced by employees must be done, if it is to be accomplished effectively, on daily, weekly, and monthly bases. The culmination of this continuous process is the completion of a written report or form. The completion of the formal document, however, is not performance appraisal. Rather, it is a recapitulation of the many individual evaluations of how an employee has carried out the duties and responsibilities of his or her job over the entire period covered by the report. In fact, if it were not for the continuous evaluations made of performance, the formal report could not be completed accurately.

Performance appraisal is, or should be, *systematic* in nature. It should be a logical, objective assessment of how well an employee has performed a job. Effective performance appraisal depends upon well-defined standards of accomplishment that are measured in accordance with a systematic approach that eliminates—or severely reduces—subjectivity. Job standards are the yardsticks by which job accomplishments are measured; a consistent methodology for comparing accomplishments with standards establishes the system necessary for accurate, effective performance appraisal.

Performance appraisal is an *evaluation*. To evaluate means to determine the amount of; in this case, the amount of work actually accomplished. Measurements are critical to evaluation. Standards of performance, as mentioned above, establish the expectations. Measurements are the means by which job results are ascertained. Without measurements and standards, there can be no evaluation. There can only be guesses, subjective opinions, and estimations.

Finally, performance appraisal, if it is to be fully effective as an internal staffing tool, must include a *development* aspect. The focus of development is twofold: identifying current needs for employee growth and improvement on the present job and identifying employee potential for promotion to positions of higher responsibility. The developmental aspect of performance appraisal looks at what the employee has done and seeks to determine what he or she needs to be able to perform the job better, while at the same time it seeks to determine how the employee could be better utilized to his or her own personal advantage as well as the organization's benefit.

Performance appraisal, in essence, has a bi-directional focus. It objectively evaluates what has been accomplished in the job by the employee and then looks to the future by describing individual developmental needs.

USES OF PERFORMANCE APPRAISAL

Unfortunately, most managers—and employees, too—have a very restricted view of performance appraisal, visualizing it as merely the means whereby increases in compensation are awarded. But performance appraisal, used to its fullest extent, is much more than a wage and salary administration device. It can be used as a mechanism for:

* Providing feedback to employees on how well they are accomplishing job duties and responsibilities.
* Identifying individuals whose present performance and future potential warrant promotion to positions of greater responsibility.
* Identifying individuals whose inability to perform on the present job indicates the need for demotion to a position of lesser responsibility, lateral transfer, or termination.
* Identifying the need for training of individual employees or work units.
* Verifying the effectiveness of the selection process. (If new hires consistently perform below expectations, inappropriate selection criteria are possibly being used.)
* Determining the need for disciplinary action because of low output, poor quality of work, or frequent infractions of company rules, procedures, or policies.
* Determining the extent of employee progress in performing job duties.
* Identifying employees who have potential that may be significantly increased through additional training or other developmental activities.
* Increasing communication between the supervisor and the employee relative to job performance.
* Providing a basis for determining which employees should be granted pay increases and which should not.[3]

Relating these uses of performance appraisal to the staffing process, it is apparent that performance appraisal yields data valuable for decision making in such staffing activities as human resources planning, recruiting, selecting, career planning and development, and human resource administration.

Human Resource Planning

To assess accurately an organization internal supply of human resources for planning purposes, data must be available that describe the promotability and potential of all employees, especially high level professionals and managers. An effective performance appraisal system is one means by which these data are derived. In short, a well-designed appraisal system provides a profile of an organization in terms of the strengths, weaknesses, and potentialities of its current work force and establishes a basis for filling future personnel needs.[4]

Recruiting

Performance evaluations can provide information that may be used to improve an organization's recruiting efforts. For example, an analysis of high performing employees or managers may reveal that they received their training at particular schools, majored in certain disciplines, or were recruited from the same sources. Such information could certainly influence a firm's approach to recruiting, allowing it to concentrate more of its efforts on sources and approaches that have been the most productive.

Selecting

Performance appraisal is crucial to validating the use of certain selection standards. Validation requires the identification of successful and non-successful performers and a correlation between success on the job and the selection standard or test used. An accurate performance appraisal system is essential not only for identifying successful and non-successful performance but also for establishing a reliable database to make the required correlations. If the performance appraisal system is not accurate, attempts to validate selection devices will not produce usable results.

Career Planning and Development

Whether viewed from an individual or an organizational perspective, effective career planning and development is heavily dependent upon performance appraisal information. Managers need information relative to the strengths, weaknesses, and potentialities of their subordinates in order to counsel and assist them in developing and implementing their career plans. Likewise, employees need the information provided by performance appraisal to make personal decisions about their career aspirations.

Human Resource Administration

Performance appraisal data are used as the basis for making a number of administrative decisions in an organization. Decisions concerning promotions, transfers, demotions, terminations, and layoffs are frequently based on performance appraisals.

Promotions. While an individual's performance in one position is not necessarily an accurate predictor of success in a position of greater responsibility, it is a useful indicator that is widely used. Through performance appraisal an employee's ability to handle particular types of tasks well is identified, as are other kinds of skills. This "track record" gives an organization a reasonable basis for making promotion decisions.

Transfers. As with promotion decisions, an employee's performance record in one job may be useful in determining his or her ability to perform in another job of equal importance. While this may not be a prime factor when transfers are used solely for the purpose of employee development, it is important when making lateral moves to fill job vacancies.

Demotions. Unfortunately, an employee is sometimes placed in a position that requires greater skill than the employee possesses, a fact that is revealed through performance appraisal. Demotion to a job more commensurate with the employee's level of skills and abilities may be in order when this happens. It is important to remember that inability to perform one particular job well does not mean that an employee is incapable of performing other jobs successfully. Demotion can be a viable means of salvaging the organization's investment in a person.

Terminations. Performance appraisal data are frequently used to make termination decisions. When an employee cannot perform and there are no lower level jobs to which he or she can be demoted, when work is of a totally inferior quality, when there are serious or repeated violations of company rules, termination may be called for. Because of the increasingly complex legalities involved in discharging employees, an accurate performance appraisal system is rapidly becoming necessary as a factual basis to support a termination action.

Layoffs. When it becomes necessary for an organization to reduce the size of its work force because of economic factors, performance appraisals provide a rational basis for determining which employees will be laid off and which will not. Obviously, the marginal performers are the ones who should be laid off and the more productive workers are the ones who should be retained.

When employees are working under a labor agreement, however, layoffs are determined on the basis of seniority, not performance, and management is deprived of its flexibility in deciding which people to lay off.

PERFORMANCE APPRAISAL METHODS

Over the years several different methods of formally appraising performance have been developed. The seven most commonly used approaches found in organizations today are: (1) rating scales, (2) ranking, (3) checklists, (4) behaviorally anchored rating scales, (5) work standards, (6) essays, and (7) management by objectives.

Rating Scales

The single most widely used method of appraising the performance of non-exempt employees is some form of rating scale. Perhaps as many as 50 percent of all organizations with performance evaluation systems use this approach.[5] One reason for the popularity of this method is its simplicity; another is the quickness with which it can be used to evaluate employees.

With rating scales, employees are evaluated according to a set of predetermined factors such as quantity of work, quality of work, and absenteeism. Each evaluation factor is divided into a number of degrees—five is a very common number although some scales use as many as fifteen—ranging from the lowest level of performance to the highest. In some instances, definitions of the evaluation factors are printed on the evaluation form itself; in other instances, only the factor title is shown.

To complete a performance appraisal using a rating scale, the evaluator simply checks the degree of each factor that is most descriptive of the employee's performance during the period covered by the appraisal. Figure 11-1 shows a fairly typical rating scale. Often, numerical values are assigned to each degree of each factor so that the evaluator can quickly compute a numerical average performance rating for the person being evaluated.

Many rating scale forms also include a comments section below each factor so that the appraiser can provide written justification for the factor degree assigned. Other rating scale forms provide a comments section at the end of the form, allowing the evaluator to make general comments supporting the overall appraisal.

Advantages. There are several advantages to rating scales as a method of performance appraisal: (1) they are easy to use, (2) they do not take much time to complete, (3) a set of standardized factors can be developed to cover all jobs in an organization, and (4) when numerical values are assigned to factor degrees, an average performance rating can be calculated quickly.[6]

Disadvantages. Although rating scales are probably the oldest approach to performance appraisal in existence, they do have significant disadvantages: (1) factors and degrees are often vaguely defined, if they are defined at all; (2) lack of factor and degree definitions may produce highly subjective evaluations by supervisors; (3) there is usually no factual basis for the evaluation; (4) factors used frequently contain items that are, at best, tangentially related to the job; (5) central tendency errors are likely to occur because it may be difficult for the appraiser to factually justify a rating above or below acceptable performance; and (6) the courts have usually taken a jaundiced view of rating scales because the factors used often include personality traits.[7]

Ranking

The simplest approach to performance appraisal is the ranking method. In its most elementary form, ranking entails placing all employees into a specific order based on their overall performance, from the highest or best performer all the way down to the lowest or worst performer. In a group of seven employees, for example, the best performer would be designated as a one, the next best performer a two, and so on. To determine the rankings,

Figure 11.1
Typical Rating Scale

PERFORMANCE FACTORS	Below Minimum (unacceptable)	Below Expectations (marginal)	Meets Expectations (normal)	Exceeds Expectations	Clearly Outstanding
JUDGMENT	☐	☐	☐	☐	☐
INITIATIVE	☐	☐	☐	☐	☐
CREATIVENESS	☐	☐	☐	☐	☐
PROBLEM SOLVING	☐	☐	☐	☐	☐
THOROUGHNESS & ACCURACY	☐	☐	☐	☐	☐
QUANTITY	☐	☐	☐	☐	☐
COMMUNICATION	☐	☐	☐	☐	☐
JOB KNOWLEDGE/SKILL IMPROVEMENT	☐	☐	☐	☐	☐
WORKING WITH OTHERS	☐	☐	☐	☐	☐
LEADERSHIP ABILITY	☐	☐	☐	☐	☐
ADVANCEMENT POTENTIAL	☐	☐	☐	☐	☐
ADAPTABILITY	☐	☐	☐	☐	☐
ABSENTEEISM/PUNCTUALITY	☐	☐	☐	☐	☐
ATTITUDE	☐	☐	☐	☐	☐

evaluators frequently use an alternation ranking procedure: the evaluator first selects the best performer and then identifies the worst performer; next, the second best performer is selected and the second worst performer is identified. This alternation is continued until all employees have been put into rank order.

As typically used, ranking involves no specific criteria or performance guidelines; it relies entirely upon the appraiser's judgment for determining the order of employee performance.

Advantages. Ranking, it is claimed, has several advantages as a performance appraisal method: (1) it is inexpensive to install, (2) it is easy to use, (3) it eliminates the problem of central tendency error because it forces the appraiser to place employees into a ranking based on overall performance, (4) it does not require extensive training of evaluators, and (5) since employees and supervisors naturally tend to rank individuals in some order of performance anyway, it legitimatizes an already existing informal procedure.[8]

Disadvantages. Unfortunately, no simple approach to dealing with a complex process is without limitations or shortcomings. The disadvantages to ranking are: (1) there are usually no objective criteria for determining an employee's position in the rank order, (2) it may be difficult to explain to an employee his or her ranking since most employees consider themselves to be above average in performance, (3) ranking may produce morale problems among employees who are not rated at or near the top of the list, (4) performance comparisons across departmental lines are impossible since a lower ranking employee in one unit may actually be superior in performance to a higher ranked employee in another work group, (5) ranking forces a distribution of performance that may not fit a work group in that it is possible that all employees may be superior or all may be inferior, and (6) ranking provides the evaluator with no information that may be useful in counseling employees about their performance.[9]

Checklists

Performance appraisal checklists provide the evaluator with a series of statements, phrases, or adjectives that describe employee performance. These statements may be subdivided into specific factors such as quantity of work, quality of work, and so forth, with the descriptors listed under each category. Occasionally, the phrases or adjectives are simply listed without categorization. Using the checklist method, the appraiser checks off the statement or adjective considered to be most descriptive of the employee's performance during the period covered by the appraisal. Figure 11-2 shows a typical checklist.

Figure 11.2
Typical Checklist

QUALITY OF WORK (Disregard Quantity)

____Extremely neat and accurate.
____Good accurate worker. Makes few mistakes.
____Adequate but some improvement would be desirable.
____Barely up to minimum standards. Often inaccurate.
____Below minimum standards. Complete checking required.

QUANTITY OF WORK (Disregard Quality)

____Outstanding volume.
____Well above average volume.
____Adequate volume.
____Barely up to minimum standards.
____Below minimum standards. Needs much improvement.

JOB KNOWLEDGE (Technical)

____Expert. Has superior knowledge.
____Well rounded knowledge. Seldom needs assistance.
____Possesses acceptable knowledge.
____Knowledge is adequate to perform minimum job requirements.
____Very limited knowledge. Needs frequent assistance.

RESPONSIBILITY (Ability to Plan and Direct Work)

____Plans and carries out own work in superior manner.
       Self Sustaining..
____Plans and carried out work well. Requires little supervision.
____Requires occasional work direction.
____Carries out only the most obvious tasks without follow-up.
____Always waits to be directed.

There are two variations to the straight checklist method. One variation is the forced choice technique. In this approach, the appraiser reviews a series of statements about an employee's performance and indicates which statement is most descriptive or least descriptive of that individual's performance. Figure 11-3 is an example of a forced choice checklist. After the checklist is completed, the items are reviewed to determine a composite view of performance.

A second variation of the checklist is the weighted checklist performance evaluation form. It is very similar to the forced choice method except that weights have been assigned to each of the various responses. Normally the weights, developed by the human resource group, are not known to the evaluator. This approach, it is believed, tends to reduce bias on the part of the person conducting the appraisal.

Advantages. Proponents of checklists claim that this method offers the following advantages: (1) the evaluation is not as vague as in the rating scale approach because actual job behaviors are described in the checklists, (2) evaluator objectivity is greater than with rating scales or ranking because

Figure 11.3
Forced Choice Checklist

MOST DESCRIPTIVE	LEAST DESCRIPTIVE	
☐	☐	SELDOM MAKES MISTAKES
☐	☐	FAILS TO FOLLOW THROUGH ASSIGNMENTS COMPLETELY
☐	☐	ALWAYS MEETS DEADLINES
☐	☐	CONSTANTLY SEEKS HELP ON ROUTINE ASSIGNMENTS
☐	☐	DOES NOT PLAN AHEAD
☐	☐	GRASPS INSTRUCTIONS QUICKLY
☐	☐	SELDOM WASTE TIME
☐	☐	COMMUNICATES WELL
☐	☐	LEADER IN GROUP ACTIVITIES
☐	☐	SPENDS TOO MUCH TIME ON TRIVIAL MATTERS
☐	☐	PATIENT WITH OTHERS
☐	☐	INDUSTRIOUS WORKER

appraisers have to evaluate specific job performance behaviors, (3) the evaluator tends to act more as a recorder of observed behaviors than as a judge, and (4) checklists are typically developed for groups of similar jobs so that evaluation factors are more job specific than the general ones used in rating scales.[10]

Disadvantages. The shortcomings of checklists include: (1) the time and expense of developing statements for various job groups that are actually reflective of job performance; (2) appraisers often have difficulty in interpreting the statements because some items appear to be virtually identical; (3) where the weighted checklist is used, the appraiser has no knowledge of the assigned weights and may give an employee a different evaluation than intended; (4) factual data to support the assigned evaluation is usually lacking; (5) lacking knowledge of which items are the most heavily weighted, the appraiser may be at a disadvantage in counseling the employee relative to his or her job performance; and (6) there is little evidence to indicate that checklists are an improvement over other appraisal methods.[11]

Behaviorally Anchored Rating Scales

Behaviorally anchored rating scales (BARS) are basically a more detailed and refined version of the traditional rating scale. The development of BARS begins with a detailed analysis of a job and a precise identification of specific job behaviors, both effective and ineffective ones. Once each performance factor has been identified, descriptive statements for each level of performance for each job factor is then arranged on a scale in rank order. Typically, the scale provides for seven descriptive statements for each performance factor, although sometimes points along the scale will not have a behaviorally descriptive statement attached to them. Figure 11-4 provides an example of a behaviorally anchored rating scale for the performance factor "Customer Relations" in a payments cashier's job.

BARS was developed to overcome weaknesses in other performance appraisal methods by addressing specific job behaviors and performance expectations. While research has been conducted on the effectiveness of BARS as compared to other methods, such as rating, the results appear to be mixed.[12] It does not appear, though, that this approach has fulfilled earlier expectations concerning its effectiveness.

Advantages. Proponents of BARS claim several advantages for this method: (1) it is job based inasmuch as each job must be carefully studied to identify specific behaviors that will be used to assess performance, (2) it is more objective than other methods because specific behavioral statements rather than vague descriptions of performance are used, (3) its validity is superior to methods that rely on worker traits or personality factors that may not be job related, and (4) it provides for an easier communication of

Figure 11.4
Behaviorally Anchored Rating Scale

Job: Payments Cashier

Factor: Customer Relations--includes all those behaviors the cashier demonstrates when dealing with the customers.

Clearly Outstanding Performance	7	Carefully explains company services to customers and attempts to cross-sell services whenever possible.
Excellent Performance	6	Answers all questions knowledgeably and occasionally attempts to cross-sell one or two services.
Good Performance	5	Answers most customer inquiries knowledgeably and courteously.
Neither Good Nor Bad Performance	4	Is friendly toward customers and answers some questions correctly.
Slightly Poor Performance	3	Answers questions by referring customer to another department.
Poor Performance	2	Responds to customer inquiries grudgingly, but lacks adequate knowledge of company services.
Very Poor Performance	1	Indifferent to customer needs.

job expectations to employees since these expectations are specifically identified in advance.[13]

Disadvantages. As a performance appraisal device, BARS have the following disadvantages: (1) they are expensive and time consuming to develop since each job must be studied in detail; (2) their development normally requires professional expertise because of the extensive job analysis entailed; (3) there are usually little or no backup data collected to support the evaluator's assessment of performance; (4) problems of evaluator bias are not eliminated because judgment still plays a significant part in the evaluation; and (5) there is no clear-cut evidence that this method, although more detailed and expensive, is superior to other commonly used approaches.[14]

Work Standards

The work standards approach to performance appraisal is one in which each employee's output is compared to a predetermined level of output of acceptable quality. Standards, established through work measurement techniques such as time study, work sampling, or predetermined time systems, reflect the amount of work that a qualified employee working at a normal rate of speed under normal conditions could produce within a specified period of time.[15] This method is most commonly used in manufacturing where output is readily quantifiable, but is also found in banking and other non-manufacturing environments.

Advantages. Where work standards can be used, they offer distinct advantages: (1) they are objective, quantifiable criteria for determining performance; (2) they provide for the easy identification of high as well as low performers; (3) they establish a definitive basis for relating merit pay increases to performance; and (4) they set expectations that can readily be communicated to employees.[16]

Disadvantages. Some of the drawbacks to work standards include the following: (1) the standards used to measure output must be very accurate,[17] (2) standards cannot be applied to jobs where there is lack of a readily quantifiable output, (3) this approach typically provides no developmental data that are useful for a supervisor in counseling employees, (4) workers must believe that the standards are fair, and (5) any changes made in the standards may have an adverse impact on employee morale.

Essays

Free-form essays are another performance appraisal method. In their simplest form, the evaluator merely writes a brief narrative describing the employee's performance, usually elaborating on strengths as well as indicating areas where the individual needs to make improvement. This method tends to focus on extreme behaviors in the employee's behavior rather than routine, day-to-day performance because extremes are more easily remembered by the appraiser. Evaluations of this type, obviously, depend quite heavily upon the writing ability of the evaluator. However, some managers believe that this approach is perhaps the best approach to performance appraisal,[18] undoubtedly because the evaluator is not constricted or limited as to what might be covered in the evaluation. Essays are most often used in conjunction with other appraisal methods rather than as the sole method.

Advantages. The advantages claimed for the essay approach include: (1) the thoughtful attention an appraiser must give to writing a report that is truly reflective of the employee's performance, (2) the wide latitude given to the evaluator to cover items that may not be included in a set of predetermined evaluation factors, (3) the attention that must be given to citing specific examples of demonstrated performance in order to compose an accurate narrative, and (4) the kind of information provided to the employee may be extremely useful to the individual in improving his or her performance.[19]

Disadvantages. Essays have several inherent drawbacks when used as the only means of performance appraisal. Among these are: (1) the quality of the evaluation is more often than not a function of the appraiser's ability to write well than it is of the employee's ability to perform a job successfully; (2) the method can be very time consuming if it is given the attention it deserves; (3) inasmuch as essays require time, supervisors may be inclined to perform them perfunctorily if several employees are being appraised at once; (4) the evaluator tends to concentrate more on behavioral extremes than examples of day-to-day performance; and (5) comparisons of employee performance across departmental lines is difficult because appraisers do not all cover the same aspects of performance nor possess the same writing skills.[20]

Management by Objectives

Management by objectives (MBO) is both a management philosophy and an approach to performance appraisal. As a management philosophy, it utilizes employee participation in setting meaningful, attainable goals for each individual. These individual goals are directed toward departmental goals and ultimately toward the overall goals of the organization.

As an approach to performance appraisal, MBO is a results centered technique that does not attempt to evaluate traits or personality characteristics; its focus is entirely on actual achievements measured in terms of expected achievements as set by employees themselves. With MBO the focus of the appraisal process shifts from evaluation of the worker's personal attributes or tangentially related job factors to actual job accomplishments. The appraiser's role changes from that of performance judge to one of counselor and performance facilitator. The employee's involvement in the appraisal function becomes one of active participator rather than one of passive bystander.

In an MBO appraisal system, the employee and his or her supervisor mutually set goals that the employee will achieve during the next evaluation period. These goals then become the standards by which the employee's performance will be measured. While goals are normally set in terms of quantitative terms that lend themselves to clear-cut measurement, qualitative goals that are not as easily measurable are often used, too. At the conclusion of the appraisal period, the employee and the supervisor meet to discuss the extent to which stated goals have been achieved and review further actions that may be necessary to accomplish goals that were not met in the current appraisal period. In this review session, goals for the next period are also normally established. With MBO, the supervisor keeps communication channels open and attempts to assist in any way possible to see that the employee actually achieves the goals that have been set.

Advantages. MBO has been touted as a performance appraisal system for over thirty years. Among the advantages claimed for it are: (1) it increases the employee's involvement in setting performance objectives and concommitantly increases the motivation required to reach those objectives; (2) it offers an objective, factual basis for measuring accomplishments; (3) it emphasizes results, not traits or personality characteristics; (4) it is entirely job centered; (5) it establishes the appraiser as a facilitator of performance rather than as a critic of performance; (6) it assures the organization that all employees are working toward a common purpose; and (7) it supports the psychological concept that people will exercise self-direction and self-control in the accomplishment of organizational aims that they have participated in setting.[21]

Disadvantages. While the advantages of management by objectives as a performance appraisal system are real, it also has disadvantages that are just as real. For example: (1) MBO is incompatible with certain managerial styles—it will not work under authoritarian conditions; (2) it is an organizational philosophy—it cannot operate at one organizational level without operating at all levels; (3) installing a truly effective MBO approach is time consuming—it requires an installation period of at least five years before it can permeate the entire organization; (4) MBO cannot be implemented at all organizational levels simultaneously nor can it be implemented from the bottom up—it must begin at the very top of the organization and work its way down; (5) it requires a total and sizable commitment of management support, interest, and time if it is to succeed; (6) it does not lend itself to all types of jobs—individuals performing routine, repetitive, or machine-paced jobs are better appraised by another method; and (7) employees require extensive training before they normally will respond in a positive fashion to MBO.[22]

It is hoped that this brief discussion of performance appraisal methods has illustrated that there is no perfect approach to assessing employee job performance. Some approaches are decidedly better than others; some are clearly deficient. Specific approaches employed by an organization must take into consideration several factors: the uses that will be made of the results, the organization's philosophy and climate, the types of jobs being evaluated, and the time and expense that will be required to furnish the organization with a system that it can use effectively.

PROBLEMS IN PERFORMANCE APPRAISAL

As pointed out in previous chapters, many human resource practices and procedures, unfortunately, are imperfect at best. Performance appraisal is no exception. Many of the problems in performance appraisal occur not so much from the method used—although some methods are more susceptible to problems than others—but from the way in which the approach is used. Many problems stem from the fact that supervisors and managers are largely untrained in how to appraise employee performance. Even when appraisers are trained, they often find it difficult to accurately and effectively assess the accomplishments of their subordinates. Some of the most common problems encountered in performance appraisal are described below.

Perfunctoriness

For many supervisors, performance appraisal is a task they find difficult and, consequently, do not like to perform. Some view it as too time consuming; some see it as an unnecessary administrative function the human resource department requires to be performed; others do not relish the thought of having to explain or discuss an evaluation with an employee. Consequently, it is not unusual to find the appraisal handled very superficially. The form is completed without a great deal of thought; any discussion with the employee is cursory. While it is a matter of importance to both employee and employer, performance appraisal is often handled in a fashion that suggests it is not important.

One of the authors once witnessed an annual performance review discussion with a relatively high level professional employee that took place in a hallway and occurred in no more than thirty seconds! Granted, this is an extreme example of perfunctoriness, yet it is indicative of the superficiality with which many appraisals are handled. The fact that it transpired in one of the largest companies in the country is even more astonishing.

Lack of Objectivity

An obvious weakness in many performance appraisal systems in use today is their lack of objectivity. Rating scales, for example, commonly use personality traits or characteristics such as attitude, loyalty, appearance, resourcefulness, and personal conduct that are not only difficult to measure, but are also open to completely subjective interpretation by the evaluator. In addition, these and similar factors may have little or nothing to do with job performance. As discussed in Chapter 3, the courts have taken a dim view of subjective appraisal systems.

While it is true that some element of subjectivity will probably exist in even the best of systems, a definite attempt must always be made to ensure that objective factors—quantifiable, measurable, and job related—are stressed in the appraisal method used. Lack of objective criteria place the evaluator and the employer in untenable positions relative to both employees and the EEOC.

Central Tendency

Perhaps one of the most common errors in appraising performance is central tendency: rating all employees as average or at the middle value of a numerical scale. This problem may occur for three reasons. First, it is the most expedient way to do appraisals, especially when many employees have to be evaluated at the same time. Two, rating scales have a built-in tendency that forces ratings toward the center rather than toward the extremes. Three, evaluating an employee as average relieves the appraiser of having to explain or justify high or low evaluations because there is no need to offer substantial justification as to why the rating is other than average. Appraisers committing this type of error are probably seeking to avoid controversy, criticism, or lengthy discussions associated with either high or low evaluations.

Halo and Horns Effect

A halo effect refers to the tendency to rate an employee high on all aspects of performance, even though actual performance has not been uniformly high, because the evaluator places an extraordinary importance on one factor where performance has been high. For example, if an evaluator places great importance on quantity of work produced, the employee who turns out the most items will tend to receive a higher rating on quality of work than is justified by the actual quality level. Likewise, other factors will receive a higher rating than can be factually supported due to the extreme importance the appraiser attaches to work quantity.

The horns effect is the direct opposite of the halo effect. Poor performance on one highly valued aspect of performance tends to lead to lower than deserved ratings on all other performance factors.

Leniency and Strictness

Leniency, sometimes referred to as "evaluation inflation," is the giving of undeserved high ratings. Research on performance appraisal suggests that where the evaluators are required to discuss evaluations with employees there is a tendency to overrate actual performance.[23] In many instances, the evaluator simply gives the employee the benefit of the doubt about performance. In one study it was discovered that more than 50 percent of the employees in a particular organization were rated in the most favorable category possible, "Excellent."[24] Leniency obviously eliminates the necessity to discuss any unpleasant aspects of performance with the employee. The problem of overrating is more apt to occur when subjective appraisal factors are used.

Strictness refers to the problem of being unduly critical of an employee's work performance. Supervisors sometimes use performance reviews, unfortunately, as an opportunity to enumerate all of an individual's deficiencies, weaknesses, and developmental needs—ostensibly, of course, for the employee's own good. When performance appraisal is used in this manner, the result is likely to be a much lower than warranted evaluation.

Personal Biases

An evaluator's personal feelings about the person being appraised can significantly affect the result of a performance appraisal. Appearance, mode of dress, hair styles, mannerisms, and a host of other factors may cause an evaluator to like or dislike particular employees and produce negatively or positively skewed appraisals. Individuals of particular religious affiliations, ethnic groups, sex, age, or handicap status, although protected by law, do not always receive fair evaluations because of personal biases extant on the part of the supervisor conducting the appraisal. Exacerbating the problem of personal biases is the fact that these biases are often subconscious prejudices and are, therefore, difficult to eliminate or control.

Recent Behavior Bias

This type of bias occurs when the appraiser takes into account only the latest performance of the employee and fails to consider the performance that has occurred over the entire evaluation period. Since the normal appraisal period is one year, it is difficult in the absence of detailed documentation to remember what has happened in the earlier part of the period;

thus, the appraiser tends to focus on the most recent and easiest to remember aspects of performance.

Employees, too, contribute to this problem. Most employees are very aware of when they are scheduled for a performance review, and while their actions may not be conscious, their behavior and productivity tend to improve before the scheduled evaluation; consequently, the supervisor's remembrance of recent behavior tends to be even more positively reinforced.

Guessing

In the absence of quantitative, objective performance measures, evaluators may resort to guessing about what an employee has or has not done during the appraisal period. Lacking sufficient documentation relative to accomplishments, appraisers may simply make assumptions about an individual's performance. Often these guesses are incorrect.

Use Bias

The way in which performance appraisal is used in an organization may introduce another form of bias into the process. If the primary purpose of the evaluation is for awarding merit pay increases, appraisers may display a tendency to rate poor performers as average so as not to deny raises to these employees. In times of high inflation, supervisors also tend to overrate performance so that employees receive raises that are more commensurate with inflation rates.[25]

On the other hand, where the emphasis of performance appraisal is on helping the employee to develop and improve his or her job skills, evaluators may tend to be more realistic or even stringent in their performance assessments because they are concerned with helping employees develop their talents more fully.

Lack of Documentation

A major problem with most appraisal systems is that they do not require any form of continuous documentation of employee performance. In instances where documentation does exist, it is often inadequate to support an accurate assessment of employee accomplishments. Nonexistent or inadequate documentation leads supervisors to commit many of the performance appraisal errors described above.

CHARACTERISTICS OF AN
EFFECTIVE APPRAISAL SYSTEM

It is highly unlikely that any performance appraisal system will be totally free from criticism or immune to legal challenge. However, systems that possess certain characteristics are apt to be more defensible legally as well as produce useful results for an organization, its managers, and its employees. Described below are eleven characteristics that an effective performance appraisal system should have.

Consideration of these characteristics will make another significant point abundantly clear: development of an effective appraisal system is not an easy task nor does it happen overnight. A performance appraisal system that does its job well is the result of hard and careful thinking.

Formalized

The first requirement for any effective performance appraisal system is that it be formalized in writing. There should be definite policies, procedures, and instructions for its use. Written guidance should be furnished to all appraisers, either as part of the organization's personnel policy handbook or as a separate document. General information about the system should be given to all employees via an employee handbook where there is one or by a separate memorandum if there is no handbook.

Formalizing the system forces an organization to think through all facets of performance appraisal and to clarify what it wants the system to achieve and how it will achieve it. Many potential problems can be eliminated by reducing the system to writing.

Job Related

All factors used to evaluate performance must stem from the jobs that are being appraised. Inasmuch as performance appraisal is an employment test according to the definition of test given in the *Uniform Guidelines on Employee Selection Procedures*, general traits, personality characteristics, and tenuously related job factors should be scrupulously avoided. Only appraisal factors that account for success or lack of success in performing a job should be used. These factors must be susceptible to standardized definition and uniform interpretation by appraisers.

Developing job-related performance factors may, obviously, necessitate creating different sets of factors for different groups of jobs. Because jobs are dissimilar in content and expected results, it is difficult to develop a single set of performance appraisal factors that will adequately cover every job in an organization.

Standards and Measurements

Standards are expectations, norms, desired results, or anticipated levels of job accomplishment that express the organization's concept of acceptable performance. To set standards an organization must carefully examine each of its jobs and determine reasonable expectations that are acceptable to both the institution and the employees performing the jobs. By no means is this an easy task, but it is one that must be accomplished if performance is to be evaluated on any kind of meaningful basis.

Once standards have been set, some method of measuring actual results has to be developed. In many cases, measurements are difficult to establish because jobs do not lend themselves to easy or meaningful quantification. Yet if comparison with an established standard is to be accomplished, measurements must be developed. Even an imperfect measurement will be better than no measurement at all.

Establishing standards and measurements is a difficult and challenging task, but it is one that must be accomplished if job performance is to be evaluated accurately.

Valid

Any test is valid if it measures what it purports to measure. As far as performance appraisal is concerned, the system employed or the method used is valid if it measures what it is designed to measure—actual job performance.

Establishing the validity of performance appraisal actually begins with job analysis, the process wherein job performance factors are clearly identified. These factors may include quantity of work, quality of work, meeting deadlines, adhering to prescribed procedures, and so forth. Whatever the specific factors are, they are items that directly and specifically reflect the outcomes expected of the individual performing the job. They are also items that are subject to explicit definition and measurement.

As far as performance appraisal is concerned, there should be a reasonably high relationship between the evaluation an employee has received on a particular performance factor and the actual results the individual has achieved as measured by that factor. Employees who consistently produce high volumes of output should consistently receive a higher rating on this performance factor than employees whose output is lower.

Unfortunately, most performance appraisal systems in use today have not been subjected to statistical validity studies as required by the *Uniform Guidelines*.

Reliable

Reliability, statistically speaking, refers to the ability of any test or measure to yield consistent results. A performance appraisal system that does not consistently measure work performance accurately cannot be considered an effective one. Assume, for example, that an employee's actual work performance on a particular job factor or even a whole series of factors is, in fact, considerably above expectation for three evaluation periods, but that the individual receives an average rating on the job factor or factors for the first period, a high rating for the second period, and a below average rating for the third period. A performance appraisal system producing such results could not be considered a reliable one—there is an absence of consistency. High performance must consistently receive a high rating, just as low performance must consistently receive a low rating for the measurement system to be considered reliable.

Where definitive standards and measurements are not used, reliability problems often arise in performance appraisal because supervisors lack objective criteria for evaluating performance, thus opening themselves to committing performance evaluation errors that produce inconsistent, unreliable results.

Open Communication

All employees have a strong psychological need to know how well they are performing. An effective performance appraisal system ensures that feedback is provided on a continuous basis—not in the form of a written evaluation, but in the form of daily, weekly, and monthly comments from the supervisor. For any performance appraisal system to be effective, the ongoing aspect of its nature must be emphasized to supervisors and the necessity of providing continuous feedback information on job performance must be underscored. The annual evaluation and its accompanying interview or performance discussion must be devoid of "surprises." While the interview presents an excellent opportunity for both parties to exchange ideas in depth, it is not a substitute for day-to-day performance communications.

Trained Appraisers

Essential to the effectiveness of performance appraisal is thorough training—as well as updating and retraining—of all individuals in the organization who conduct evaluations. Classroom training is especially important when a new or revised system is being installed; it is also essential for all new managers and supervisors. An organization must not assume that, because performance appraisal information is contained in a supervisory handbook or is included in the company personnel policy manual, supervisors will automatically learn how to conduct effective appraisals.

In addition to formalized training sessions, opportunities for coaching and counseling by the appraisers' immediate supervisors should also be incorporated into the system's procedures. Such personal sessions often permit the discussion and resolution of appraisal problems in their incipiency. Moreover, by actively involving each level of management in teaching performance appraisal, the system becomes more strongly imbedded in the organization as a vital function of human resource management.

Easy to Use

A performance appraisal system does not have to be complex to be effective. In fact, the simpler the system, the easier it is to use, the more readily it can be understood by evaluators, and the more likely it is to be used in the manner intended. If the system is firmly based on standards and measurements, it will probably be not only easier to use but also more valid, reliable, and so on than many of the performance appraisal approaches used in industry today.

Employee Access to Results

As a result of the Federal Privacy Act of 1973, employees of the federal government as well as federal contractors must be given access to their personnel records, including all files or other data pertaining to their performance appraisals. Presently, this requirement does not apply to employees in the private sector at large, but there are several reasons, totally aside from the potential extension of legislative coverage to private industry, that suggest the necessity of allowing employees to examine any records that are maintained about their job performance. First, secrecy breeds suspicion about the fairness of the system. Second, concern about the fairness of the system could possibly lead to lawsuits. Third, fairness in dealing with employees suggests that they have an implicit right to certain kinds of information that directly affects them on their jobs. Fourth, permitting employees to review their performance records builds a safeguard into the system in that employees have the opportunity to detect errors that may have been made in the evaluations. Finally, since one of the espoused purposes of performance appraisal is employee development, employees must have access to performance records if they are, in fact, to initiate efforts to improve the way they carry out their job duties and responsibilities.

Review Mechanism

To eliminate any problems of bias, discrimination, favoritism, or the like, a performance appraisal system should contain a review mechanism.

Each evaluation of an employee should be automatically reviewed by the next higher level of management—usually the evaluator's immediate supervisor. The purpose of this review is not to have the superior perform a second appraisal; rather, it is for the purpose of auditing the evaluation for fairness, consistency, accuracy, and making certain that the evaluator has carried out his or her function objectively. While review by the immediate superior increases the time that must be devoted to the performance appraisal process, it protects both the employee and the organization by ensuring fairness and consistency in employee evaluations.

Appeal Procedure

An accepted principle of American jurisprudence is the right of due process. Unfortunately, in a number of organizations there is no procedure whereby an employee can appeal what he or she considers to be an unfair or inaccurate performance appraisal. The employee is simply "stuck" with the immediate supervisor's evaluation. In such situations, the employee has few options other than living with the unfavorable review or leaving the organization for employment elsewhere. There have even been instances where employees whose performance was acceptable for years were summarily discharged on the basis of one bad performance appraisal. Now that an employer's right to fire at will is being challenged in the courts—often successfully—the need for a clearly delineated appeal procedure in the performance appraisal system seems imperative. (It should be noted that organizations having to deal with unions have long had well-established appeal mechanisms in the form of grievance procedures.)

The number of steps that should be contained in an appeal procedure depends on the size of the organization. As a minimum, there should be two steps: an appeal to the next higher level of management and an appeal to the level above that. In larger organizations, the human resource department would be included at some point in the process—possibly the third or fourth step. The procedures by which an employee can appeal an unfavorable review should be clearly spelled out in the formalized policies and procedures of the performance appraisal system as well as specified in the employee handbook.

An appeal process serves three purposes: it protects the employee, it protects the organization, and it helps ensure that supervisors do a more conscientious job of evaluation since they know that their appraisals are subject to scrutiny and interpretation by others in the organization.

THE PERFORMANCE APPRAISAL INTERVIEW

Once the appraisal forms have been completed and the necessary documentation prepared, the evaluator faces what is often the most difficult of all performance appraisal tasks: the appraisal interview.[26] Many evaluators consider the interview or performance discussion an unpleasant task, particularly if the employee has not performed up to standard. Others view the discussion as simply an organizational requirement that should be disposed of as quickly as possible. A more realistic perspective of the interview, however, would suggest that it is an opportunity for *both* evaluator and evaluatee—an opportunity for the evaluator to coach, counsel, and assist the employee to improve his or her performance; an opportunity for the evaluatee to recognize his or her areas of strength and areas of growth and development possibilities. Conducted properly, the performance appraisal interview is a means of increasing organizational effectiveness.

Preparing for the Interview

An effective performance appraisal interview is not something that just happens; it is an event that must be carefully planned for if it is to achieve its purposes. To prepare for the interview, the evaluator must clarify in his or her own mind and outline the following:

- The favorable aspects of performance that will be covered in the discussion.
- The areas of performance deficiencies or areas where improvement is needed.
- The anticipated reaction of the employee to both areas of strengths and areas of improvement.
- The employee's likely emotional or personal reaction to the performance discussion.
- The specific facts relative to the discussion and the order in which they will be presented.
- The specific suggestions and assistance that will be offered to the employee.
- The follow-up action that will be taken to ensure that improvements in performance will take place.[27]

Types of Performance Appraisal Interviews

Performance appraisal interviews are of two types: the direct method and the indirect method.[28]

The direct method is more structured, deals primarily with facts, and is closely controlled by the supervisor through the use of direct questions or statements. The tone of the interview is set by the evaluator and the employee has little opportunity to do much more than answer questions or respond to statements. Specific areas of interest to the employee are covered only to the extent that the supervisor's structured questions permit. Frequently, this type of performance interview places the employee in a defensive position and the interviewer in a judgmental role. Yet the direct method is commonly used because supervisors find it easier to discuss performance when they are in control of the direction of the discussion. The biggest drawback to the direct interview method is that little is learned of the employee's ideas about areas of desired personal growth, development, and improvement.

The non-directive interview, on the other hand, is an interactive approach that encourages the employee to talk as much as possible. It is an attempt to explore performance areas with the employee, to uncover reasons for good as well as poor performance, and to discover the employee's ambitions and perceived developmental needs.

Comparing the two types of interviews, it is obvious that improvements in performance are more likely to come from the indirect approach than they are from the direct approach. Since the employee is an active participant in the indirect interview, he or she is more apt to accept suggestions for improvement and recognize developmental needs. Additionally, a sense of joint responsibility for performance may develop from the discussion. The non-directive interview will, however, require a much greater amount of time than the direct interview, but it is time that will be well spent if performance actually improves as a result of the discussion.

Guidelines for Conducting the Interview

Performance appraisal interviews are not easy tasks. They have to be well planned and carefully thought out. If handled improperly, they can create poor morale, misunderstanding, or even outright hostility on the part of the employee. Some suggestions for conducting an effective performance interview include the following:

- *Prepare the employee.* Notify the individual in advance so that he or she can come to the interview prepared to discuss performance in a meaningful fashion.
- *Establish the proper climate.* Create an atmosphere that suggests that the discussion is important.
- *Compare actual performance to standards or expectations.* Use specific examples. Avoid vague generalities about performance.
- *Bite the bullet.* If performance has not been satisfactory, address the subject directly. Don't try to evade the issue by attempting to cover up poor performance with insignificant items of good performance.
- *Comment on improvements.* Recognize areas where the individual has improved and express appreciation for the improvements.

- *Avoid sitting in judgment.* The rightful role of the evaluator is coach, counselor, and facilitator, not judge.
- *Listen and ask questions.* Give the employee ample opportunity to discuss areas that he or she thinks are important.
- *Ask what you can do to help the person improve.* Offer whatever assistance you can to facilitate performance and growth.
- *Work with the person to establish new performance goals.* Make this a joint effort so that the employee becomes more committed to actually achieving the goals.
- *Allow sufficient time.* Never rush the interview. Make certain that the discussion will not be interrupted.[29]

Keeping these points in mind when discussing a performance appraisal will help ensure that the discussion achieves its objectives.

OTHER PERFORMANCE APPRAISAL CONSIDERATIONS

Three final considerations that must be taken into account in designing and operating an effective performance appraisal system are: assigning the responsibility for conducting the appraisal, determining the length of time to be covered by the appraisal period, and establishing the point in time at which the appraisal will occur.

Responsibility for Appraisal

Typically, the human reource department is responsible for designing and administering the performance appraisal program. The responsibility for actually conducting the appraisals, however, is assigned to others within the organization. Several possibilities exist for fulfilling this responsibility.

Immediate Supervisor. The most logical choice for conducting a performance appraisal is the employee's immediate supervisor since this is the individual in the best position to know the most about the employee's degree of performance. The immediate supervisor is also the most common choice in organizations. One study disclosed that 96 percent of the firms surveyed assign the responsibility for appraisal to the immediate supervisor.[30] Three reasons favor the supervisor's handling of the appraisal: (1) he or she is in the best position to observe the employee's performance on a day-to-day basis, (2) assigning the responsibility to someone else seriously erodes the supervisor's authority as manager of a work unit, and (3) one of the primary functions of any supervisor is training and development of his or her people—a function that is inextricably tied to performance appraisal. Throughout this chapter it has been assumed that the immediate supervisor will be the person conducting the evaluation. This assumption reflects the authors' views as to who should perform the appraisal.

Subordinates. Can a supervisor or manager be effectively evaluated by his or her subordinates? The conclusion reached by a very limited number of firms is that they can. Subordinates are in a unique position to view the overall effectiveness of their managers; they can sometimes recognize strengths or weaknesses not seen by others. Managers who advocate this approach suggest that evaluations by subordinates will make supervisors more conscientious in carrying out their responsibilities effectively. On the negative side, ratings by subordinates may cause a supervisor to become excessively concerned with popularity rather than effective performance of the work unit.

Peers. Evaluation by one's peers may be feasible in limited instances. Where employees must work closely together as a team, it is possible that coworkers would know more about an individual's work performance than the unit supervisor. The fact that evaluation is seldom performed by peers would seem to suggest that this approach is not considered a viable alternative by the vast majority of managers.

Team Appraisal. This form of evaluation occurs when two or more supervisors who are familiar with an employee's performance jointly appraise his or her performance. In many instances, an employee actually works for two or more supervisors; in other cases, the employee works for one supervisor but interfaces across organizational lines with several supervisors or managers. Under these conditions, a collective appraisal would probably be more accurate and objective than one by a supervisor who has not had sufficient opportunity to observe the employee's work in all areas. Perhaps the biggest disadvantage to this approach is that it undermines supervisory authority and responsibility.

Self-appraisal. Another appraisal possibility is to have each employee evaluate his or her own performance. If individuals truly understand the objectives they are expected to reach and the standards by which their accomplishments will be measured, they may well be in the best position of all to appraise their performance.[31] Moreover, since development is essentially self-development, appraisal by employees themselves may lead to greater levels of motivation.

Combinations. Often, some combination of the approaches mentioned above is used. The combination used most frequently is some form of self-appraisal and appraisal by the supervisor. With this approach, the employee is asked to complete an evaluation form and the supervisor does likewise. Then the two parties meet to discuss their separate appraisals, resolve any discrepancies, and complete a mutually agreed upon evaluation. This approach has a great deal of merit because it involves the employee in the process and reemphasizes the joint responsibility for effective performance.

The Appraisal Period

Annual is usually a word that is attached to performance appraisal and is probably a fairly good indicator of how often appraisals are conducted. But is an annual appraisal frequent enough? There are two schools of thought on this matter. One maintains that performance feedback should be given on a more frequent basis, especially if the primary purpose of the appraisal is employee development. The other school of thought maintains that if the system is operating effectively, feedback will be provided on daily, weekly, and monthly bases and that there is no need for a formal appraisal more than once a year.[32] It would appear in most instances that an annual formalized appraisal is sufficient, provided that ongoing feedback is furnished to the employee.

In the case of new employees, exceptions should be made to the annual review. Good human resource practice suggests that a new employee should be given a formal evaluation at the end of his or her probationary period—the juncture at which the organization makes the decision as to whether the individual will be retained. A review at this point can also relieve anxiety on the part of employees who become permanent members of the organization's staff because they know that they are performing at an acceptable level.

When to Appraise

Assuming that formal evaluations will occur annually, there is still the question of precisely when the evaluations will take place. There are two approaches to solving this problem: evaluate all employees on a fixed date or evaluate each employee on the anniversary date of his or her employment. The latter approach appears to be the most feasible. Conducting a performance appraisal properly and discussing it thoroughly with the employee is a time-consuming matter. For a supervisor to have to evaluate all employees on a fixed date leads to rushing through the process and not accomplishing it effectively. Consequently, the recommended approach is the employment anniversary date method since the supervisor will have fewer evaluations to conduct at any specific time and can give each one the thorough attention it deserves.

NOTES

1. Donald L. Caruth, *Compensation Management for Banks* (Boston: Bankers Publishing Company, 1986), p. 206.

2. Don Caruth, Bill Middlebrook, and Frank Rachel, "Performance Appraisals: Much More Than a Once-a-Year Task," *Supervisory Management*, September 1982, pp. 28–36.

3. Caruth, *Compensation Management*, p. 208.

4. Charles J. Fombrun and Robert J. Laud, "Strategic Issues in Performance Appraisal: Theory and Practice," *Personnel*, November-December, 1983, p. 24.

5. Caruth, *Compensation Management*, p. 212.

6. Ibid.

7. Ibid.

8. Ibid., p. 216.

9. Ibid.

10. Ibid., p. 214.

11. Ibid., p. 215.

12. Stephen J. Carroll and Craig E. Schneier, *Performance Appraisal and Review Systems: The Identification, Measurement, and Development of Performance in Organizations* (Glenview, Ill.: Scott, Foresman and Company, 1982), p. 117.

13. Caruth, *Compensation Management*, pp. 216, 218.

14. Ibid., p. 218.

15. Donald L. Caruth, *Work Measurement in Banking*, 2nd ed. (Boston: Bankers Publishing Company, 1984), p. 206.

16. Ibid., p. 28.

17. Ibid., p. 73.

18. R. Wayne Mondy and Robert M. Noe III, *Personnel: The Management of Human Resources* 3rd ed. (Boston: Allyn and Bacon, 1987), p. 384.

19. Caruth, *Compensation Management*, p. 218.

20. Ibid., pp. 218-219.

21. Ibid., p. 219.

22. Ibid., p. 220.

23. Hubert S. Field and William H. Holley, "Subordinates' Characteristics, Supervisors' Ratings, and Decisions to Discuss Appraisal Results," *Academy of Management Journal*, June 1977, pp. 315-321.

24. William H. Holley, Hubert S. Field, and Nona J. Barnett, "Analyzing Performance Appraisal Systems: An Empirical Study," *Personnel Journal*, September 1976, p. 458.

25. Caruth, *Compensation Management*, p. 211.

26. Caruth, Middlebrook, and Rachel, "Performance Appraisals," p. 32.

27. Don Caruth, Frank Rachel, and Bill Middlebrook, *Management Dynamics II* (Carrollton, Tex.: Spinnaker Publications, 1983), p. 65.

28. Caruth, Middlebrook, and Rachel, "Performance Appraisals," pp. 33-35.

29. Ibid., pp. 35-36.

30. Fombrun and Laud, "Strategic Issues," p. 27.

31. Margaret A. Bogerty, "How to Prepare Your Performance Review," *S.A.M. Journal*, Autumn 1982, p. 12.

32. Caruth, *Compensation Management*, p. 235.

12

Career Planning and Development

Rising educational levels and higher occupational expectations in today's work force coupled with slower economic growth and reduced promotion opportunities in contemporary organizations are factors that suggest the need for formalized career planning and development activities.[1] Additionally, compliance with equal opportunity and affirmative action requirements necessitates that positive steps be taken to ensure adequate career progression for minorities and women. Once considered a luxury that was within the purview of a limited number of large organizations, career planning and development is now becoming an essential activity for companies of all sizes and types.

CAREER PLANNING AND DEVELOPMENT DEFINED

Several definitions are in order before examining this process in detail.[2] A *career* is a course of occupational action pursued by a person over the span of his or her working life. *Career planning* is the procedure whereby an individual establishes career goals and identifies ways these goals can be accomplished. The organization's role in career planning is one of helping the individual achieve a better match between personal aspirations and opportunities that are available in the organization. One way of doing this is by developing *career paths* or lines of job progression through which employees typically move. *Career development* includes all of those activities undertaken by the organization or the individual to prepare a person for successful progression along a particular career path.

As the preceding definitions suggest, effective career planning and development is, ideally, a joint effort. While the primary responsibility for career planning rests with the individual inasmuch as work choices and occupational pursuits are matters of a personalized nature, organizations can help employees make better decisions by acquainting them with various options and providing avenues through which their choices can be pursued. Although each individual has a personal responsibility for undergoing the preparation required for a particular line of work, career development can be facilitated by the organization as it offers formal and informal means of acquiring needed skills and experience. Organizations that assist their employees in career planning and development benefit themselves as well as their employees.

PURPOSES OF CAREER PLANNING AND DEVELOPMENT

As interesting as it would be to explore how people make career choices and prepare themselves for occupations, the concern of this chapter is the organization's role in career planning and development. Organizations typically have several purposes in mind when they implement career planning and development programs—purposes that serve institutional needs as well as the needs of employees. These basic purposes are described below.

Organizational

There are eight specific organizational purposes that are served through career planning and development programs. These purposes, in general, center around having sufficient numbers of qualified people available so that the company can fulfill its mission and goals.

Improve Utilization of Personnel. Talent is not always obvious. Often, developmental activities are necessary to bring out the latent abilities within people. The first purpose of career planning and development, therefore, is to ensure that an organization is effectively utilizing the human resources already employed with the firm.

Reduce Turnover. Another reason for career-centered programs is turnover reduction. Companies that display an active interest in fostering career development stand a much greater chance of retaining skilled personnel. Employees are more likely to remain with a firm that is genuinely interested in providing opportunities for career advancement. Thus, the organization benefits in two ways: turnover expenses are reduced and qualified employees are available for advancement to positions of greater responsibility when vacancies occur.

Increase Motivation and Commitment. The provision of opportunities to gain new skills and experiences enhances employee motivation and loyalty to the organization. Knowing that their efforts will be recognized and rewarded with chances to further their careers, employees are apt to perform at higher levels and remain committed to an organization. The organizational payoff is increased productivity and job tenure.

Reduce Employee Obsolescence. Because of technological and scientific advancements, many careers for which people spend years in training become obsolescent in a relatively short period of time. Unless an organization takes positive developmental actions to counter this possibility, it may find itself with a number of employees whose skills are no longer appropriate for organizational tasks that must be performed. In effect, a company may find itself burdened with employees who can no longer make a contribution to achieving the objectives of the enterprise. Career planning and development is one solution to this problem.

Increase Organizational Effectiveness. The effectiveness of any institution is increased by having thoroughly trained individuals continuously available to perform necessary activities. Career enhancement is a means of accomplishing this. Developmental activities improve the utilization of employees, reduce turnover, increase motivation and commitment, alleviate obsolescence, and substantially improve the company's effectiveness in accomplishing its objectives.

Assist in Recruiting Highly Talented People. Given a choice, talented individuals will seek employment with a firm that offers opportunities for advancement and growth. Career planning and development thus becomes a recruiting tool that aids a company in attracting skilled applicants. The selection process also benefits in that a better pool of applicants is available from which to hire the employees a firm needs.

Assist in Equal Employment Opportunity and Affirmative Action. Goals in these areas include more than merely hiring sufficient numbers of protected class applicants. Objectives also include upward mobility for minorities and women. Career planning and development is one means an organization can use to assist minorities so that they can progress within the company. In fact, programs may make special efforts to address specific training and experience needs of minorities.

Eliminate Barriers to Upward Mobility. In many organizations, there are often subtle, or even not so subtle, barriers to progression. (These barriers will be identified in a subsequent section.) One purpose of career planning and development is to find and remove these obstacles so that sufficient progression opportunities are available for qualified employees.

Individual

When an organization implements career planning and development it normally does so because it desires to achieve the purposes described above. At the same time, it generally has in mind some other purposes that directly relate to satisfaction of the needs of its employees. As far as the individual employee is concerned, career planning and development programs serve four essential purposes.

Encourage Growth. Developmental activities cause employees to grow, to acquire new abilities, and to become more capable than they presently are. Career focused activities help bring out the full potential in an employee.

Develop New Skills. Systematic career planning and development, working in conjunction with human resource planning, seeks to identify the kinds of skills that employees will need in the future and provide opportunities to acquire these skills. As new skills are acquired, further growth is also encouraged.

Alleviate Plateauing. In any organization there are always employees who seem to progress well up to a certain point and then remain at that plateau. Certainly, it is true that there is a point beyond which some people will not be able to advance, but it is also possible that these same individuals could be utilized more effectively in other laterial positions and some, through training and development directed to their specific needs, might even be capable of further advancement. Career planning and development addresses this problem and attempts to make certain that employees are not victims of artificial plateauing.

Satisfy Employment Expectations. Every employee entering a firm has certain expectations about his or her employment opportunities. These expectations may involve advancement, learning and growing in the job, or opportunities for new experiences. Career planning and development can assist in satisfying these desires.

A well-planned, carefully designed career planning and development program can produce substantial benefits for an organization as well as its employees; it can increase organizational effectiveness while at the same time it can satisfy basic psychological needs of the firm's employees.

BARRIERS TO UPWARD MOBILITY

In the absence of career planning and development, there are usually a number of barriers that impede upward mobility in an organization. The major barriers are described below.[3]

Lack of Career Paths

One of the major limiting factors to employee progression in a company is lack of career paths. When organizations have not thought about how jobs relate to each other and the sequence in which employees should move from one job to another to gain experience, progression opportunities are often severely limited. Promotions or transfers are likely to be made on a haphazard basis. Higher level positions are apt to be filled externally because current employees have not been trained sufficiently to move into jobs of greater responsibility.

Inflated Job Specifications

The necessity for developing realistic job specifications that set forth the minimum human qualifications for satisfactory job performance has been addressed in a previous chapter. Unfortunately, specifications are sometimes inflated. If this occurs, it can seriously inhibit promotional opportunities for employees and result in positions of higher responsibility being continuously filled from outside since insiders do not meet the overstated specifications.

Lack of Internal Recruiting Programs

In the absence of career planning and development programs, organizations are unlikely to have definite procedures for recruiting current employees to fill job vacancies. Skills and management inventories, two basic tools for internal recruiting, may not be utilized at all. If so, systematic identification of internal talent is impossible and the organization will have to look outside for the talented human resources it needs when new jobs are created or vacancies occur.

Lack of Job Posting and Bidding

A common complaint of employees in many companies is that they did not know that a higher level position for which they considered themselves qualified was vacant until someone was brought in from outside to fill it. Lack of job posting and bidding precludes most employees from applying for other positions in the organization because they do not have information on what positions are available. It has already been suggested in this book that present employees are the greatest potential source of candidates for higher level jobs, but if they lack knowledge of these jobs they are barred from upward mobility opportunities.

Lack of Training and Development Programs

Training programs impart skills for performing the present job or another job. Development programs, in essence, are attempts to bring out the full potential in individuals so that they can progress within the organization. Where these kinds of efforts are lacking, another barrier to upward mobility exists.

Inadequate Performance Appraisal

Failure of the performance appraisal system to accurately evaluate performance on the present job or to identify areas where an employee needs to improve creates a mobility barrier. An inadequate system provides no real basis for making promotion or lateral transfer decisions. Excellent performers may be completely overlooked along with poor performers.

Managerial Indifference

One of the most important tasks of a manager, but one that is often overlooked, is training and development of subordinates so that they can be fully productive in their present jobs and be prepared to move up to other jobs when vacancies arise. When managers are indifferent to the training and development task, mobility is hampered tremendously. Employees are effectively "stuck" in their present positions.

Career planning and development is an effective way of eliminating the foregoing mobility barriers. Indeed, they must be eliminated if the program is to be successful.

CONSEQUENCES OF NOT PLANNING AND DEVELOPING CAREERS

Organizations that do not make conscious efforts to assist their employees in planning and developing careers suffer several deleterious consequences that have an impact on overall effectiveness and directly affect the staffing process.[4] Excessive turnover, increased recruiting costs, underutilitization of talent, employee dissatisfaction, stymied progression, and poor promotion are some of the most significant effects on the staffing process.

Excessive Turnover

Employees who find themselves in dead-end jobs or who discover that promotional or lateral movement opportunities are too limited are prone to leave an organization fairly early in their employment experience, usually within the first six months or so. In one organization that did not have a career planning and development program, turnover of hourly personnel ran as high as 250 percent annually.[5] Certainly, not all of this turnover was the result of not having a program, but undeniably the existence of a number of dead-end jobs and lack of promotional opportunities was a contributing factor to the conservatively estimated $6 million that turnover was costing the company each year.

Increased Recruiting Costs

Excessive turnover increases recruiting costs because constant, and sometimes intensive efforts, are required simply to keep positions filled. If the company gains a reputation for lack of interest in the careers of its employees, the recruiting task becomes even more arduous as well as expensive.

Underutilization of Talent

In the absence of career-centered developmental activities, available talent is highly susceptible to underutilization. Employees may be hired to do a particular job, with little or no thought given to other jobs for which they could be trained and developed. Under these conditions, overall organizational effectiveness sufers and staffing bears the burden of excessive turnover and increased recruiting expenses.

Employee Dissatisfaction

When employment expectations are not adequately fulfilled, employees become dissatisfied, motivation decreases, and productivity may decline. The chances of the dissatisfied employee becoming a turnover statistic are reasonably high if he or she is short tenured. Longer-tenured employees may simply become organizational deadwood.

Stymied Progression

For every employee whose upward mobility is precluded, there is one or more other employees who cannot progress. Often, organizations hold an employee in a particular position because "there is no one else to take your place." The truth of the matter is that there are probably several others who could fill the position, but the organization has not taken steps to develop replacements. By holding one individual in place, promotional opportunities are being denied to other employees—a situation that may cause dissatisfaction and increased turnover.

Poor Promotion Decisions

Lack of career planning and development may result in poor promotion decisions. Decisions as to who will be promoted are prone to be based on favoritism, politics, and inconsequential factors rather than on performance, preparation, and organizational needs. When the wrong people are promoted—and for the wrong reasons—there will be a negative impact on institutional effectiveness. Morale is apt to decrease while motivation and commitment drop.

This brief review of the consequences of not engaging in career planning and development should have underscored the need for having a formalized program. Career management should not be left to chance because the organizational risks of doing so are too great.

RESPONSIBILITY FOR CAREER PLANNING AND DEVELOPMENT

It was mentioned earlier that career planning and development is a joint responsibility involving the individual employee and the organization. We will now turn our attention to the roles each party must fulfill for this activity to be accomplished effectively.

Organizational

The organization's principal responsiblities are to develop and implement the program, ensure that it produces results, and assist the employee through formal as well as informal means. Top management, human resource management, and the firm's immediate supervisors each play an important part in seeing that the program is successful.

Top Management. Although not involved in the day-to-day operation of the program, top management's role in career planning and development is a crucial one. Management must recognize the need for the program, contribute its support to the concept, commit adequate resources to its operation, and evaluate the overall results produced. The program will not work without this kind of backing from the top echelon of the organization.

Human Resource Management. Personnel specialists have a number of responsibilities in career planning and development. These include: (1) designing the overall system, (2) developing policies and procedures, (3) formulating career paths in conjunction with other managers, (4) selecting the developmental methods that will be used, (5) training managers and supervisors for their responsibilities in career management, (6) designing and maintaining replacement tables, (7) designing and maintaining skills and management inventories, (8) designing the performance appraisal system and instrument, (9) designing and offering training and development programs, (10) counseling employees, (11) coordinating the program, and (12) evaluating program effectiveness.

Immediate Supervisors. Much of the success of a career planning and development program rests with the organization's supervisors. Supervisory support and action are requisites to making the program work. The employee's immediate superior must be able to counsel the individual about career opportunities and developmental needs; the supervisor must be committed to providing needed training; the supervisor must recognize his or her essential role of talent developer even though the work unit may lose a number of employees to promotional or transfer opportunities. Obviously, a career planning and development program places an additional training burden on first-line management. It seems incumbent that upper level management find means of rewarding those supervisors who do an outstanding job of developing their employees for progression through the organization.

Individual

Ultimately, the one individual who has the greatest responsibility for career development is the employee. As Peter Drucker says so succinctly, "Development is always self-development."[6] This is not to say that the organization cannot assist development through work experiences, courses, seminars, or other actions. It does suggest, however, that whether the developmental opportunities are successful depends upon the individual and his or her willingness to respond positively to the organization's actions by recognizing the personal reponsibility to learn and grow. The organization can provide guidance and assistance, but the employee must recognize the responsibility for undertaking the training and development necessary to progress along a chosen career path.

A formalized career planning and development program properly operated can help stimulate employee interest in development by emphasizing the necessity for learning and growing in a particular job. Training opportunities can also stimulate interest in career management. Reward systems that recognize developmental efforts of employees can, additionally, encourage employees to prepare themselves for current and future opportunities. But ultimately the burden of development rests with the employee.

CAREER PLANNING AND DEVELOPMENT TOOLS

There are many tools or methods that can be used in the career planning and development process. These devices run the gamut from very structured, formal approaches such as career paths and replacement tables to unstructured, informal approaches such as coaching and counseling.

Career Paths

The most basic career management tool for organizations is the career path—that line of job progression along which an employee typically moves during his or her tenure with a company. Depending upon the organization and the nature of the jobs involved, one of three types of career paths may be used: traditional, network, or dual. Examples of these types of paths are illustrated in Figure 12-1.

Figure 12.1
The Three Types of Career Paths

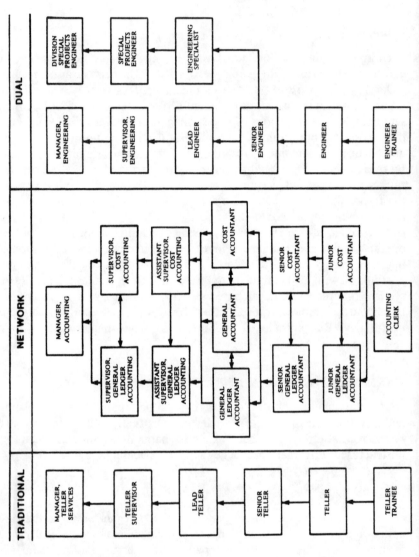

Traditional. The traditional career path is one wherein an employee moves along a vertical line of progression from one specific job to the next specific job. In Figure 12-1 we see the route a person may take from an entry level position of teller trainee to an ultimate position of manager, teller services. The traditional career path assumes that each preceding job is essential preparation for the next higher level of job; consequently, an employee must move step by step from one job to the next to gain any needed experience and preparation. This type of career path is most likely to be found in clerical or production operations functions.

One of the biggest advantages of the traditional career path is its straightforwardness: the path is clearly laid out and the employee knows the specific sequence of jobs through which he or she must progress. A primary disadvantage of this type of progression ladder is that it fails to recognize that other organizational jobs may provide equivalent or even more substantial experience that could enable an employee to advance without having performed certain jobs in the specified linear sequence. Another potentially serious disadvantage of the traditional career path is that of blockage; that is, a long-tenured employee at one level who is not capable of being promoted to the next level may retard the progress of other employees in lower positions.

Network. The network career path, or lattice as it is sometimes called,[7] contains not only a vertical sequence of jobs, but a series of horizontal options as well. Figure 12-1 shows a fairly typical network career path for jobs in an accounting department. Vertically, there are seven levels of jobs through which an employee progresses before becoming manager of the accounting department. At five of these levels there may be lateral movement between two or more jobs before moving upward to the next level, or there may be no lateral movement before progressing vertically. The network career path recognizes two things: the interchangeability of experience at certain levels and the need to broaden experience at one level before promotion to a higher level.

The network path is a more realistic representation of jobs in an organization than is the traditional career path. Moreover, it provides more opportunities for employee development. Because of the vertical and horizontal options in the network, the problem of a particular employee blocking the progression for other employees is lessened. One disadvantage of this type of career path, albeit a minor one, is that it is more difficult to explain to employees the specific route their careers may take within a given line of work.

Dual. The dual career ladder was originally developed to deal with the problem of technically trained employees who had no desire to move into management—the normal procedure for upward mobility in an organization. The dual career path recognizes that technical specialists can and should be allowed to continue to contribute their expertise to a company without having to become managers; consequently, it provides an alternative progression route whereby an employee such as a scientist or engineer can increase his or her knowledge of a specialized field and make contributions to an organization that are just as valuable as those made by managers. This type of path is shown in Figure 12-1. Note that after an individual reaches the position of senior engineer, his or her career can be pursued vertically along a management path or it can be pursued vertically along a technical path. Whether on the management or technical side of the path, compensation would be the same at each level.

The dual career path is becoming increasingly popular today. In a high-tech world, intense specialized knowledge is as important as managerial skill. Rather than creating poor managers out of competent technical specialists, the dual career path permits an organization to have both skilled managers and highly competent technical people.

Career paths are very important to successful career planning and development. Not only do they indentify typical lines of progression, but also they suggest kinds of developmental experiences and activities that are needed for employees. They are essential for preparing today's employees for tomorrow's job openings.

Replacement Tables

Another career management tool—one that is often valuable in human resource planning—is the replacement table. Due to the time and expense involved, replacement tables are usually prepared only for management or high level professional positions. Replacement tables generally resemble an organizational chart in that they identify positions and reporting relationships. But the resemblance ends there for the replacement table contains substantial evaluative information that is used to identify potential successors, assess their current performance, estimate when they may be ready for promotion, and specify developmental needs. Figure 12-2 presents such a table for the position of division manager. The sensitive nature of the information displayed practically dictates that some type of coding system be used.

Information for developing a replacement table may come from several sources: the performance appraisal system, reports from a manager's superior, or assessments made by the human resource department. To be used effectively in career planning and development, the information must be updated at least annually.

Replacement tables require an organization to analyze its previous employee developmental efforts and evaluate the extent to which specific individuals have responded to those efforts. In addition, they help an

Figure 12.2
Typical Replacement Table

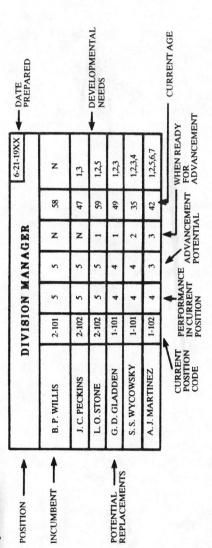

	DIVISION MANAGER					6-21-19XX	
B. P. WILLIS	2-101	5	5	N	58	N	
J. C. PECKINS	2-102	5	5	N	47	1,3	
L. O. STONE	2-102	5	5	1	59	1,2,5	
G. D. GLADDEN	1-101	4	4	1	49	1,2,3	
S. S. WYCOWSKY	1-101	4	4	2	35	1,2,3,4	
A. J. MARTINEZ	1-102	4	3	3	42	1,2,5,6,7	

POSITION →

INCUMBENT →

POTENTIAL REPLACEMENTS →

DATE PREPARED

DEVELOPMENTAL NEEDS

CURRENT AGE

WHEN READY FOR ADVANCEMENT

ADVANCEMENT POTENTIAL

PERFORMANCE IN CURRENT POSITION

CURRENT POSITION CODE

EXPLANATION OF CODES

CURRENT POSITION		PERFORMANCE IN CURRENT POSITION		ADVANCEMENT POTENTIAL		WHEN READY FOR ADVANCEMENT		DEVELOPMENTAL NEEDS	
2-101	DIVISION MANAGER	5	EXCELLENT	5	UNLIMITED	N	NOW	1	CONTRACT ADMINISTRATION
2-102	ASSISTANT DIVISION MANAGER	4	OUTSTANDING	4	EXCELLENT	1	WITHIN 1 YEAR	2	CONTRACT NEGOTIATION
1-101	DEPARTMENT MANAGER	3	ACCEPTABLE	3	GOOD	2	WITHIN 2 YEARS	3	COST CONTROL
1-102	ASSISTANT DEPARTMENT MANAGER	2	NEEDS IMPROVEMENT	2	LIMITED	3	WITHIN 3 YEARS	4	DELEGATION
		1	UNSATISFACTORY	1	NONE	4	OVER 3 YEARS	5	MOTIVATION
								6	COMMUNICATION
								7	PLANNING

255

organization discover other experience and training individuals may need to prepare those individuals for upward progression.

Skills Inventories

Skills inventories were discussed in Chapter 6 as a human resource planning tool; they are also useful devices for career planning and development. Where skills inventories are maintained on a current basis, they can be used as a means of internal recruiting, thereby ensuring that current employees are not overlooked when promotional opportunities arise. Analysis of the data maintained in the inventories can also be useful for determining what kinds of training or developmental experiences should be provided specific employees or groups of employees.

Management Inventories

Management inventories were also discussed previously as a human resource planning tool. They, too, are extremely beneficial in career planning and development. In fact, they are essential in developing replacement tables inasmuch as some of the information needed for construction of the table is derived directly from the inventory, Additionally, they serve the same basic career management functions as skills inventories, except at a higher level where development may be extremely crucial to organizational success.

Job Rotation

Job rotation, if it is done on a planned basis, is an excellent means of developing both employees and managers. Through rotation of job assignments, individuals can be given experience in areas or fields where personal knowledge or expertise is lacking; their backgrounds can be broadened so that they gain a better perspective of company operations. For example, an engineer who knows little about marketing may be given an assignment in the marketing department so that he or she can gain insight into how products are sold or how customers use the products and the problems customers may encounter in using them.

For job rotation to be used successfully as a development tool, several principles must be observed. First, each assignment must be planned so that it adds to or fills in gaps in the person's background. Accomplishing this means that the individual's previous education and experience has to be analyzed carefully so that the rotational assignment increases the employee's capabilities in some way. Job rotation that adds little in the way of new skills and experiences is of dubious value. Second, assignments must entail responsibility and the requirement for performance on the job. Rotation that is merely an observational tour, while interesting to the person involved, is not development. Real training and development comes only through a responsibility for performance. Third, each assignment must be of long duration so that the person actually gains an in-depth knowledge of the job and the department. While short assignments may be helpful in understanding what goes on in a particular area, and their use for this purpose should not be precluded, assignments for longer periods of time are required if significant development is to take place.

Coaching

Coaching is an on-the-job development approach in which a supervisor teaches, trains, counsels, and explains how things are done and why they are done that way. It differs from the typical job instruction approach in that it is highly interactive in nature; the supervisor shares his or her experiences with the employee and the employee asks questions and shares viewpoints with the supervisor.

Because effective coaching is time consuming, it is not used with all employees in a work group; it is normally reserved for those who show the greatest potential for career development and advancement.

At the managerial level, coaching is frequently referred to as mentoring. An experienced manager takes a subordinate manager under his or her "wing" and attempts to impart insights and techniques that will make the subordinate a better manager.

Counseling

Closely allied to coaching is counseling. As counseling is used in career planning and development, it differs from coaching in that it is specifically related to career opportunities or discussion of areas in which an employee needs to make improvement efforts. Much of the responsibility for this kind of counseling falls on the first-line supervisor. However, the human resource department should also be involved in the process, especially as it relates to career progression or development.

Training and Development Programs

Another essential career development tool is training and development. Programs offered in this area may be related directly to employees' jobs or they may be oriented to career-related topics. Obviously, job-related programs could cover almost every aspect of a person's duties and responsibilities. Career programs are usually directed to increasing a person's knowledge of self, aptitudes, interests, and so forth. The purpose of job-related programs is to increase present or future work performance; the purpose of career programs is to make the employee more aware of his or her potential so that appropriate career fields within the organization can be pursued.

Performance Appraisal

A performance appraisal system that encourages employees to work toward specific goals, identifies areas of strengths and weaknesses, and accurately measures current performance is important to career development. Feedback from the system may lead to a great deal of self-development or it may require the organization to initiate specific training activities to assist in developing employees.

Ideally, any organization that is truly interested in furthering the careers of its employees would use all of the career planning and development tools available. Use of all the tools would ensure that the organization is fulfilling its role and would ensure that managers and supervisors are prepared to carry out their roles in support of the career management endeavor.

REQUIREMENTS FOR A SUCCESSFUL PROGRAM

Most of the requirements for a successful career planning and development program can be deduced from the material that has already been presented in this chapter. But for the sake of emphasis, the essential ingredients for an effective program will now be delineated specifically.

- *Top management commitment.* No major organizational program can be successful without the full support and commitment of top management. This commitment is more than just allocating resources to implement and operate the program. It entails a belief in the value of human resources and a recognition of the organization's responsibility to itself and its people to take positive steps to help employees reach their full potential.
- *Formulation.* Career planning and development is too important and too complex an activity to be handled on an informal basis. The program must be carefully thought out, policies and procedures developed, responsibilities assigned, and so forth. Needless to say, it must be reduced to writing and communicated to all concerned parties.
- *Promotion from within policy.* Such a policy must be considered one of the cornerstones of effective career planning and development. This policy must be adhered to as assiduously as possible. Failure to follow the policy will cast serious doubts on the organization's interest in the careers of its employees.
- *Job posting and bidding system.* Concommitantly with promotion from within, the organization must have an effectively functioning job posting and bidding

system that clearly gives current employees the right and opportunity to apply for vacancies, promotional or lateral, before efforts are initiated to fill a position from external sources. The right to bid for job openings signifies the organization's interest in the progression of its employees.

- *Training and development programs.* Training and development opportunities of all kinds are requisites for effective career planning and development. Workshops, seminars, skills training sessions, educational assistance, and many similar endeavors are necessary to develop employees to their fullest potential. Such programs are also tangible evidence of the organization's commitment to its human resources.

- *Training of managers and supervisors.* Support for a career planning and development program must not only come from the top of the firm, it must also come from the operating managers and supervisors who coach, counsel and assist employees in their development. All managers must be thoroughly trained to carry out fully and effectively their responsibilities relative to the program.

- *Communication.* Communication of the program must be accomplished through any and all means possible—personnel policy manuals, supervisory handbooks, employee handbooks, bulletin boards, periodic announcements, and so on. Free and open communication is another indication of the company's interest in and commitment to the program.

NOTES

1. Wayne F. Cascio, *Managing Human Resources*, (New York: McGraw-Hill Book Company, 1986), p. 326.

2. R. Wayne Mondy and Robert M. Noe III, *Personnel: The Management of Human Resources*, 3rd ed. (Boston: Allyn and Bacon, 1984), pp. 336–337.

3. Adapted from Linda Gail Christie, *Human Resources: A Hidden Profit Center* (Englewood Cliffs, N.J., Prentice-Hall, 1983), p. 127.

4. Adapted from William F. Glueck, "Career Management of Managerial, Professional, and Technical Personnel," in Elmer H. Burack and James W. Walker, eds., *Manpower Planning and Programming* (Boston: Allyn and Bacon, 1972), pp. 242–243.

5. Based on one of the author's experiences as a manager with this organization.

6. Peter F. Drucker, *Management: Tasks, Responsibilities, Practices* (New York: Harper & Row, 1974), p. 427.

7. Elmer H. Burack and Nicholas J. Mathys, *Career Management in Organizations: A Practical Human Resource Planning Approach* (Lake Forest, Ill., Brace-Park Press, 1979), p. 141.

13

Human Resource Administration

The bulk of the duties of human resource administration begins when an employee is hired and then continues throughout the person's tenure with the organization. Human resource administration encompasses a multitude of activities: issuing payroll checks, processing insurance claims, maintaining time and attendance records, updating employee files, revising compensation rates, and so forth. Every functional area in an organization's personnel system affects, and is in turn affected by, human resource administration. This chapter, however, will deal only with those administrative activities directly related in a major way to the staffing function. These activities are: (1) employee orientation, (2) promotion, (3) transfer, (4) demotion, (5) resignation, (6) layoff, (7) termination, and (8) retirement. While line management has the responsibility for carrying out most of these activities, the personnel department develops the policies, procedures, and guidelines for ensuring that the activities are accomplished in a logical, consistent, equitable, and legally defensible fashion. Personnel also has the responsibility for maintaining adequate records relative to these activities.

EMPLOYEE ORIENTATION

Orientation is the process whereby a new employee is familiarized with the organization, job, and work group. It is both a formal and an informal process. On the formal side, the human resource department may conduct classes that introduce the worker to company history, policies, codes of conduct, health and insurance benefits, and other items of importance; or the new worker's supervisor, following a prescribed format, may introduce the employee to the requirements of the job, departmental operations, and other employees. On the informal side, personnel may conduct no classes, but simply explain on the new worker's first day, in one-on-one fashion, major items of importance and furnish the worker an employee handbook. Or the supervisor may, without adhering to any formalized procedure, explain the job and introduce the worker to others in the work group.

Purposes of Orientation

Whether it is accomplished formally or informally, employee orientation has four purposes: to help the employee adjust to the organization, to provide information about the job and performance expectations, to create a favorable impression of the organization, and to furnish information on policies, rules, employee services, benefits, and similar items. For orientation to be effective, it must accomplish each of these purposes.

Adjustment to the Organization. For many people, the first few days on a new job can be a frightening, tension producing, or anxiety laden experience.[1] There is much to be learned (new procedures, new methods, new requirements); there are new people to be met; there are new customs and traditions to be absorbed. The new employee may well feel at a loss unless the organization makes a deliberate attempt to ease the transition into the new job and surroundings.

The immediate supervisor plays a large role in helping the employee make the initial adjustment to the organization. Explanations concerning the job, introductions to members of the work group, familiarization with the physical surroundings, and information regarding break times, lunch times, and so forth are a few of the basic things a supervisor is expected to do to make the new worker feel more comfortable with the job and organization.

Integration of the new employee into the informal work group is also important. Often, this can be accomplished best by assigning the new person to work with a senior employee who not only trains the new hire, but also introduces him or her to the other workers and generally sees that the person is made to feel part of the total work group.

Of special concern is easing the adjustment of women or minorities to the work group, particularly where the group has been predominantly white males. Without proper introduction to the work group, employee turnover may be higher for members of protected classes than those in the more traditional work group.[2] A supervisor's responsibility in this case is to prepare the work group in advance for the arrival of the protected class employee. The supervisor should reiterate the organization's policy on equal employment and state his or her expectations of behavior from current employees.

Provide Information about the Job and Performance Expectations. A second purpose of orientation is to give the new employee specific information about how the job is to be performed, the quantity of work expected, and levels of quality that must be maintained. It is axiomatic that people cannot be fully productive unless they fully understand what is expected of them. Not knowing what is expected, they may set their own unrealistic performance standards, either too high or too low. Or they may quickly become frustrated with the job and become another number in the organization's turnover statistics. It is clearly the responsibility of the immediate supervisor to ensure that each new employee has a thorough understanding of what is to be done, how it is to be done, why it is to be done, when it is to be done, and where it is to be done. Proper explanation of these matters not only reduces turnover, but also assists the employee to become a productive worker as rapidly as possible.

Create Favorable Impression. A third purpose of orientation is to create a favorable impression of the organization and the job. It is not unusual for a new employee to have doubts about the new organization and the new job. Consequently, the orientation process should attempt to demonstrate that the organization is a good place to work and that each job is important to successful operation of the firm. A word of caution is in order, however. It is very easy, and perhaps too tempting, to go overboard in this area. The impression conveyed to the new worker should be an honest one. If it is not, the employee will all too soon discover the truth for himself or herself and likely become disillusioned.

Provide Information on Rules, Policies, Benefits, and so Forth. The final purpose of orientation is to furnish the worker information concerning a host of items that are important not only to the employee but to the organization as well. Among these are: (1) policies relative to promotion consideration, vacation eligibility, outside employment, ethics, and the like; (2) work rules such as time clock procedures, labor hour reporting, absence reporting, and so forth; (3) employee services such as discounts on merchandise, tuition refund programs, recreational opportunities, child care centers, and so forth; and (4) benefits such as health insurance, life insurance, profit sharing, retirement plans, and other forms of indirect compensation. Some of this information will come from the supervisor, while other parts will come from the human resource department.

It is estimated that between 60 and 80 percent of the current work force in an organization is not only new to the organization but to the job market as well. The new work force with which many companies have to deal includes either late entries or reentries of women, people who were formerly self-employed, recent high school and college graduates, and individuals who have made career changes.[3] Undoubtedly, many of these individuals have anxieties about entering an organization—anxieties that can be alleviated through an effective orientation program.

Figure 13.1
New Employee Induction Checklist

EMPLOYEE _____ EMPLOYMENT DATE _____
JOB TITLE _____ DEPARTMENT _____
PAY GRADE _____ SUPERVISOR _____

I. INFORMATION PROVIDED
    ☐ 1. COMPANY ORGANIZATION
    ☐ 2. BASIC INSURANCE BENEFITS
        ☐ Medical   ☐ Dental   ☐ Life
        ☐ Disability   ☐ Travel
    ☐ 3. OPTIONAL INSURANCE BENEFITS
        ☐ Additional Life Insurance
        ☐ Comprehensive Medical
    ☐ 4. PAYMENTS FOR TIME NOT WORKED
        ☐ Holidays   ☐ Vacations
        ☐ Sick Leave   ☐ Miscellaneous Time Off
    ☐ 5. EMPLOYEE SERVICES
        ☐ Tuition Reimbursement   ☐ Product Discounts
        ☐ Recreational Facilities   ☐ In-House Medical Services
        ☐ Training Programs   ☐ Retirement Program
    ☐ 6. COMPENSATION
        ☐ Salary Range   ☐ Performance Review
        ☐ Pay Periods
    ☐ 7. OTHER
        ☐ Equal Employment Opportunity
        ☐ Promotion Policy
        ☐ Suggestion System

II. MATERIALS PROVIDED
    ☐ 1. Orientation Packet
    ☐ 2. I.D. Card
    ☐ 3. Employee Handbook
    ☐ 4. Labor Agreement
    ☐ 5. Insurance Handbook

The employee has been given the information and materials indicated above.

_____   _____
Human Resource Representative   Date

I have received the information and materials indicated above.

_____   _____
Employee   Date

Stages in Effective Orientation

An effective employee orientation program encompasses four stages. These are described below in the chronological order in which they typically occur.

Personnel Department Overview. For the vast majority of employees, the first day on a new job starts in the human resource department. There are forms to be completed, insurance options to be exercised, beneficiaries to be designated, and other administrative details to be attended to just to get a person on the payroll and enrolled in an organization's programs. At this time, the employee is also given some general information about the company, its policies, procedures, compensation, and benefits. An employee handbook may also be given to the new hire. Some companies use new employee checklists such as the one shown in Figure 13-1 to ensure that personnel representatives cover all basic information with the worker. Additionally, information may be provided about the company's products, services, locations, subsidiaries, and other matters pertaining to the overall organization.

Supervisory Indoctrination. The employee's supervisor is responsible for the second stage of the orientation program. Items covered include an overview of the department, job requirements, safety procedures, break and lunch times, specific work rules, location of restrooms and cafeterias, a tour of the department, and personal introductions to other employees. It is beneficial to use a checklist here, too, so that the supervisor does not neglect to mention any item that may be important. A supervisory orientation checklist is shown in Figure 13-2. Comparing this figure with the previous one reveals that the immediate supervisor must explain a number of job-related details, whereas the human resource department is basically concerned with benefits, services, and company overview. It cannot be emphasized too strongly that the key role in successful orientation is performed by the supervisor.

Formal Orientation. Formal orientation takes place in a classroom and is conducted by a member of the human resource staff. These sessions may be as short as one or two hours or as long as a full day, depending upon the importance attached to orientation. Shorter sessions generally focus on benefits and employee services; longer sessions tend to include company history, products, processes, and even presentations by high ranking departmental representatives. Orientation classes fulfill two general purposes: they provide for in-depth explanation and discussion of matters that new employees may deem important, and they introduce new employees to each other so that the new person's acquaintances are not limited merely to his or her department or sphere of operations.

Figure 13.2
Supervisor's Orientation Checklist

EMPLOYEE _____ EMPLOYMENT DATE _____

JOB TITLE _____ DEPARTMENT _____

PAY GRADE _____ SUPERVISOR _____.

I. GENERAL INFORMATION
  ☐ Departmental Organization
  ☐ Products or Services
  ☐ Relationship To Other Departments
II. EMPLOYEE'S JOB
  ☐ Job Description
  ☐ Relationship To Other Jobs
  ☐ Performance Expectations
III. WORKING CONDITIONS
  ☐ Hours of Work   ☐ Time Cards
  ☐ Employee Entrances   ☐ Lunch Hours
  ☐ Break Periods   ☐ Restroom Locations
  ☐ Cafeteria Location   ☐ Overtime Requirements
IV. WORK RULES
  ☐ Absences   ☐ Tardiness
  ☐ Personal Phone Calls   ☐ Safety Procedures
  ☐ Probationary Period
V. INTRODUCTIONS
  ☐ Co—Workers
  ☐ Trainer
  ☐ Union Representative

_____   _____
      Employee   Supervisor

_____   _____
       Date   Date

Employee orientation classes generally take place after a person has been on the job for a while—at least a few days and sometimes several weeks. Some experience on the job and with the organization affords the new worker time to formulate questions that might not otherwise surface if formal orientation were held the first day. While it is critical that an employee be given adequate information about the company and job on the first day, information overload can occur if too much is given at that time.

Follow-up. For orientation to be completely effective, there must be some form of follow-up and evaluation. During the first few weeks on the job, the immediate supervisor should work very closely with the employee to clarify misunderstandings and see that the employee is properly integrated into the work group. The human resource department also plays a part in follow-up, either by working with the supervisor or by directly contacting the employee.

Training Supervisors for Their Role in Orientation. Of critical importance to any successful orientation program is training for supervisors so that they can carry out their key role. The human resource department can provide the new employee with a great deal of organizational information, but only the supervisor can fulfill the function of integrating the employee into the work group.

In training supervisors, the following points about orientation should be emphasized:

- Orientation is an investment in people since it prepares them for organizational entry.
- Effective orientation reduces employee turnover, thereby saving money for the organization.
- Proper orientation enables employees to become productive more quickly.
- Both positive and negative features of the job should be explained to the employee.
- Orientation is not limited to the employee's first day on the job—nurturing and support may be needed for several weeks.
- The supervisor should explain his likes and dislikes relative to job performance.
- All questions, comments, and concerns on the part of the employee should be considered important and addressed appropriately.
- Introductions to other employees are crucial and should not be handled perfunctorily.
- Details—location of restrooms, lunch periods, time clock procedures, and so forth—should not be overlooked because little things can make a big difference to the new employee and his or her adjustment to the organization.

PROMOTIONS

Promotion, the upward movement of an employee to a position of greater responsibility and compensation, is another crucial human resource administration activity. Promotions have a direct impact on staffing because they are signals to employees that growth and advancement are realities within an organization. Decisions as to promotion criteria and who will be promoted are made by line management, but often with assistance from human resource specialists. In a unionized environment, seniority is normally the ruling criterion; in a nonunionized organization, performance appraisal—or some combination of performance appraisal and seniority— is generally the basis for making such decisions.

One major problem associated with promotions—one that may necessitate counseling with employees or other efforts to retain productive workers—is that not everyone can or will receive a promotion. It has been estimated that once beyond entry level positions, only one out of every seven employees will receive a promotion.[4] Thus, for every elated employee who is promoted, there may be six others for line management and the human resource department to deal with. Promotion decisions can be made more palatable to those who are not promoted by having clear promotion policies and criteria. It is here that personnel can be of invaluable assistance to supervisors and managers who must make promotion decisions.

In the future, promotions may be even harder to obtain than they are to-day. Changes in work force demographics, removal of the mandatory retirement age, organizational downsizing to reduce costs, and international competition that retards the growth of some firms are factors that may substantially restrict the number of higher level positions to which employees can be promoted. Additionally, greater numbers of women and minorities vying for positions denied them in the past will place limitations on promotional opportunities for white males.[5]

Considering the changes that are likely to occur in promotional opportunities, human resource specialists may be well advised to consider two alternatives to traditional promotions. First, place a greater emphasis on learning, growth, and development in the present job through various types of training efforts. Second, develop "dual promotion" ladders that reward creative, technical, or professional personnel with financial rewards similar to those people who advance into management positions. The dual promotion ladder supports the first alternative by allowing individuals to grow in their own fields without having to make a switch into management positions—the typical promotion route for many employees. The individual can advance in his or her own area of expertise and reap the normal rewards of promotion, but continue doing the same type of work. Currently, this concept of dual ladder promotion is being used in high-tech companies to keep engineers and scientists in areas where they are vitally needed, but it is also being increasingly used in other industries such as publishing and banking.[6]

TRANSFERS

A transfer is a lateral movement of an employee from one job to another job of equal responsibility and compensation. Transfers may be initiated by the organization or by the employee. They are neither promotions or demotions, simply shifts in jobs.

Transfers serve several useful purposes. First, they are a means of developing employees by giving them experience in different functional areas. The employee's knowledge of the organization can be broadened or the employee's skills can be sharpened by lateral movement through meaningful job assignments. In essence, transfers may serve training as well as career development purposes.

Second, transfers are often necessitated by reorganizations. As offices and departments are created or eliminated, it may be imperative to transfer employees to fill positions. By the same token, when positions are eliminated, management may find transfers a good way to retain valued employees who might otherwise be terminated.

A third reason for transfers is to satisfy needs or desires of employees. Personal reasons for wanting to transfer are numerous: to reduce commuting time, to learn a new job, to use different skills, and so on. By accommodating the employee's wishes, the organization can hold on to productive workers who might quit if the transfer is not forthcoming.

Another reason for using transfers is to open up promotional opportunities. Productive, but unpromotable employees may retard the upward mobility of lower level workers who are qualified for advancement. In order not to lose these qualified workers, it may be necessary to resort to transfers to create promotion vacancies for them.

Finally, transfers may be utilized to eliminate personality clashes. An employee may not be able to work effectively for a particular supervisor or with other members of a work group. By shifting the person to another position, the problem may be eliminated.

Transfers can serve the best interests of both employee and organization. However, there should be definite policies developed that clearly spell out the conditions under which transfers will be used or granted. Development of these policies is, obviously, one of the functions of human resource administration.

DEMOTIONS

A demotion is the movement of an employee to a job of lesser responsibility or lower level duties. Typically, a reduction in compensation accompanies a demotion. There are basically three conditions that may require the use of demotion as a staffing tool: promotion of an individual beyond his or her level of capabilities, reduction of the organization's work force, or an alternative to discharge.

Promotions are normally made on the basis of performance or seniority in one's current job—neither of which are necessarily valid indicators of how a person will perform in a higher level position. It may turn out that the employee simply cannot perform satisfactorily at a higher level of responsibility. In this case it is not the worker's fault; it is management's fault. To terminate an employee who was productive in his or her previous job would be unjust to the employee and could even result in other employees becoming reluctant to take promotions. Consequently, it is better to move the employee back to the level at which performance was satisfactory.

Work force reduction may also involve demotions. For example, where two similar sections are combined into one to reduce the total number of workers, one supervisory position will be eliminated. Instead of terminating the unneeded supervisor, the organization may elect to demote that person to retain his or her skills and abilities so that if expansion does occur in the future a qualified person is already available for a higher level job.

Where long-tenured employees are involved, demotion may be used successfully as an alternative to termination. An employee may have performed well in a position for a number of years but due to physical or other reasons is no longer capable of performing at the same level. Demotion can be used to deal with this problem.

In a unionized environment, demotion policies and procedures are delineated clearly in the labor-management agreement. In a nonunionized organization, they may or may not be, depending upon the consideration that has gone into formulating comprehensive personnel policies. Demotion, however, is too much of an emotionally charged process to be handled on a case-by-case basis; there should be definitive policies defining its usage.

RESIGNATIONS

Even in the best of organizations, it is inevitable that employees will resign. A certain amount of turnover is beneficial for a company because it provides an opportunity to bring in new people with fresh ideas and approaches, creates promotional opportunities for current workers, rectifies poor selection and placement decisions, and helps prevent organizational stagnation. But too much turnover can be disruptive and expensive for a firm. Unfortunately, no one has yet established how much turnover is good and how much is bad. The Bureau of National Affairs (BNA), however, does publish a quarterly report on job absence and turnover that provides baseline information that organizations can use to compare their turnover rates with other institutions. BNA's report shows turnover by organizational size, industry, and region. While these figures encompass both voluntary and involuntary turnover, the report offers data that a company can use to establish what it considers to be a reasonable resignation rate.

Why Employees Leave

Employees may choose to leave an organization for a variety of reasons. Table 13-1 shows the major causes of resignations and suggests actions that can be taken to deal with each cause of turnover.

While understanding the general causes of resignations is an excellent starting point, an organization should conduct its own analyses to isolate specific causes so that it can initiate specific corrective actions to eliminate excessive resignations.

Analyzing Resignations

Two techniques for determining the reasons behind voluntary resignations are the exit interview and the post-exit questionnaire. Frequently, they are used in combination with each other.

Exit Interview. An exit interview is conducted while the employee is still on the payroll. It is normally the last formal contact the employee has with the organization. The responsibility for conducting the interview usually rests with the human resource department inasmuch as the employee is more likely to respond in a free and open fashion to a personnel specialist than he or she would to an immediate supervisor or other manager. In conducting the interview, the interviewer typically adheres to the following pattern:

- Establishes rapport with the employee.
- Explains the purpose of the interview.
- Assures the employee of confidentiality.
- Solicits attitudes relative to the old job.
- Solicits attitudes relative to the company.
- Explores the employee's reasons for leaving.
- Asks the employee to compare the old job with the new job.
- Asks the employee to suggest any changes he or she would recommend for the job or the organization.
- Concludes the interview on a positive note.[7]

An effective exit interview focuses on job-related factors and probes in depth for the real reasons the employee is leaving the company. While one specific interview may not provide much eye-opening information, a series

Table 13.1
Why Employees Leave and What to Do About It

1. Poor Selection or Mismatching
   o Develop job descriptions and job specifications.
   o Train interviewers.
   o Use appropriate selection tests.
   o Check references carefully.
   o Use employment agencies for screening.

2. Lack or Opportunity for Advancement
   o Use realistic job previews.
   o Develop career progression ladders.
   o Use a job posting and bidding system.
   o Provide training and development opportunities.

3. Poor Supervision
   o Provide interpersonal skills training.
   o Reward supervisors for turnover reduction.
   o Replace ineffective supervisors.

4. Inadequate Compensation
   o Implement a compensation plan.
   o Conduct compensation surveys to assure competitiveness.
   o Review compensation and benefits on a regular basis.
   o Use a performance appraisal system.

5. Insufficient Training
   o Provide thorough orientation.
   o Implement formal training programs.
   o Train supervisors to be trainers and coaches.

6. Monotonous Work
   o Use realistic job previews.
   o Redesign jobs to enrich content.
   o Use a job rotation system.
   o Pay premium compensation.

7. Inadequate Grievance Procedures
   o Implement a formal system for handling complaints.
   o Maintain open communications.
   o Develop an open door policy.
   o Use an ombudsman.

8. Personal Problems
   o Train supervisors to be listeners and counselors.
   o Train supervisors to watch for warning signs.
   o Implement an employee assistance program.

9. Low Work Group Morale
   o Provide interpersonal skills training for supervisors.
   o Train supervisors to be listeners.
   o Train supervisors to watch for warning signs.
   o Conduct attitude surveys on a regular basis.
   o Maintain good physical surroundings.

10. Labor Market Conditions
   o Stay attuned to changes in supply and demand for various skills.
   o Implement a compensation plan.
   o Conduct compensation surveys to assure competitiveness.
   o Review compensation and benefits on a regular basis.

Source: Don Caruth and Frank Rachel, "Why Employees Leave and What to Do About It," unpublished paper, November, 1986.

of interviews conducted over time may reveal patterns that indicate weaknesses in the human resource management system or the organization's methods of operating. On the basis of this kind of information, appropriate corrective actions can be taken.

Post-exit Questionnaire. The second method for uncovering causes of resignations is the post-exit questionnaire. When this approach is used, former employees are sent a questionnaire to complete and mail back to the company. The instrument is usually sent two or three weeks after the employee has terminated. The advantage of this method is that, since the person is no longer with the organization, he or she may respond more candidly, thereby revealing the real reasons for leaving. When a questionnaire is used, it should be carefully constructed so that it provides sufficient information and is designed so that it can be completed fairly quickly. Ample blank space should also be included to allow the former employee to express his or her feelings about the job, supervisor, or company.

To obtain the most complete information possible, the interview and the questionnaire should be used in conjunction with each other.

Resignation Policies

Two policy areas that merit attention are advance notification of intent to resign and whether the terminating employee will be allowed to remain on the job until the resignation is effective. Organizational practices in these areas vary considerably.

Normally, organizations request that employees give two weeks notice when resigning. It is not unusual to find firms that request a month's notice from professional or managerial employees. Advance notice gives the organization time to seek a replacement. When advance notice is requested, the organization typically pays the individual for the stipulated period even if it does not allow the person to remain on the job. Of course, the employee is always free to quit without any notification whatsoever, in which case the company is not obligated to compensate the employee further.

Should the departing employee be allowed to remain on the job for the length of the notification period? There are two sides to this question. On the one hand, the employee may be needed to perform important work or to help train a replacement. On the other hand, a resigned worker can create problems by becoming non-productive; or the worker, if resentful of the company or the supervisor, can be a disruptive force that causes morale problems among other employees. As a general policy, it is preferable to keep the worker in the job, but exceptions will have to be made if problems arise.[8]

LAYOFFS

A layoff is a temporary or indefinite termination of an employee because of economic reasons. Although being laid off is not the same as being fired because the worker does have the hope of being recalled at some future time, the short-term effect is the same: the worker is unemployed.

In a sense, a layoff can be more devastating to an individual than a termination. When a person is terminated, the relationship with the organization is permanently severed and the former employee is completely free to seek other employment. In the case of a layoff, the individual still has ties to the company, Moreover, the person may find job search opportunities hampered because other organizations are unwilling to hire someone who may leave shortly to return to his or her former job.

In a labor-management agreement layoff and recall procedures are clearly spelled out. Employees are laid off in inverse order of seniority and recalled on the basis of seniority. Typical contract procedures provide for "bumping rights" or job regression; that is, when a senior level position is eliminated, the person occupying the position has the right to bump an employee with less seniority from a lower level position. The worker who is bumped may, in turn, bump another worker. Thus, in a unionized company, a layoff may drastically alter the composite of the work force.

In a nonunion environment, layoff policies and procedures are more likely to be ill defined, with factors other than seniority deciding the question of which workers go and which workers stay. Productivity or performance may be the biggest consideration. To avoid charges of favoritism or discrimination, union-free organizations should establish definitive policies and procedures regarding layoffs—the need is no less pressing here than it is in a unionized situation.

An emerging trend is a "no layoff" policy.[9] Some companies have had such a policy for many years, but so far these organizations have been the exception rather than the rule.[10] Spurred by the success of Japanese companies in providing what is tantamount to life-time employment, we can expect to see more and more companies in this country adopting such a policy.

TERMINATIONS

Termination, the permanent severing of the relationship between organization and employee, is the most severe penalty a company can impose on an individual. It is usually a drastic step for the organization and a traumatic experience for the employee. The employee is likely to feel angry, hurt, depressed, shocked, or fearful of the future. The supervisor or manager making the termination is apt to be tense or anxious as well.

While there are a number of similarities in the termination of employees at any level in the organization, there are also distinct differences that exist between the firing of operative level employees, executives, and managers and professionals.

Termination of Operative Employees

Generally, the policies and procedures for terminating operative employees are well defined and outlined in personnel policy manuals or employee handbooks. Most organizations are careful to delineate the types of offenses or behavior that will result in immediate discharge of an employee. These may include items such as the following:

- Theft of company or another employee's property.
- Appropriation or misappropriation of company funds.
- Possession, use, or being under the influence of alcohol or drugs on the organization's premises.
- Deliberate falsification of personnel records such as employment applications or time cards.
- Willful abuse or deliberate damage of company property.
- Immoral conduct or indecency.
- Insubordination or willful failure to perform assigned tasks.
- Fighting on company premises.
- Absence without notice or approval for three consecutive working days.
- Revealing proprietary information to a competitor.

Repeated violations of other work rules may also constitute grounds for immediate termination; for example, sleeping on the job, soliciting political contributions, or leaving the premises without permission during working hours.

Termination of Executives

Discharging an executive is quite different from terminating an employee. In most instances, there are no identified policies, procedures, or grounds for termination, nor is there an appeal mechanism the executive can use. The primary reasons for firing an executive are:

- Lack of "fit"—the executive has a personality conflict with another executive, is not considered a "team player," or has philosophical differences with other officials relative to operation of the company.

- Reorganization—mergers, acquisitions, or realignments may result in elimination of the position.
- Economics—adverse business conditions may force the elimination of a high level job.
- Decline in performance—inability to produce the results desired by the organization, inability to generate new business, failure to meet deadlines, and the like may necessitate the removal of an individual.

Of all of the above cited reasons for executive terminations, the major one is usually "lack of fit."[11] At the operative level, people are terminated because of poor performance or job elimination, whereas at the executive level personality, politics, and other personal factors are the predominant causes of discharge.

Increasingly, contemporary organizations are taking a socially responsible attitude concerning executives—and other personnel, for that matter—who are terminated by assisting them in finding further employment. This effort, known as outplacement, will be discussed in a subsequent section.

Termination of Managers and Professionals

Perhaps the most vulnerable group of organizational employees subject to termination are lower level managers and professionals. These individuals may be discharged for any number of reasons—the ones that apply to operative level employees or the ones that apply to executives. They lack the political clout that executives have; they are not protected by labor agreements; the reasons for their terminations are not clearly defined; and they often are not inclined to seek protection under anti-discriminatory statutes. Undoubtedly, individuals in this group are the organizational members most likely to be fired on the basis of whim or caprice.[12] It would appear that definitive policies are needed for the termination of managers and professionals.

General Guidelines for Termination

There is no question that terminating an employee, regardless of the individual's level in the organization, is a necessity at times—a necessity that is in the best interests of the organization as well as the employee. The basic problem is how to go about it in a manner that preserves the dignity of the person and the reputation of the organization. The starting point is the development of policies concerning termination—policies that state the organization's position concerning termination. Next is the establishment of procedures on how the actual termination will be handled. The most difficult part of terminating anyone is the face-to-face meeting in which the person is informed that his or her services are no longer required by the organization. Here are some guidelines for handling a termination:

1. Do not terminate an employee on Friday afternoon (the most typical termination time) because the individual cannot initiate efforts to secure new employment over the weekend and may even resort to forms of non-productive behavior—excessive consumption of alcohol, for example—to relieve his or her frustrations. The individual's family may also have to suffer through a weekend of anxiety, dread, and tension.

2. Do terminate early in the week, preferably on a Monday or Tuesday, and early in the morning. This gives the individual the opportunity to begin a job search immediately.

3. Always terminate an employee in the superior's office, not at the person's work station or at a neutral site. This practice ensures more privacy in handling a delicate matter.

4. Once the interview begins, terminate the employee quickly—in the first five minutes or so—and leave the remainder of the time for the employee to talk.

5. Do not become emotional; be businesslike and to the point.

6. Explain the termination decision, but don't attempt to justify it or defend it since such action is likely to result in argumentation.

7. Be prepared and organized; know in advance what you are going to say.

8. Keep the interview short—thirty minutes should be the maximum time allotted.

9. If assistance is to be provided for securing further employment, outline what the organization is prepared to offer.[13]

As these guidelines suggest, termination should be planned in advance, given thoughtful consideration, and concluded as quickly as possible. In addition to what is recommended above, the terminated employee should be escorted from the premises as soon as the meeting is over to avoid any problems that might be caused by the discharged worker talking with other workers.

Outplacement Services

When terminations occur because of management decisions and not because of violations of work rules (theft, drunk on the job), many organizations assist the terminated employee, especially at the executive or managerial level, in the search for new employment. Outplacement, the term used to describe such assistance, is a systematic process designed to help the discharged employee find suitable employment with another organization within a reasonable length of time and with a minimum of psychological trauma.[14] This process normally utilizes an outside consultant who counsels the former employee, assists in determining job interests, helps prepare resumés, offers training in how to be interviewed, assists in identifying potential employers, and is available to assist the individual in other ways.[15]

Outplacement services are provided on an individual basis to executives and managers and on a group basis to operative level employees. Outplacement services tend to take some of the sting out of termination, while creating a favorable reputation for the company. The benefit for the individual is that professional assistance and support is available to reduce the trauma of termination and aid in locating a new job. The benefit for the organization is that it is acting in a socially responsible manner that enhances its image as an employer.

Employment at Will

Under common law the courts have traditionally held that an employer could discharge an employee for any one of three reasons: good cause, bad cause, or no cause. This, in essence, is the concept of employment at will. The U.S. legal system has long held that the employment relationship is a tenuous one subject to severance at any time by either party with or without reason.[16] Consequently, employment has been viewed as an agreement rather than a contract; the employee agrees to work for an employer for a stipulated amount of compensation, but neither party makes a commitment as to how long the agreement is expected to remain in force.

With the exception of South Dakota, the employment at will concept is still the standard interpretation of the employment relationship in this country.[17] However, there is an emerging trend that is redefining what is meant by employment at will. In almost thirty states judicial interpretation or legislative intervention has affected the application of the employment at will concept.[18] So far, four exceptions to the rule have been identified. These involve terminations that are contrary to public policy, abusive discharge, the implied guarantee of employment unless there is just cause for discharge, and the theory that there is an implied covenant of good faith and fair dealing contained in the employment relationship.[19] Additionally, of course, if a discriminatory motive is involved in discharge, exceptions to employment at will can be made under federal statutes.

Public Policy. In many instances, state courts have ruled that when an employee is discharged under conditions that are contrary to established public policy, the concept of employment at will does not apply. The most frequent application of this exception has been in cases where an employee has been terminated for filing a worker's compensation claim.[20] The exception has also been applied where so-called whistle-blowing has been involved; that is, reporting violations of state or federal statutes by the organization or by fellow employees.

The public policy exception is generally interpreted very narrowly and is applied only where the discharged worker can establish that his or her termination was contrary to some well-established public policy and that no other remedy is available to protect either the individual involved or society.[21]

Abusive Discharge. Retaliatory discharges have also been the basis for exceptions to employment at will. If, for example, an employee is terminated for refusing to do personal favors for a supervisor that are outside the scope of normal job duties, the courts may rule that wrongful discharge has occurred.[22] Today, abusive discharge would probably be covered more effectively under federal discrimination laws than under state laws.

Implied Guarantee of Employment. While heretofore the employment relationship has been viewed as an agreement, the courts are increasingly interpreting it as a form of contract that requires just cause for termination. In some cases, statements made by the hiring manager or contained in company personnel policies have been cited as evidence that discharge can occur only for just cause and not at the whim or caprice of the employer. Essentially, either oral or written statements to the effect that the employee has a job as long as he or she performs satisfactorily have been viewed as implying a continuation of employment that can only be broken for good cause.[23]

Good Faith and Fair Dealing. In the employment relationship, it is assumed that each party will deal fairly and in good faith with the other. Where organizations have acted conversely, state courts have held that an exception to employment at will has occurred. In *Fortune* v. *National Cash Register Co.*, the firm allegedly terminated a salesman in order to deny him bonuses and other benefits that were due him. A Massachusetts court ruled that the company had acted in bad faith and solely for its own benefit in discharging the employee.[24] Consequently, an exception to the employment at will concept was allowed.

Federal Statutes. As illustrated in earlier chapters, there are numerous statutes that protect employees from termination on various kinds of discriminatory bases. Thus, federal law provides a firm, identifiable foundation for exceptions to the employment at will doctrine if protected classes are involved.

In summary, employment at will has long been considered legally acceptable. This is no longer the case. It is not an inviolable concept in today's employment environment. To withstand legal challenges, organizations must develop policies that specifically state their position on job security or permanent employment. If the organization chooses to follow an employment at will policy, it must clearly identify its intentions and avoid any implications suggesting job security or permanent employment. A statement to this effect on the application form is a starting point. Training of those involved in the hiring process is another step.

RETIREMENT

Since employee turnover rates decrease as length of service with the organization increases,[25] the majority of long-term employees will leave a company through retirement. Although under the 1986 amendments to the Age Discrimination in Employment Act most employees cannot be forced to retire at any age, organizations usually stipulate that an employee may elect to retire at a certain age or after a certain number of years with the company, or at some combination of age and years of service. Upon retirement, former employees, provided the firm has a pension or retirement system, receive a pension each month for the remainder of their lives.

It is too early to speculate what impact removal of the mandatory retirement age will have on organizations and the composition of their work forces. Certainly it will have an effect. Conceivably it could clog promotion channels, making it more difficult for younger workers to advance; or, it could increase insurance costs. This issue is one that staffing specialists should watch very closely because it may affect the manner in which traditional staffing activities are conducted.

Two other issues that must be addressed in the retirement area are early retirement and retirement planning.

Early Retirement

A policy that permits workers to retire before reaching the customary age or length of service requirements serves five purposes. First, early retirement can be used as an alternative to an extended layoff. When a product line is discontinued, a plant is closed, or economic conditions take a downturn, an organization may, of necessity, have to lay off employees for an indefinite period of time. Allowing eligible workers to retire early benefits both employees and the organization. The employee is ensured some continuity of income, although at a reduced rate, and the organization enhances its reputation as a socially responsible institution that cares about its workers—a positive image that may affect future staffing efforts in a positive manner.

Second, early retirement may be used to cut an organization's operating expenses. Firms with many long-tenured employees may find that their compensation costs are higher than other companies in the same line of business, thereby placing the firm at a competitive disadvantage in pricing its goods or services or eroding profit margins if competitive pricing is maintained. A solution to this problem is often one of encouraging early retirement so that the cost structure can be adjusted.

Third, early retirement is an alternative to termination. When a long-term employee's peformance falls below an acceptable level, an organization may find itself in a dilemma. Termination of the individual may result in discrimination charges, seriously affect work group morale, or tarnish the company's reputation in the human resource area. Rather than discharge such an individual, the person may be encouraged to retire early.

Fourth, too many long-service employees in an organization may seriously hamper promotional opportunities for highly qualified employees—a blockage that can be alleviated through an early retirement option.

Finally, early retirement benefits the employee by providing him or her with a means of making a career change without having to undergo severe financial strain. Second careers are becoming more common and popular—a trend that early retirement has certainly contributed to and one that human resource planning must take into consideration.

Retirement Planning

Although a worker may have happily looked forward to retirement for many years, the actual experience of retiring may be an emotion-laden one. Leaving one's career, friends, and familiar organizational environment behind can be a frightening experience. Questions concerning money, how time will be spent, and whether the adjustment to retired life can be made successfully may be of concern to the employee as the retirement date approaches. Just as a well-planned and executed orientation program eases the transition of a new hire into the organization, organizations are finding that company-sponsored retirement planning programs help ease the transition of the employee from work to leisure.[26]

Retirement planning programs provide information on finances, housing, relocation, family relations, adjustment to a nonorganizational setting, legal affairs, and similar matters.[27] In large organizations where groups of employees may be retiring at essentially the same time, formal classroom sessions may be conducted. In small organizations, retirement planning is more likely to be a one-on-one situation handled by a member of the personnel department.

Retirement is a major event in a person's life. Organizations can help the individual make the transition more smoothly by offering the assistance needed to make the change.

NOTES

1. One of the authors vividly recalls, even some twenty-odd years later, his first

day on the job with a Fortune 500 company. The normal tension and anxiety were further heightened by the fact that no one explained where the restrooms (situated in a nonconspicious location) were.

2. R. Wayne Mondy and Robert M. Noe III, *Personnel: The Management of Human Resources*, 3rd ed. (Boston: Allyn and Bacon, 1987).

3. Mark S. Tauber, "New Employee Orientation: A Comprehensive Systems Approach," *Personnel Administrator*, January 1985, p. 65.

4. Peter F. Drucker, film series, *The Manager and the Organization: How to Make the Organization Work for You* (Washington, D.C.: BNA Communications, 1977).

5. Mondy and Noe, *Personnel*, p. 652.

6. Susan Dillingham, "Rewarding Expertise," *Insight*, January 19, 1987, p. 49.

7. Adapted from Wanda R. Embrey, R. Wayne Mondy, and Robert M. Noe, "Exit Interview: A Tool for Personnel Development," *Personnel Administrator*, May 1979, p. 46.

8. Mondy and Noe, *Personnel*, p. 649.

9. John Naisbitt, *Megatrends* (New York: Warner Books, 1984), p. 100.

10. Dale S. Beach, *Personnel: The Management of People at Work*, 5th ed. (New York: Macmillan Publishing Company, 1985), pp. 585–586.

11. William J. Morin, *Successful Termination* (New York: Drake Beam Morin, 1981), p. 2.

12. Mondy and Noe, *Personnel*, p. 645.

13. Adapted from Morin, *Successful Termination*, pp. 7–27.

14. Morin, *Successful Termination*, p. iv.

15. William J. Morin, "Outplacement Counseling: What Is It?" *The Personnel and Guidance Journal*, May 1977, p. 555.

16. Lawrence Z. Lorber, J. Robert Kirk, Kenneth H. Kirschner, and Charlene R. Handorf, *Fear of Firing: A Legal and Personnel Analysis of Employment at Will* (Alexandria, Va.: ASPA Foundation, 1984), p. 1.

17. Mondy and Noe, *Personnel*, p. 646.

18. David P. Twomey, *A Concise Guide to Employment Law* (Cincinnati: South-Western Publishing Co., 1986), p. 97.

19. Ibid., pp. 96–97.

20. Ibid., p. 99.

21. Ibid.

22. *Monge* v. *Beebe Rubber Co.*, 114 N.H. 130, 316A. 2d 549, 1974.

23. Twomey, *A Concise Guide*, p. 99.

24. *Fortune* v. *National Cash Register Co.*, 373 Mass. 96, 364 NE 2d 1251, 1977.

25. Guvenc G. Alpander, *Human Resources Management Planning* (New York: AMACOM, 1982), p. 115.

26. Mondy and Noe, *Personnel*, p. 653.

27. Marilyn Merikangas, "Retirement Planning with a Difference," *Personnel Journal*, May 1983, p. 420.

14

Evaluating the Staffing Function

The success of any organization depends not only on the formulation and execution of well-thought-out plans, but also on the continuous evaluation of progress toward accomplishment of specified goals and objectives. For an organization as a whole, evaluation may be performed in terms of profitability ratios, sales increases, market penetration, and a host of other factors. For individual functional units within the organization, such as the human resource department, evaluation may be more difficult because of the absence of absolute measures that indicate whether the unit is fulfilling its mission. Yet the need for evaluation is just as important in these areas as it is in other areas.

How should an organization go about evaluating its staffing function? Are there particular measures or indicators that reveal how well this function is carrying out its responsibilities and supporting the overall organization's efforts to reach planned objectives? These are the two questions this chapter will attempt to answer.

There are two basic methods that may be used to evaluate how well staffing activities are accomplished in a company: checklists and quantitative measures. The checklist approach poses a number of questions that can be answered either "yes" or "no." This method is concerned with whether important activities have been recognized and, if so, whether they are being performed. Essentially, the checklist is an evaluation in terms of what should be done and the extent to which it is being done. The more "yes" answers the better the evaluation; "no" answers indicate areas or activities where follow-up or additional work is needed to increase the effectiveness of staffing. The checklists presented below should be viewed as representative, not inclusive. Organizations deciding to use this evaluation approach will, undoubtedly, discover many questions of their own that can be added. The checklist method is purely an internal evaluation device; it is not a vehicle for comparing the company with other companies, rather, it is strictly a means of internal analysis.

The second method for evaluating the performance of staffing activities is a quantitative one that relies on the use of various numerical data that can be accumulated and ratios that can be computed from this data. Numerical data is mainly useful as an indicator of activity levels. From these numbers important trends can be identified. Ratios show the results of activities or volumes—numbers that in themselves are important, but also reveal, when maintained over a period of time, trends that may be extremely critical. In some instances, quantitative measures may be used for external comparisons with other organizations; however, since very few standards of performance exist for the human resource function, external comparisons should always be interpreted in light of the organization's own situation. For example, the one area in which the greatest amount of external comparative data is probably available is employee turnover. While it may be tempting to evaluate a specific organization's turnover in terms of industry average or size of work force, such a comparison may be meaningless because of the variables that affect a specific organization's turnover such as the nature of the local labor market, the number of long-tenured employees on the staff, the ability of the firm to pay competitive rates of compensation, the reputation the company has gained as an employer, and so forth. On the other hand, there is one measure that can truly be considered a standard one: the four-fifths or 80-20 rule that measures the selection rate of protected class employees against other employees. Generally, as discussed in an earlier chapter, this ratio should approximate 80 percent; but even so, there are exceptions to this standard based on the specific situation with which an organization is faced. In short, while quantitative data may be useful for external comparisons with other similar companies, it is probably most helpful in establishing internal baselines that show direction of movement from those baselines.

It is not the intent of the authors to promulgate or even suggest performance standards for the staffing function. Our purpose is, simply, to enumerate various criteria that may be useful in determining how well staffing is performed in an organization. The qualitative and quantitative factors outlined below should be viewed in light of the organization's specific goals and situation. Some of the evaluation criteria will be pertinent to all organizations; other criteria will not. Each company must make its own determination as to what is relevant; each company must make its own determination as to what answers to the checklists actually mean; each company must decide for itself what the quantitative data and ratios really indicate.

In the following sections both checklists and quantitative measures for each of the various staffing activities described in this book, as well as the legal compliance area, will be presented. A total of 153 questions and 70 statistical items are suggested for use. The suggestions offered should encourage human resource practitioners to undertake a needed, but often neglected task: the evaluation of staffing activities.

LEGAL COMPLIANCE

The risks associated with compliance to various federal (as well as state) statutes dealing with employment practically dictate that this area be the first one evaluated for effectiveness. Deficiencies that show up in the evaluation should be addressed immediately.

Checklist

The following questions indicate the areas and activities to be addressed in evaluating the legal compliance portion of the staffing function.

1. Have all managers and supervisors been informed of their responsibilities under federal and state equal employment opportunity and anti-discriminatory statutes?
2. Are all legally mandated reports submitted to requiring agencies on time?
3. Are all jobs properly classified as to exempt and non-exempt status?
4. Are data necessary for filing EEO-1 reports, if required, maintained on a current basis?
5. Is an applicant flow analysis conducted on a periodic basis?
6. Where required, does the organization have a current affirmative action plan?
7. Is progress toward accomplishing affirmative action goals evaluated on a regular basis?
8. Does recruitment advertising conform to applicable legal and affirmative action standards?
9. Is a four-fifths rule analysis performed on a regular basis?
10. Is the organization's policy concerning equal employment opportunity posted in conspicuous places?
11. Are adequate safeguards taken to ensure non-discrimination against protected classes?
12. Is executive level management committed to and fully supportive of equal employment opportunity?
13. Has a policy on sexual harassment been developed?
14. Have managers and supervisors received training concerning their responsibilities relative to enforcing the sexual harassment policy?
15. Have policies and procedures been developed to ensure reasonable accommodation of the religious practices of employees?

16. Has information on the organization's affirmative action program been disseminated to all appropriate parties?
17. Is a utilization analysis of minorities and females conducted on a regular basis?
18. Have the causes of underutilization of minorities and females been identified?
19. Have appropriate corrective actions been taken to remedy any underutilization problems?
20. Have all selection tests and procedures been validated as required by the *Uniform Guidelines*?

Quantitative Measures

Compliance with federal statutes and regulations necessitates the accumulation of various kinds of data; consequently, organizations may have a good deal of quantitative information already available for evaluating this area of staffing. Some of the data that are useful in evaluation would include the following:

1. Total number of applicants
2. Number of applicants classified by protected group status
3. Total number of employees hired
4. Number of employees hired classified by protected group status
5. Total number of employees promoted
6. Number of employees promoted classified by protected group status
7. Total number of employees terminated
8. Number of employees terminated classified by protected group status
9. Number of discrimination charges filed
10. Number of wage and hour complaints filed

The preceding kinds of data provide an organization with the raw material it needs to analyze trends and perform other analyses in the compliance area.

The following ratios provide additional means of evaluation:

$$1. \quad \frac{\text{Protected Group Selection Rate}}{\text{Best Achieving Group Selection Rate}} = \text{Protected Group Selection Ratio}$$

$$2. \quad \frac{\text{Protected Group Promotion Rate}}{\text{Best Achieving Group Promotion Rate}} = \text{Protected Group Promotion Ratio}$$

$$3. \quad \frac{\text{Protected Group Termination Rate}}{\text{Majority Group Termination Rate}} = \text{Protected Group Termination Ratio}$$

4. $\dfrac{\text{Number of Minorities and Women Hired}}{\text{Total Number of Employees Hired}} \times 100 = $ Minority and Female Hiring Percentage

5. $\dfrac{\text{Number of Minority and Female Employees}}{\text{Total Number of Employees}} \times 100 = $ Minority and Female Work Force Percentage

JOB ANALYSIS

The criticality of job analysis has been emphasized numerous times throughout this book. As the cornerstone on which many other human resource activities depend, it is important that the effectiveness of this process be carefully evaluated.

Checklist

Here are some questions that may be used to assess the effectiveness of job analysis.

1. Have formalized procedures and methods been developed for conducting a job analysis?
2. Is the most appropriate method or combination of methods being used to conduct job analyses?
3. Have all jobs in the organization been analyzed?
4. Are standardized job titles from the *Dictionary of Occupational Titles* used to identify all jobs?
5. Have job descriptions been prepared for every job in the organization?
6. Are all job descriptions current?
7. Have job specifications been prepared for every job in the organization?
8. Are all job specifications current?
9. Do all job specifications reflect minimum rather than ideal human qualifications necessary for satisfactory job performance?
10. Do all employees have a copy of their job description?
11. Are all job descriptions reviewed at least annually to determine if they are accurate and up to date?
12. Are all job specifications reviewed at least annually to determine if they are accurate and up to date?
13. Have procedures been developed whereby managers and supervisors can request re-analysis of a job when changes occur in that job?
14. Are job descriptions and specifications written in a readable, easy-to-use format?
15. Is the job analysis process effectively integrated with other human resource management processes?

Quantitative Measures

Suggested quantitative evaluations of job analysis include:

1. Total Number of Jobs Analyzed
2. Number of New Jobs Created
3. Number of Job Analysis Requests from Managers and Supervisors

4. $\dfrac{\text{Number of New Jobs Analyzed}}{\text{Number of New Jobs Created}} \times 100 =$ Percentage of New Jobs Analyzed

5. $\dfrac{\text{Number of Job Analysis Requests Completed}}{\text{Number of Requests for Job Analysis}} \times 100 =$ Percentage of Job Analysis Requests Completed

HUMAN RESOURCE PLANNING

Perhaps one of the most difficult areas of staffing to evaluate is human resource planning. Even though planners customarily deal with statistical data in forecasting requirements and availability, a great amount of subjectivity is also involved. Moreover, the best laid plans may be negated by unanticipated changes in the economy, technology, or other outside forces. Yet, despite the difficulties, this area needs to be evaluated as much as, or even more so, than the other staffing processes.

Checklist

There are some essential questions that must be asked about human resource planning. Among these are:

1. Is human resource planning interactively involved with the strategic business planning process?
2. Are human resource requirements forecasts made at least annually?
3. Are appropriate quantitative and subjective techniques used in conjunction with each other to forecast human resource requirements?
4. Do operating managers participate in the development of requirements forecasts?
5. Are requirements forecasts used to develop a pro forma organization structure?
6. Are requirements forecasts used to develop staffing tables that reflect human resource needs at various levels of organizational activity?
7. Are human resource availability forecasts made at least annually?
8. Are skills inventories maintained on all employees?

9. Are management inventories maintained on all managerial personnel?

10. Are skills and management inventories updated at least annually?

11. Are skills and management inventories used in the human resource planning process to assist in determining the internal availability of personnel?

12. Are sufficient demographic, economic, and other data maintained in current fashion for forecasting the availability of personnel from external sources?

13. Does the organization have standing plans, policies, and procedures for dealing with anticipated shortages or surpluses of personnel?

Quantitative Measures

The effectiveness of human resource planning, from a quantitative viewpoint, can best be judged by the accuracy of the requirements and availability forecasts made. The closer the forecasts approximate reality, the more effective the planning process is. Two key measures seem to suggest themselves.

1. Requirements forecast compared to actual personnel needs

2. Availability forecast compared to actual availability of personnel

RECRUITING

Recruiting is generally the most publicly visible of all staffing activities. By its very nature it is concerned with making known the availability of positions to many individuals and agencies. Recruiting, in a sense, is much like advertising and public relations in that it creates both an image and awareness of the organization in the external environment. Obviously, the high visibility of this function warrants a careful evaluation of its effectiveness.

Checklist

In evaluating recruiting it is necessary to examine its internal as well as external effectiveness. The following questions may be helpful.

1. Does the organization have policies and procedures governing the use of alternatives to recruiting?

2. Is the recruiting process effectively integrated with human resource planning?

3. Does the organization have a promotion from within policy?

4. Does the organization typically adhere to the promotion from within policy before looking to external sources to fill vacancies?

5. Is a job posting and bidding system used to fill vacancies from internal sources?

6. Have all recruiters been thoroughly trained?

7. Have the most likely external sources from which candidates may be recruited been properly identified?

8. Have each of the most likely external sources of candidates been evaluated to determine their effectiveness in furnishing qualified candidates?

9. Is there a formal procedure whereby managers and supervisors may request authorization to hire an employee?

10. Have appropriate recruiting methods been identified and analyzed?

11. Have each of the various recruiting methods been evaluated to determine their effectiveness in generating sufficient quantities of qualified candidates?

12. Are recruiting methods effectively matched to sources of qualified candidates?

13. Have sources of minority and female candidates been properly identified?

14. Have sources of minority and female candidates been evaluated to determine their effectiveness in furnishing qualified candidates?

15. Are special methods used to reach minority and female applicants?

16. Does the recruiting program utilize affirmative action to attract minority and female applicants?

17. Are minorities and females used as recruiters?

18. Does recruitment advertising conform to applicable legal and affirmative action standards?

19. Is recruitment advertising done in a fashion that creates a favorable image for the organization?

20. Are different advertising media used in conjunction with each other?

Quantitative Measures

Because many organizations are required to maintain data on applicant flow, statistical information may already be available to assist in evaluating recruiting effectiveness. Additionally, segregation of recruiting costs can also provide relevant analysis data. Items that may be used for evaluation purposes include:

1. Total Number of Job Applicants

2. Number of Applicants Classified by Protected Group Status

3. Employment Advertising Expenses

4. Employment Agency Fees

5. Executive Search Firm Fees

6. Number of Applicants Generated by Source

7. Number of Applicants Classified by Protected Group Status Generated by Source

8. Total Recruiting Function Costs

9. $\dfrac{\text{Total Recruiting Costs}}{\text{Number of Applicants}} = \text{Average Recruiting Cost per Applicant}$

10. $\dfrac{\text{Total Recruiting Costs}}{\text{Number of Employees Hired}} = \text{Average Recruiting Cost per Employee Hired}$

11. $\dfrac{\text{Employment Agency Fees}}{\substack{\text{Number of Employees Hired} \\ \text{from Agencies}}} = \substack{\text{Average Cost per Employee Hired} \\ \text{from Agencies}}$

12. $\dfrac{\text{Number of Applicants Hired by Source}}{\text{Number of Applicants Generated by Source}} \times 100 = \substack{\text{Recruiting Source} \\ \text{Hiring Percentage}}$

SELECTING

One of the most sensitive areas of staffing is selection. It is here that an organization most frequently opens itself to charges of discrimination. In fact, the majority of the court cases examined in Chapter 3 center on charges of discrimination that occurred during the selection process. Consequently, this area of staffing should be subjected to rigorous evaluation concerning not only its effectiveness but also its adherence to statutory and regulatory requirements.

Checklist

A great many questions can be asked about selection, beginning with the employment application and proceeding all the way through the organization's ability to retain the employees it hires. Here are a few of the questions that could be posed.

1. Does the application form conform to applicable legal and affirmative action standards?

2. Has the feasibility of using a weighted application blank been investigated?

3. Does the employment application contain an employment at will clause?

4. Are references systematically checked before an employment offer is extended?

5. Where appropriate, are physical examinations of potential new hires required before an employment offer is extended?

6. Have policies and procedures for conducting employment interviews been developed?

7. Have all managers and supervisors received training in interviewing?

8. Do all managers and supervisors understand the legal ramifications of employment interviewing?

9. Do all managers and supervisors understand the types of questions that can, cannot, or should not be asked in an employment interview?

10. Is an applicant evaluation form used in the interviewing process?

11. Are realistic job previews given during the employment interview?

12. Are job descriptions and specifications used during interviewing to assist in determining an applicant's qualifications?

13. Are rejected candidates notified promptly of the organization's decision not to extend an employment offer?

14. Are candidates who are rejected for one job encouraged to apply for other organizational jobs for which they may be qualified?

15. Are selection ratios calculated on a regular basis?

16. When necessary, is selection ratio information used to evaluate and revise selection criteria?

17. Are all selection criteria used realistic and job related?

18. Are all selection criteria reviewed on a regular basis to ensure that they are non-discriminatory?

19. Are appropriate selection tests used to evaluate candidates?

20. Where tests are used, are the results utilized as one of several selection criteria and not as the sole basis for selection?

21. Have all employment tests used been validated in accordance with the requirements of the *Uniform Guidelines*?

22. For all employment tests used, have reasonable cut-off scores been established?

23. Is a four-fifths rule analysis performed on a regular basis to determine how protected classes succeed in the selection process?

24. Are turnover statistics used to evaluate or revise selection criteria?

Quantitative Measures

As in recruiting, the necessity of maintaining statistical records for EEO, OFCCP, or other reporting purposes means that quantitative data may be readily available for analyzing and evaluating selection activities. Potential evaluative data would encompass such items as:

1. Total Number of Employees Hired

2. Number of Employees Hired Classified as to Protected Group Status

3. Number of Positions Filled Internally

4. Number of Positions Filled Externally

5. Number of Employment Offers Extended
6. Number of Employment Offers Accepted
7. Total Testing Costs

8. $\dfrac{\text{Protected Group Selection Rate}}{\substack{\text{Best Achieving Group Selection} \\ \text{Rate}}}$ = Protected Group Selection Ratio

9. $\dfrac{\text{Number of Employees Hired}}{\text{Number of Applicants}}$ = Selection Ratio

10. $\dfrac{\text{Number of Positions Filled Internally}}{\text{Number of Positions Filled}} \times 100 =$ Percentage of Positions Filled Internally

11. $\dfrac{\text{Number of Positions Filled Externally}}{\text{Number of Positions Filled}} \times 100 =$ Percentage of Positions Filled Externally

12. $\dfrac{\text{Total Testing Costs}}{\text{Number of Applicants Tested}}$ = Average Testing Cost per Applicant

13. $\dfrac{\text{Total Testing Costs}}{\substack{\text{Number of Tested Employees} \\ \text{Hired}}}$ = Average Testing Cost per Employee Hired

PERFORMANCE APPRAISAL

Possibly one of the most neglected areas of evaluation is performance appraisal. It is not unusual for organizations to develop and implement an appraisal system and subsequently do little or no follow-up on the system to determine if it is working as planned or if it is producing the results that it is supposed to produce. Furthermore, few organizations recognize performance appraisal as a type of employment test that should be validated in terms of job content. Effective evaluation of this staffing area is long overdue.

Checklist

Insight into performance appraisal effectiveness can be gained by simply asking questions about the system and the instrument used. Some relevant questions are as follows:

1. Are all employees and managerial personnel appraised at least annually?
2. Are all new employees appraised at the end of their probationary period?

3. Are performance appraisal results integrated with the human resource planning process?

4. Are performance appraisal results used in the career planning and development process?

5. Is performance appraisal information used to assist in evaluating the recruiting and selecting processes?

6. Have formalized policies and procedures been developed for using performance appraisal?

7. Have all appraisers received training in performance appraisal?

8. Has the performance appraisal instrument used been validated in terms of actual job content?

9. Are different appraisal instruments used for different levels of jobs such as operative employees, professionals, and managers?

10. Does the performance appraisal instrument rely on standards and measures rather than subjective factors such as worker traits or personality characteristics?

11. Does the system and the instrument produce reliable results?

12. Is a periodic audit of performance appraisal results performed to determine if evaluation inflation or deflation is occurring?

13. Is the performance appraisal instrument easy to understand and use?

14. Are promotion, transfer, demotion, termination, and layoff decisions based on performance appraisal information?

15. Does the system contain an appeal procedure whereby an employee may challenge an unfavorable review?

16. Does the system contain a review procedure wherein the next higher level of management is required to review the results of each employee's appraisal?

17. Are managers and supervisors required to discuss appraisal results with employees?

18. Do managers and supervisors spend sufficient time discussing appraisal results with employees?

19. Do employees have proper access to their performance records?

20. Are appraisals conducted in accordance with a predetermined schedule?

Quantitative Measures

While performance appraisal may not be as amenable to statistical evaluation as other staffing areas, there are some indicators that can shed light on how well the system is working. Among these are:

1. Correlation of Performance Appraisal Results with Actual Job Performance Measures

2. Average Performance Ratings by Job, Work Unit, and Department

3. $\dfrac{\text{Number of Appraisals Performed}}{\text{Number of Appraisals Scheduled}} \times 100 =$ Percentage of Required Appraisals Actually Completed

4. $\dfrac{\text{Number of Employees Rated at Below Standard}}{\text{Number of Employees Appraised}} \times 100 =$ Percentage of Employees Rated Below Standard

5. $\dfrac{\text{Number of Employees Rated as Excellent}}{\text{Number of Employees Appraised}} \times 100 =$ Percentage of Employees Rated in Highest Performance Category

6. $\dfrac{\text{Number of Appraisals Appealed}}{\text{Number of Appraisals Completed}} \times 100 =$ Percentage of Appraisals Appealed

CAREER PLANNING AND DEVELOPMENT

Assessing the effectiveness of career planning and development is sometimes difficult to do. This is particularly true of the developmental portion of the process. Since development is essentially self-development, results are not always obvious in the short run. Years may elapse before it becomes apparent that development is actually occurring. But if an organization is going to invest time and money in efforts to assist employees in their careers, this activity must be examined carefully to determine whether it is producing the desired results.

Checklist

The following questions are representative of the ones that can be posed to evaluate career planning and development.

1. Have career paths or ladders of job progression been identified?
2. Where appropriate, have dual career ladders been developed?
3. Is career planning and development integrated with human resource planning as a means of identifying personnel available in the organization for promotion or transfer?
4. Are skills inventories maintained on all employees?
5. Are management inventories maintained on all managerial personnel?
6. Are skills and management inventories used to assist employees and managers in developing their careers with the organization?
7. Are career opportunities communicated clearly to all employees and managers?
8. Is a promotion from within policy used to foster career development with the organization?

9. Does the organization typically adhere to the promotion from within policy?

10. Does the organization offer formal career planning and development assistance to employees?

11. Do managers and supervisors understand their roles in career planning and development?

12. Are replacement tables used to assist in career planning and development?

13. Is job rotation used as a means of developing employees and managers?

14. Are employees and managers encouraged to participate in in-house and external workshops, seminars, or other programs to enhance their career potential?

Quantitative Measures

Quantitatively, some indication of the effectiveness of career planning and development can be ascertained through measures of employee retention and upward mobility. These include:

1. Number of Positions Filled Internally

2. Number of Promotions Made

3. Number of Employees Promoted Classified as to Protected Group Status

4. Number of Transfers Made for Developmental Purposes

5. Number of Employees Transferred for Developmental Purposes Classified as to Protected Group Status

6. Number of Voluntary Terminations

7. Number of Voluntary Terminations as a Percentage of Total Terminations

8. Number of Employees with One or More Years Service as a Percentage of Total Employees

9. Employee Turnover Rates by Job, Work Unit, and Department

10. Number of Employees and Managers Attending Workshops, Seminars, and Other Developmental Programs

11. Number of Positions Filled Internally as a Percentage of Total Positions Filled

12. Number of Positions Filled Externally as a Percentage of Total Positions Filled

HUMAN RESOURCE ADMINISTRATION

As discussed in the preceding chapter, human resource administration encompasses a broad range of activities. While the performance of each of these activities is important, this section will focus only on those functions related to staffing.

Checklist

Human resource administration is very susceptible to evaluation by checklist. A performance audit of this area would involve asking the questions listed below.

1. Does the organization have a formal employee orientation program?
2. Are orientation checklists used by the human resource department to provide new employees with an overview of the organization?
3. Are orientation checklists used by the immediate supervisor of the new employee to ensure that the employee is familiarized with the job, the work unit, and other items of importance?
4. Have supervisors received training in how to carry out their role in orientation?
5. Does the human resource department have policies and procedures for orientation follow-ups after new employees have been on the job for a stipulated period of time?
6. Have policies and procedures on promotions been developed?
7. Have policies and procedures on transfers been developed?
8. Have policies and procedures on demotions been developed?
9. Have policies and procedures on layoffs been developed?
10. Have policies and procedures on involuntary terminations been developed?
11. Have policies and procedures on promotions, transfers, demotions, layoffs, and terminations been communicated clearly to all employees?
12. Have the reasons for termination of employees been identified and stipulated?
13. Have the reasons for voluntary terminations been identified and analyzed?
14. Are exit interviews used to identify causes of resignations?
15. Are post-exit questionnaires used to identify causes of resignations?
16. Have appropriate corrective actions been taken on the basis of information gathered from exit interviews and post-exit questionnaires?
17. Are outplacement services provided for employees?
18. Are outplacement services provided for managers and professionals?
19. Are outplacement services provided for executives?
20. Have policies, programs, and procedures on retirement been developed?
21. Have policies, procedures, and programs for early retirement been developed?
22. Are retirement planning programs and services provided for employees and managers?
23. Are organizational climate surveys conducted on a regular basis?
24. Is the information from organizational climate surveys used to take appropriate corrective action?
25. Are employees, supervisors, and managers informed of the results obtained from organizational climate surveys?

26. Is employee turnover data maintained on job, work unit, departmental, functional, and organizational bases?
27. Is employee turnover analyzed on a regular basis?
28. Is appropriate corrective action taken on the basis of analysis of employee turnover data?
29. Are all personnel records maintained in accordance with a prescribed records retention schedule?

Quantitative Measures

Because of the all-inclusive nature of human resource administration, many measures can be used to evaluate the performance of this activity. In fact, most of the quantitative measures suggested for the evaluation of other staffing processes can be used, to some extent, to evaluate the effectiveness of the administrative function. Thus, rather than repeat previously enumerated measures, this section will present only a few critical indicators relative to employee turnover and retention.

1. $$\frac{\text{Number of Terminations from All Causes}}{\text{Average Number of Employees}} \times 100 = \text{Turnover Percentage}$$

2. $$\frac{\text{Number of Terminations from All Causes} - \text{Number of Voluntary Terminations}}{\text{Average Number of Employees}} \times 100 = \text{Unavoidable Turnover Percentage}$$

3. $$\frac{\text{Number of Voluntary Terminations}}{\text{Average Number of Employees}} \times 100 = \text{Avoidable Turnover Percentage}$$

4. $$\frac{\text{Number of Employees with One or More Years Service}}{\text{Total Number of Employees}} \times 100 = \text{New Hire Retention Percentage}$$

5. $$\frac{\text{Number of Employees Leaving within First Year}}{\text{Number of Employees Hired in One Year}} \times 100 = \text{Percent of New Hires Lost}$$

SUMMARY

Staffing is critical to the success of contemporary organizations. It promises to become even more so in the future as international competition heightens and American enterprises endeavor to remain leaders in effectiveness and efficiency. Having the right people in the right places at the right time—the basic objective of staffing—is imperative in the rapidly increasing competitive struggle.

For staffing to be fully effective, it must be viewed as a system that is fully integrated within itself and also fully integrated within the total human resource management system of an organization. Each staffing activity must be performed as effectively as possible; each staffing activity must be continuously evaluated to eliminate deficiencies and enhance strengths. This is the challenge of today and this is the challenge of tomorrow. It is a challenge that can and will be met as the cruciality of staffing is recognized.

Bibliography

The following bibliography has been compiled for the reader who wishes to pursue staffing further. The references cited will enable the reader to acquire more detailed, technical information as well as gain a better understanding of staffing problems and their potential solutions. This bibliography is intended to be representative rather than exhaustive and contains only references to what we consider major works in the field. Journal articles have been purposely omitted in order to reduce the length of the reference list and make it more useful to the working personnel professional.

Alpander, Guvenc G. *Human Resources Management Planning*. New York: AMACOM, 1982.

Anastasi, Anne. *Psychological Testing*. 5th ed. New York: Macmillan Co., 1982.

Anderson, Howard J. *Primer of Equal Employment Opportunity*. Washington, D.C.: Bureau of National Affairs, 1978.

Arvey, Richard D. *Fairness in Selecting Employees*. Reading, Mass.: Addison-Wesley, 1979.

Baird, Lloyd S., Richard W. Beatty, and Craig Eric Schneier. *The Performance Appraisal Sourcebook*. Amherst, Mass.: Human Resource Development Press, 1982.

Beach, Dale S. *Personnel: The Management of People at Work*. 5th ed. New York: Macmillan Co., 1985.

Bemis, Stephen E., Ann Holt Belenky, and Dee Ann Soder. *Job Analysis: An Effective Management Tool*. Washington, D.C.: Bureau of National Affairs, 1983.

Burack, Elmer, and Nicholas J. Mathys. *Career Management in Organizations: A Practical Human Resource Planning Approach*. Lake Forest, Ill.: Brace-Park Press, 1979.

Burack, Elmer H., and James W. Walker, eds. *Manpower Planning and Programming*. Boston: Allyn and Bacon, 1972.

Carrell, Michael R., and Frank Kuzmits. *Personnel: Human Resource Management*. 2nd ed. Columbus, Ohio: Merrill Co., 1986.

Carroll, Stephen J., and Craig E. Schneier. *Performance Appraisal and Review Systems: The Identification, Measurement, and Development of Performance in Organizations.* Glenview, Ill.: Scott, Foresman and Company, 1982.

Caruth, Donald L. *Compensation Management for Banks.* Boston: Bankers Co., 1986.

Caruth, Donald L. *Work Measurement in Banking.* 2nd ed. Boston: Bankers Co., 1984.

Caruth, Don, Frank Rachel, and Bill Middlebrook. *Management Dynamics II.* Carrollton, Tex.: Spinnaker Publications, 1983.

Cascio, Wayne F. *Applied Psychology in Personnel Management.* 2nd ed. Reston, Va.: Reston Co., 1982.

Cascio, Wayne F. *Managing Human Resources.* New York: McGraw-Hill Book Company, 1986.

Christie, Linda Gail. *Human Resources: A Hidden Profit Center.* Englewood Cliffs, N. J.: Prentice-Hall, 1983.

Chruden, Herbert J., and Arthur W. Sherman, Jr. *Managing Human Resources.* 7th ed. Cincinnati: South-Western Co., 1984.

Day, Virgil B., Frank Erwin, and Alan M. Koral, eds. *A Professional and Legal Analysis of the Uniform Guidelines on Employee Selection Procedures.* Berea, Ohio: American Society for Personnel Administration, 1981.

Douglas, John, Stuart Klein, and David Hunt. *The Strategic Managing of Human Resources.* New York: John Wiley & Sons, 1985.

Dreher, George F., and Paul R. Sackett. *Perspectives on Employee Staffing and Selection*: Readings and Commentary. Homewood, Ill.: Richard D. Irwin, 1983.

Drucker, Peter F. *Management: Tasks, Responsibilities, Practices.* New York: Harper & Row, 1974.

Fear, Richard A. *The Evaluation Interview.* New York: McGraw-Hill Book Company, 1973.

Fear, Richard A., and James F. Ross. *Jobs, Dollars—and EEO: How to Hire More Entry-Level Workers.* New York: McGraw-Hill, 1983.

French, Wendell L. *Human Resources Management.* Boston: Houghton Mifflin, 1986.

Gael, Sidney. *Job Analysis: A Guide to Assessing Work Activities.* San Francisco: Jossey-Bass, 1983.

Gilmer, B. von Haller, and Edward L. Deci. *Industrial and Organizational Psychology.* 4th ed. New York: McGraw-Hill Book Company, 1977.

Glueck, William F. *Personnel: A Diagnostic Approach.* 3rd ed. Plano, Tex.: Business Publications, 1982.

Goodale, James G. *The Fine Art of Interviewing.* Englewood Cliffs, N.J.: Prentice-Hall, 1982.

Henderson, Richard I. *Compensation Management: Rewarding Performance.* 3rd ed. Reston, Va.: Reston Co., 1979.

Henderson, Richard I. *Performance Appraisal: Theory and Practice.* Reston, Va.: Reston Co., 1980.

Heneman, Gerbert G. III, and Donald P. Schwab, eds. *Perspectives on Personnel/ Human Resource Management*. rev. ed. Homewood, Ill.: Richard D. Irwin, 1982.

Holley, William H., and Kenneth M. Jennings. *Personnel Management*. Chicago: Dryden Press, 1983.

Latham, Gary P., and Kenneth N. Wexley. *Increasing Productivity Through Performance Appraisal*. Reading, Mass.: Addison-Wesley, 1981.

Ledvinka, James. *Federal Regulation of Personnel and Human Resource Management*. Belmont, Calif.: Kent Co., 1982.

Lorber, Lawrence Z., J. Robert Kirk, Kenneth H. Kirschner, and Charlene R. Handorf. *Fear of Firing: A Legal and Personnel Analysis of Employment at Will*. Alexandria, Va.: ASPA Foundation, 1984.

McCulloch, Kenneth J. *Selecting Employees Safely under the Law*. Englewood Cliffs, N.J.: Prentice-Hall, 1981.

Miner, John B., and Mary Green Miner. *Employee Selection within the Law*. Washington, D.C.: Bureau of National Affairs, 1979.

Miner, John B., and Mary Green Miner. *Personnel and Industrial Relations*. 4th ed. New York: Macmillan Co., 1985.

Moffatt, Thomas L. *Selection Interviewing for Managers*. New York: Harper & Row, 1979.

Mondy, R. Wayne, and Robert M. Noe III. *Personnel: The Management of Human Resources*. 3rd ed. Boston: Allyn and Bacon, 1987.

Mondy, R. Wayne, and Robert M. Noe III. *Personnel: The Management of Human Resources*. 2nd ed. Boston: Allyn and Bacon, 1984.

Morgan, Henry H. and John W. Cogger. *The Interview's Manual*. 2nd ed. New York: Drake-Beam & Associates, 1980.

Morgan, Marilyn A. *Managing Career Development*. New York: D. Van Nostrand Company, 1980.

Morin, William J. *Successful Termination*. New York: Drake Beam Morin, 1981.

Nettler, John, and William Wassterman. *Applied Linear Statistics*. Homewood, Ill.: Richard D. Irwin, 1974.

Player, Mack A. *Federal Law of Employment Discrimination*. 2nd ed. St. Paul, Minn.: West Co., 1981.

Schlei, Barbara Lindemann, and Paul Grossman. *Employment Discrimination Law*. 2nd ed. Washington, D.C.: Bureau of National Affairs, 1983.

Schneider, Benjamin, and Neal Schmitt. *Staffing Organizations*. 2nd ed. Glenview, Ill.: Scott, Foresman and Company, 1986.

Schuler, Randall S., and Stuart A. Youngblood. *Effective Personnel Management*. 2nd ed. St. Paul, Minn.: West Co., 1986.

Schultz, Duane P. *Psychology and Industry Today*. 2nd ed. New York: Macmillan Co., 1978.

Sethi, S. Prakash. *Up Against the Corporate Wall*. Englewood Cliffs, N.J.: Prentice-Hall, 1971.

Siegel, Jerome. *Personnel Testing under EEO*. New York: AMACOM, 1980.

Taylor, Benjamin J., and Fred Witney. *Labor Relations Law*. 4th ed. Englewood Cliffs, N.J.: Prentice-Hall, 1983.

Tiffin, Joseph, and Ernest J. McCormick. *Industrial Psychology.* 6th ed. Englewood Cliffs, N.J.: Prentice-Hall, 1974.

Tiffin, Joseph, and Ernest J. McCormick. *Industrial Psychology.* 5th ed. Englewood Cliffs, N.J.: Prentice-Hall, 1965.

Twomey, David P. *A Concise Guide to Employment Law, EEO & OSHA.* Cincinnati: South-Western Co., 1986.

U.S. Department of Labor, Manpower Administration. *Handbook for Analyzing Jobs.* Washington, D.C.: U.S. Government Printing Office, 1972.

U.S. Office of Personnel Management. *Equal Employment Opportunity Court Cases.* Washington, D.C.: U.S. Government Printing Office, 1979.

Walker, James W. *Human Resource Planning.* New York: McGraw-Hill Book Company, 1980.

Wanous, John P. *Organizational Entry.* Reading, Mass.: Addison-Wesley, 1980.

Yoder, Dale, and Herbert G. Heneman, Jr., eds. *ASPA Handbook of Personnel and Industrial Relations, Volume IV, Planning and Auditing PAIR.* Washington, D.C.: Bureau of National Affairs, 1976.

Yoder, Dale, and Herbert G. Heneman, Jr., eds. *ASPA Handbook of Personnel and Industrial Relations, Volume I, Staffing Policies and Strategies.* Washington, D.C.: Bureau of National Affairs, 1974.

Index

About the Authors

DONALD L. CARUTH is Professor of Management in the College of Business and Technology at East Texas State University.

ROBERT M. NOE III, is Professor of Management, and Head of the Department of Marketing and Management in the College of Business and Technology at East Texas State University.

R. WAYNE MONDY is Professor of Management and Head of the Department of Management and Marketing, College of Business Administration, McNeese State University.